THE SEA AND THE SWORD

The Sea
and the Sword

OLIVER WARNER

1965 NEW YORK

⚓ THE BALTIC

1630–1945

William Morrow and Company

TO FRANCES

Contents

Illustrations

Following page 114

Gustavus II Adolphus
Gustavus Adolphus at Lützen
Christian IV
Charles X Gustavus
Peter the Great
Charles XII
"Image and Superscription": Coins and Medals
Catherine the Great
Admiral Sir James Saumarez
Bernadotte
Bismarck in 1894
Lenin in 1922
Marshal Pilsudski
Marshal Mannerheim
Hitler as German Chancellor, 1934
The Yalta Conference, February 1945
Alexander I
Kronborg Castle

Maps

Foreword

It is now many years since an uncertain young man, looking across the waters of the Sound from Kronborg Castle to the Swedish shore, first felt wonder and enthralment at the history of those Baltic countries which have played so great a part in European affairs. Since then the northern world has been transformed, and it is the purpose of this narrative to trace in bold outline, occasionally in more detail, the chief events, and the influence of men and women on those events, which have most affected northern Europe since Gustavus Adolphus landed with his Swedes to intervene in the Thirty Years' War. As the title suggests, emphasis is upon conflict by sea and land, and upon its results, temporary or more permanent. An all-embracing history of the territories surrounding the Baltic has not been attempted and should not be looked for.

The first part of the work is largely a story of strife between potentates aspiring to gain territory, power and prestige at the expense of their neighbours. Many of the later chapters involve a close account of the diplomatic struggle, waged against the immediate background of war, for the political integrity of Poland. Although that struggle by Great Britain and the United States was in fact lost, there has probably never before in history been so protracted and comparatively disinterested an attempt by two Western powers to ensure stability in Continental Europe. This is the reason so extensive a share of the book has been given to one short phase in a continuing process.

There will be scarcely a paragraph, certainly not so much as a chapter, in such a summary which will not be wide open to dispute, or at least to question, on the part of the specialist in any given country, phase or period. No one is more acutely aware than the writer that it is the work of a lifetime to become, in any absolute sense, master of even a decade. A survey of this sort requires, therefore, temerity on the one part and a measure of forbearance on the other—not least because, by reason of scale, oversimplification can scarcely be avoided.

It also needs sustained encouragement, and in this respect, among many to whom a debt is due, first must be named Miss Frances Phillips, who suggested the scope of the work and helped it at every stage, and the Marquess of Anglesey, generous and enthusiastic, who quickened belief that the subject could be treated within limits not daunting through mere size. Visits to northern lands, always inspiriting, have been made still more rewarding by the company, conversation, and knowledge of Marika Jondal and her family, by Dr. and Mrs. Georg Svensson, Ragnar Svanstrom and his wife, Mrs. Erling Kristiansen, Professor W. R. Mead, and former colleagues serving on the overseas staff of the British Council. Thanks are also due Mrs. Peters for transcription of material often difficult, to Mr. William Myson, Chief Librarian of Wimbledon, to Captain Augustus Agar, V.C., R.N., and to patient editors on both sides of the Atlantic.

Certain other acknowledgements will be found elsewhere, where it is fitting to mention works which have proved of special value. In the case of the illustrations, the appropriate credits are, in all cases, no mere formalities, and Mr. Peter Davies, Mr. Nicholas Powell, and Mrs. Rosemary Pearce, among others, have been of particular help in channelling enquiries to the right source. Kindness has been shown by the Royal Danish Embassy in London, whose Press Counsellor went to much trouble in obtaining out-of-the-way information, and by the National Museum, Stockholm. Characteristic hospitality has been enjoyed by the writer and his wife during travels by sea and air in Sweden, Russia, and Finland.

It is difficult to be consistent in the spelling of Baltic names, which have sometimes changed confusingly in periods of struggle. This applies particularly to the former Baltic States, to Finland and to Schleswig-Holstein. Wherever possible, the version has been used which appears in the *Cambridge Modern History*, originated by Lord Acton, which, though in some respects old-fashioned, follows an honourable tradition of narrative writing. This is a predilection natural enough in one nurtured in the school which Acton encouraged.

Part One ♆ AN OLDER WORLD [1630-1917]

And here we are as on a darkling plain
Swept with confused alarms of struggle and flight . . .

MATTHEW ARNOLD: Dover Beach

I . Power in the Baltic

In general, though with exceptions, the trend of man's expansion has been westerly. The morning sun has risen at the migrant's back. In the evening its glow has brightened the horizon.

This has been so in land-bound Europe, while for centuries the ambitious looked across the Western Ocean in search of fresh wonders, finding them in ample measure. Even in the Pacific at least one movement from the American mainland towards Polynesia followed the same course.

In the European story resistance to the trend has led to recurrent crises. There have been protracted, often agonized counterthrusts from west to east, while there was an exceptional time when moves from the north towards the south and east made Sweden a force in diplomacy.

Today Russian impetus has driven farther west than at any other time in history, except for an incursion in Napoleon's era. Russia or her satellites at present command most of the eastern and southern shores of the Baltic, and the feat has been achieved within the span of a lifetime during which Poland rose phoenix-like from her own ashes, Finland, Denmark and Norway suffered invasion, while Germany and Russia twice came to death grips. The triumphs, blunders and sufferings which brought that fact about are the theme of these pages.

Although the whole aspect of the Baltic littoral has been modified within so short a period, it was seldom static, for over the generations the northern sea has had an importance in the affairs of the Western world second only to the Mediterranean, a fact which does not alter. From remote times kings and statesmen have striven for mastery within the area, not least because the lands surrounding the Baltic contained the richest available source of naval stores. Timber of all sorts, tar, hemp, iron, copper, every product of forest and mine which pertained to the equipment of a sailing fleet, could be had from the northern countries, and sometimes from nowhere else. This gave them strategic and political weight, while a lack in the north of other commodities, equally valuable, opened up golden prospects for the direct and the carrying trade of the Netherlands, Great Britain, France, Italy and Spain. It gave these countries a constantly expanding market for their staple goods.

Despite the personal ambition of a succession of rulers, the turbulent history of northern Europe was never a matter affecting crowns and dynasties alone; nor did the importance of the territories cease when navies were no longer wind-driven. As an instance, the importation of ore from Sweden was a factor vital to German strength in the wars of the present century. At least eleven million tons were required each year from this source. In summer the ore was shipped mainly across waters which Germany could command. In winter, when pack ice hindered Baltic traffic, it came by way of Narvik and Norwegian inshore channels. It became Britain's object to stop the flow, but she never could do so until, with the help of her allies, she had gained bases from which her forces could operate with effect.

The struggle for power in the Baltic has in fact been long, ramified and unceasing. Even today, in times which are nominally those of peace, interests and principles still clash. Political and other systems in Denmark, Sweden, Finland, Russia, Poland and the severed Germanies differ fundamentally in aim and widely in detail. The history of how present conditions came about is full of incident and drama, and since an arbitrary starting point needs to be chosen, there is justification for seeing in the actions of Gustavus Adolphus at least the beginnings of the modern world. Gustavus was an excellent judge of what could be attained with existing means, however modest, and he was a man who might well, had more time been granted him, have transformed the status of his country as a permanent factor in Europe.

In order to view the northern scene in a perspective by which Gustavus may be understood, it is necessary to consider broadly the evolution of affairs as it was known at the time when he succeeded to the Swedish throne. In this respect three events, the first occurring at the close of the fourteenth century, and the others in the fifteenth, were cardinal to the future of all Baltic lands. The Union of Kalmar, the result of a treaty which drew Denmark, Sweden and Norway together under the Danish crown, might, if it had held firm, have made the Baltic a Scandinavian lake. It was effected in 1397, under Queen Margaret of the Valdemar dynasty, but from the first the bond was precarious, and with the advent of Gustavus Vasa as sovereign in Sweden it broke altogether, having lasted, more in notion than in effect, for a century and a quarter. Denmark found that she could not maintain, by methods which were coercive, an authority repugnant to the Swedes.

While the Kalmar Union was failing, away to the east there had been a loosening of still greater significance. This was the disintegration of the Golden Horde, the Mongol tribe which for nearly two centuries had extended its power over most of Russia and much of Asia from a single khanate, with its capital at Sarai, on the Volga, into dispersed princedoms. The event gave the rulers of Moscow their opportunity. Ivan III, who repudiated the suzerainty of the Horde, made Moscow the centre of Russian power, brought Novgorod and other regions under his sway, and established his own independence.

From Ivan's marriage to Sophia Palaeologa, niece of the last Greek Emperor of Constantinople, dates the assumption of the Imperial double-headed eagle of the Caesars and the title of Tsar. Henceforward Tsars ruling in Moscow pursued two aims. One of them was to unite and to be at the head of all the Russias, Great, Little, Black, White, Red (names which derived from mediaeval maps showing branches of the race), and to provide their country with outlets in the Black Sea and the Baltic. The other, which was not realized, was to recover from the Turk the capital of the old Greek Eastern or Byzantine Empire, whence had

come, in the tenth century, the conversion of Russia to the Greek
Orthodox branch of the Christian Church.

The third event would have seemed at the time to be of less
far-reaching consequence than troubles in Scandinavia or hopes
in Muscovy. It was the acquisition of Brandenburg by the Margrave of Nürnberg, foreshadowing the rise of Brandenburg-
Prussia. The Margrave, a Hohenzollern, belonged to a family
with whose exploits and ambitions the world would grow increasingly, even sickeningly, familiar.

A final element, affecting the rest to a major degree, was fluc-
tuation in the affairs of the ancient kingdom of Poland, whose
stake in the Baltic was at one time considerable. By any standard,
Poland was unstable, for political and geographical reasons of
which the history of the country provides a running illustration,
and over the course of time the realm became first a provocation
to acts of aggression, and then a deepening shadow across the
consciences of statesmen. Words such as "enclave" and "corridor"
seem inseparable from Polish history, and one of the few constant
factors is that although Poles quarrelled, suffered and bled, yet
somehow, in spite of a succession of misfortunes, ineptitudes and
suppressions which would have extinguished the spark in a less
resilient nation, Poland revived.

What marked Poland from her neighbours was that even when
she had a strong ruler, which was not often enough for her welfare, rarely did he have an attainable political object, or any
long-term motive such as gave vigour to the wars and diplomacy
of Valdemars, Vasas, Romanovs and Hohenzollerns. There was
no fixed star to which Poles could look up. Even her hero, John
Sobieski, who in the seventeenth century saved Vienna from the
Turk, is remembered for this exploit, and not because he left
behind him a realm able to resist pressure from without, or united
enough to resolve its own future with any assurance.

II

If it is rulers who plan, it is their people who execute, and a
ruler who can summon a nation united in race has a paramount
advantage over one who must take serious account of minorities

or alien pockets. Herein lies the tragedy of Scandinavia. Racially and linguistically Danes, Swedes and Norwegians are akin. In combination they might have had an imperial destiny, foreshadowed by the success in raiding and to some degree in colonization of the Vikings and their successors, who, drawn to at least some extent from all three countries, practiced their skill as far away as Greenland, Africa, the coasts of Italy and Constantinople. The human material was of rare quality: energetic, tough, courageous, imaginative. Ironically, the later history of the three countries presents a succession of disputes, sometimes petty, often dynastic, and only partly to be acounted for by the fact that whereas Norway has always found scope for activities westward by sea, the aims of Denmark were divided, while Swedish energy has been confined mainly to the area of the Baltic. Few quarrels are so bitter and protracted as those which arise between kinsmen.

An ethnological map of such a span as the plain of northern Europe, however valuable at any given moment and however important that moment may be, is sure to be imperfect and liable to be impermanent. Races shift and mingle. Populations have removed or been transplanted, sometimes on a great scale. Nothing, certainly, is more complex than the racial pattern of the coast and hinterland which lies roughly between Danzig and Lake Ladoga, including as it does Prussians, Saxons, Kassubs, Poles, Lithuanians, Letts, Estonians, Finns and White Russians, with memories of earlier peoples such as the Goths and Vandals who figure in the formal title of sovereigns in Scandinavia. The most important factor actually lies beyond, and it is one which, in the long run, would control events in the European north. It is the stupendous size of the territories which, over the centuries, came to be known as Russia, and later still as the Union of Soviet Socialist Republics.

European Russia could have been containable. The Russia which stretches even beyond the limits of the Eastern Hemisphere has shown, in the last analysis, that she is unconquerable through sheer magnitude, and that when she has wished to expand, then sooner or later, sometimes after a very long wait, she has had her way. Strategically she operates from what is known as "interior lines." So does Germany. Russia's long-term advantage lies in the fact that she can not only trade space and people for time, which Germany cannot, except to a limited degree, but that she is imbued with the inexhaustible patience of the Orient. She may be defeated on a scale which would wreck most other countries. She cannot be absorbed, and she cannot be wiped out. A succession of thwarted attackers, which includes Napoleon, shows how little even the most brilliant strategist may learn from the past.

A reasonable idea of the likely trend of history may be gleaned from the facts of physical geography, and in this respect the Baltic area is of striking interest. Stretching down from the Arctic regions, the lobster claw of Norway and Sweden possesses a natural unity. This presented an obvious attraction to the eye of Bernadotte, trained to grand strategy, who became the choice of the Swedes to succeed to the throne once occupied by the Vasas. Bernadotte seized on part of the truth, though geographical unity is not always enough.

The Danish case differs. The Jutland peninsula thrusts north, almost into the lobster's claw, from the land mass of the European Continent. Aided by a series of islands made formidable by shoal waters, and by a narrow sound which for centuries brought her kings tribute in dues from the shipping which used it, Denmark holds the key to the Baltic, whose history is a succession of wars of which the world at large has sometimes heard little, largely because interested powers ensured, if necessary by force or a show of force, that purely Baltic disputes would not wholly disrupt the general movement of trade.

South and to the east of Denmark, a series of rivers, flowing seaward through the plains, provides a channel for traffic and determines the site of ports—Rostock, on the Warnow; Stettin, on the Oder; Danzig, at the mouth of the Vistula; Königsberg, on the Pregel; Memel, a depot for goods brought along the Niemen and Memel rivers; Riga, famed in days of sail for its masts and spars, and served by the Duna. These, with towns such as Lübeck, which were pillars of the mediaeval league of Hanseatic or trading cities, were and to some extent remain of importance to maritime nations of western Europe, and in particular to the Netherlands and Britain.

The northern and eastern Baltic, including the shores of the gulfs of Bothnia and Finland, is a region of lake, forest and islet.

It was in this area, from lack of choice, that Peter the Great had perforce to seek his window upon Europe. He built a capital city out of a swamp, like the Venetians in their lagoon, but at reckless cost in lives and treasure. His monument survives under the name of Leningrad.

The struggle for supremacy in the Baltic area, not so much in its maritime as in its territorial aspect, was a leading characteristic in the history of Europe throughout the sixteenth and seventeenth centuries. By the eighteenth century the result was becoming clear, and in the nineteenth it was decided. It would not lie with the Scandinavian countries, singly or together, though it became ever more essential that they should remain resilient and watchful, strong by sea, ready to take advantage whenever benefit offered through the powers by whom the broader trend of affairs would be directed. Their position was assured, but it would not be dominant.

2 . Gustavus Adolphus and Swedish aspiration

Over the centuries, out of a succession of figures with many of the necessary attributes, the Swedish people have fixed upon Gustavus II Adolphus as their pre-eminent hero. He had, indeed, the essential ingredients. Even Napoleon considered him to have been among the world's leading captains, and he may be said to have been beloved of the gods, for he died young. In so far as early training, precocious talent, confidence, the steady facing and overcoming of difficulties and a burning desire to serve his country mark out the statesman-king, Gustavus Adolphus had all these characteristics in generous measure and they made him a paragon of statecraft. Abundant energy, natural gifts for languages and war, and a charm which earned him the devotion of the common man were added to his other qualities. They made him a figure of proportions which were formidable from his boyhood.

Gustavus Adolphus was born in 1594, and when he was sixteen he inherited the Swedish throne through the death of his father, Charles IX. Charles had become Regent of Sweden when Gustavus was in the cradle, but there was a Vasa with a better title. This was Sigismund, King of Poland and Sweden, who had been deposed by his Swedish subjects in 1599, partly on the ground of his Catholicism, the Swedes adhering to the Lutheran faith.

In 1604 the Swedish Riksdag formally proclaimed Charles as king and debarred Catholics from the succession. For the remaining seven years of his life Charles strengthened the army, engaged in aggressive campaigns in Poland and Russia, and shortly before his death actually sent a force to Moscow, to press the claims of Vassili Shuisky to the throne of the Tsars. The mission failed, and the Danes under Christian IV took the opportunity to attack Kalmar and Göteborg, at first with considerable success. The house of Oldenburg had not renounced its claim to Sweden, and the accession of a sovereign who was still in law a minor seemed to Christian to offer a prime opportunity to re-establish Danish authority.

If Gustavus Adolphus succeeded to a difficult heritage, and at a critical moment in Swedish history, he felt equal to every challenge. The country was behind him. In Axel Oxenstierna he had a statesman-administrator of proved ability, while it was remembered of Charles IX how often in council, when forced to abandon designs to which he knew himself unequal, he would lay his hand on the fair head of his son and say, as if with prescience: "*He* will do it!"

There was more than simple affection to give Charles such assurance, and of the stories which derive from Gustavus's boyhood, two are significant. A nurse once tried to prevent him from going into a wood by telling him that the place was full of serpents, just as today she might warn him not to cross a busy road alone. "Give me a stick," said Gustavus firmly, "and I will kill them." Again, when asked which of the ships in Stockholm Harbour he liked best, the boy said: "The one with most guns." This answer is worth recalling because, through one of the miracles of our time, the *Vasa*, a major war vessel of Gustavus's reign, has been raised from beneath the waters off Stockholm, and the tragedy which led to her loss may partly have derived from the fact that her impressive ordnance helped to make her unseaworthy.

Charles IX could scarcely have left his son more taxing problems if this had been his intention. Gustavus Adolphus was faced with concurrent war against Denmark, Poland and Russia. Denmark then possessed territory in the south of Sweden, and Christian IV, who, like his opponent, had succeeded young to his throne, was of an ambitious disposition. Fortunately for Sweden, he was more successful as a builder and patron of the arts than as a war leader. Despite geographical advantages and Swedish

distraction in other parts of the Baltic, Christian gained no lasting profit. His principal success was the capture of the Swedish
fortress port of Älfsborg, which before the development of Göteborg was Sweden's principal outlet to the North Sea.

The Danish war was ended through the mediation of James I
of England, who had married Christian's sister, it being stipu-
lated that, in return for Älfsborg, Sweden was to be made to
pay a sum which would severely tax the finances of the country.
A lasting if not the most important result of the peace was that
the three crowns which appeared in the coat of arms of both
Gustavus Adolphus and of Christian, a relic of the days of Scandinavian union, were formally allowed to both. They are a notable embellishment of the *Vasa*.

The Swedish war with Russia continued until 1617, and was
richly advantageous to Gustavus. When, finally, the Russians appealed to James I to interpose his pacific offices once more, Gustavus was able to make satisfactory terms. Besides giving Sweden
monetary compensation, Russia ceded the provinces of Istria and
Karelia (land which included the future site of Leningrad) and
all her existing seaboard. At the conclusion of the negotiations
Gustavus unfolded a map of Europe. Pointing to the Baltic, he
said: "After this the Russians will find it hard to skip over that little brook."

The trouble with Poland was protracted over nearly a decade,
and it included four campaigns of varied fortune, nearly always
in Gustavus's favour, yet not without the stimulus of an occasional reverse, in one of which the King lost most of his artillery
and was himself nearly captured. By the end of the war Gustavus
had gained such experience and reputation that he was held to
be the equal of Maurice of Nassau, a prince from whom he himself
was proud to learn, a man whom soldiers of fortune were eager
to follow. In one of Gustavus's campaigns the Swedes landed in
Livonia, besieged Riga, took it by storm after five weeks and then
overran the entire province, a conquest which the King retained
for the rest of his life. Later he carried the war into Courland,
into Polish Prussia and to the gates of Warsaw. His pitched battles included three considerable victories, at Wallhof, Dirshau
and Stuhm respectively, while among his generals were numbered De la Gardie, who had served with distinction under

Charles IX, Banér, Torstensson, Horn and Wrangel. Most of them were older than Gustavus, but there was no doubt who was master.

The Swedish King could not dispose of vast armies. His total force seldom exceeded 80,000 men. Nearly half of them were used to garrison the home country and nearly half were mercenaries. There was a well-organized contingent from Scotland, with which country Swedish ties were close; there were a few English; the rest included Finns, Livonians and Germans: men drawn from hardy races, some with traditions of warfare stretching back to remote antiquity.

II

Gustavus Adolphus's virtues as a soldier deserve scrutiny. He was an innovator prepared to practice what he preached down to the smallest detail. He was a student of war who made himself a professional in the most absolute sense, thinking no task beneath him, and in the mines and trenches stripping to his shirt and toiling with spade or shovel. In this respect he differed so much from Christian IV and from Sigismund that his successes against them can be a matter of no surprise. "The soldier follows the example of his chief," he said to Oxenstierna when his Chancellor remonstrated with him on the occasion of one of his thirteen wounds. "A general who keeps himself out of danger can gain neither victories nor laurels." Yet he knew the risks he was running, and he said more than once: "By going to the well the pitcher will one day be broken."

Gustavus's three principles, from which other virtues stemmed, were discipline, mobility and morale. Discipline was laid down by regulations read aloud to the troops by Oxenstierna in the royal presence, and rigidly enforced. Mobility extended to every arm, while morale or élan was given strength through belief in the cause for which Gustavus fought. He and his soldiers were devout and vocal Protestants, and they had faith in themselves. It was a quality common to all ranks, and unshakable in the sovereign. Of Gustavus's countless indirect pupils, one of the most admiring and impressive was his near contemporary, Oliver Cromwell, who, though he came to war late in life, found Swedish ideas and Protestant belief a good foundation for what he called a New Model Army.

Gustavus insisted on uniform, and among his innovations was the abandonment of the traditional pike as a weapon for his infantry. In the interest of speed on the march he discarded first the pikeman's armour and then the long, heavy weapon itself, the musket taking its place, together with what was termed a "Swede's feather." This was a stake about five feet long with a pike head at each end, one struck in the ground, the other serving to keep off enemy cavalry, something like the stakes which the archers used at Agincourt with such astounding results.

Believing as he did in fire power, and rapid fire at that, Gustavus reduced his infantry files from ten deep to six deep. The depth of files was conditioned by the time taken by a musketeer to load and discharge his piece. The old plan was for the first rank to fire, then to fall back to the rear of the other nine to reload, and for the others to repeat this manoeuvre in succession. Gustavus taught his soldiers to load more rapidly, and before his death every European army except the Dutch copied his example. Even this practice was made flexible, was varied and improved to suit the occasion, and when Gustavus required massive concentration rather than a continuous succession of lighter volleys, he made three ranks fire at once—the first kneeling, the second stooping forward and the third standing upright and firing over the shoulders of the second. "One long and continued crack of thunder," wrote Sir Thomas Turner, an Englishman who saw the Swedes in action, "is more terrible and dreadful to mortals than three interrupted ones."

Gustavus made use of dragoons, or mounted infantry, and he transformed the methods of his cavalry proper by ordering them to fight three deep instead of six: he taught them to reserve their fire when they charged, to charge faster and to charge home. As for his artillery, it was a boast of the Swedish King that he led the world in gun drill and equipment, though not in weight or numbers. The batteries were "conducted by the most experienced artists in Christendom," said Turner. One way in which Sweden was fortunate was that she could mine high-grade iron for her cannon, and furnished her own powder and shot. In the person of Louis de Geer, a Dutchman naturalized in Sweden, she even had the greatest armament manufacturer of his time.

No operation of war was more wasteful and exasperating than the old formal siege of a fortified town or position. Gustavus believed in light artillery rather than in the ponderous siege pieces which were a feature of most armies, and his methods were described in the *Swedish Intelligencer*, a guide to the art of war which furnished information to all who were open to enlightenment. Although he was, in general, a great believer in the use of the spade, Gustavus knew its limitations. "This was his order, mostly, in the taking of a town," ran the *Intelligencer's* report. "He would not stand entrenching and building redoubts at a mile's distance, but clap down with his army presently, and if he saw the place was not by a running pull to be taken, he would not lose above five or six days before it, but rise and to another." Napoleon used to say: "Ask anything of me but time." Gustavus would have agreed. His five-week siege of Riga was justified, but such expenditure was seldom repeated.

III

It was his Protestantism which gave Gustavus what cause he needed for intervention at a critical moment in the Thirty Years' War, a protracted disaster which left Germany in ruins. At first all had gone well for the Catholic forces which fought in the name of Ferdinand II, head of the house of Habsburg and the first pupil of a Jesuit college to become Holy Roman Emperor. Frederick of the Palatinate, aspirant to the throne of Bohemia, had been defeated near Prague, and with his wife, Elizabeth, daughter of King James, that "Queen of Hearts" in whose honour Shakespeare staged *The Tempest*, had been driven from his capital. Everywhere Protestant princes had met with reverses, among the most humiliating being that of Christian IV, whose ineffective intervention in Germany in 1626 had led to defeat and to the occupation of all his mainland territory by the forces of the Imperial generals, Wallenstein and Tilly.

Ferdinand vested Wallenstein with the Duchy of Mecklenburg and gave him the title—insulting to Scandinavians—of "Gener-

alissimo of the Oceanic and Baltic Seas." Wallenstein proposed
to the Hanse towns that he should equip Wismar, in his Mecklenburg duchy, as a naval base and that, in return for their
support, the Hanse should be given a monopoly in trade with
Spain. The prospect of intervention in northern affairs by a mag-
nate of Bohemian origin, however successful in war, had no appeal for the trading cities, and when Wallenstein moved against
Stralsund, in western Pomerania, the Stralsunders appealed in
their plight to Gustavus. The Swedish King at once sent a force
from Poland. Swedes and Scots, with aid by sea from the Danes,
raised the siege and pushed Wallenstein back. This was one of
the various factors which helped to bring about the general's
dismissal from command of the Imperial Army. It seemed a small
check, but it led to great consequences.

It had been the aim of Richelieu, at that time effective ruler
of France, to support Protestants in Germany as a balance to
Habsburg power, for by land France was ringed by territory controlled by her two great rivals in Europe, the Holy Roman Empire and Spain, Catholic though they were, like Richelieu and
his King. With his usual acumen, Richelieu saw an instrument
for his purpose in the Swedish King. Gustavus had considered
many proposals, but felt no compulsion to go to the aid of the
Protestant princes when their forces were ill conducted, when
the Polish war was still on his hands and when he had seen
Christian worsted. French encouragement and subsidy was another matter, and when Richelieu's ambassadors in Warsaw managed to persuade the Poles that they were being used as cats-
paws by the Emperor, and that it was to their advantage to make
peace with Sweden, the intervention of Gustavus in the affairs
of the empire became certain. He was smarting under the fact that
the Emperor continued to refuse him acknowledgement as King
of Sweden, preferring the claims of the Catholic Sigismund, to
whose aid a force of Imperialists had actually been sent.

Assured of French backing and money, Gustavus lost no time in
returning to Stockholm to request approval from his people for a
campaign in Germany. "Estate of Burghers," he said to those of
whom he would ask much, "my wish for you is that your little log
huts may turn into large stone houses, your boats into big ships,
and that your cruse of oil may never fail. Such is my blessing."

Enthusiasm was such as, in another northern kingdom, had spurred on Henry V's preparations for his invasion of Normandy two centuries earlier.

> They sell the pasture now to buy the horse,
> Following the mirror of all Christian kings . . .

And when Gustavus commended his four-year-old daughter Christina to his countrymen as their future Queen, it was with a presentiment that he was not only offering them a living token of remembrance, but bidding them farewell. Assured of popular backing, he then embarked his army for Rügen, intending to make a limited force do the service of a mighty one, and in the process to give Europe lessons in the art of war.

On 4 July, 1630, the world learned with astonishment that some 13,000 men had landed in territory which, with the exception of Stralsund, was in Imperial hands. The Swedish force was racially mixed. The cavalry and artillery were mainly Swedes: these were tall, fair men from the south of the country; and there were squat Laplanders on their shaggy ponies, whom the Germans imagined to be only half human. There were lean, muscular Finns. There was the usual contingent of Scots; there were Germans, Dutch and soldiers of fortune of other nations. All were officially Lutherans, and all were well clothed, with fur cloaks, gloves, woollen stockings and boots made of waterproof Russian leather. They were not regularly paid, but at least they were well fitted out.

"So we have another little enemy," said Ferdinand complacently when he heard the news. "Never fear," said his courtiers, "the Snow King will melt when he nears the Southern Sun." Others were of a different mind. "The King of Sweden," wrote Richelieu, "is a Sun which has just risen; he is young, but of vast renown. The ill-treated or banished princes of Germany have turned towards him in their misfortune, as the mariner turns to the Pole Star." Tilly, though equally realistic, was less confused in his comparisons. The veteran Catholic marshal, with service behind him in many forces and under notable leaders, knew a man when he saw one. "The King of Sweden is an enemy both prudent and brave," he remarked, "inured to war and in the flower of his age. His plans are excellent, his resources considerable, his subjects enthusiastically attached to him. His army, composed of Swedes, Germans, Livonians, Finlanders, Scots and English, by its devoted obedience to its leader is blended into one nation. He is a gamester in playing with whom not to have lost is to have won a great deal." This Belgian soldier had followed the progress of Gustavus in his northern achievements and respected what he knew.

IV

Tilly, who was then occupied in southern Germany, had been shrewd to emphasize prudence in his opponent, for it was a quality which to some degree had been obscured by Gustavus's early successes. The Swedish King once remarked to Oxenstierna: "You are too phlegmatic. If somewhat of my heat did not mingle with your phlegm, my affairs would not succeed so well as they do." "Sire," answered the Chancellor, "if my phlegm did not mingle some coolness with your heat, your affairs would not be as prosperous as they are!" Both had laughed heartily, and a stage had now come when the King's heat would need to be tempered continually.

Gustavus was no impetuous amateur like Christian, but a commander who knew that if he were to strike south, towards the heart of the empire, he must first secure his base, and then his communications. He had also to gain allies in Brandenburg and Saxony. These tasks needed skill and patience, and he could afford to fail in none of them. Gustavus had engaged upon an enterprise from which most generals would have flinched. He was opposed by an Emperor whose resources far outstripped his own, whose territory was enormous, and whose authority, in a secular sense, was paramount. He would be soldiering in countries new to him, and if he had not exercised preliminary caution, his mission could have failed before it had the slightest effect on the cause of which he was champion. Though his purpose was to aid the German Protestants, he was too much of a realist to imagine that he would be welcomed unreservedly in the countries where he would need to operate. He would be judged by his actions.

His first opponent was Torquato di Conti, an Italian whose rapacity and extortions earned him the title of the Devil. Here Gustavus's discipline proved valuable, for he was stern against plunderers, and thus earned a reputation for fair dealing among the country people, who were the first to suffer from the war. Once, when he had driven deeper into Germany, he made an oration to his army on the subject. It was not his Swedes who were apt to offend, he said, but Germans in his service. "Had I known that you Germans had been of this temper," he added with the choler to which he was subject, "and of a humour that had borne no more natural affection to your own native country, I would never have saddled horses for your sakes, much less have hazarded mine own kingdom, my life and estate on your behalf." To give weight to his words, an offending lieutenant was hanged on the spot, and a soldier suffered the same fate. When Gustavus plundered and harried, it was for strategic reasons, and when his troops were allowed a limited licence to raise the necessities of life, it was because these could not otherwise be obtained.

Gustavus spent the autumn and winter of 1630 in Pomerania, suborning the old Duke, storming fortresses, winning skirmishes, adapting his strategy and tactics to the nature of the terrain. Before the end of the year he had made himself master of the province, and of as much of neighbouring Mecklenburg as suited his convenience.

As assertive in diplomacy as in war, Gustavus exacted the best possible terms from the French, insisted that his treaty with them should be openly declared rather than remain the secret arrangement Richelieu would have preferred; then he proceeded to elicit support from the Electors of Brandenburg and Saxony. In the case of Brandenburg he had the advantage of a family tie, for he was married to Princess Maria Eleanora of the Electoral house. Although his brother-in-law was no enthusiast for war and, as a Calvinist with Lutheran subjects, had his own difficulties and no army worth the name, yet Gustavus, by a mixture of persuasion, appeal and at one stage the use of force, got his way with him. Saxony was another matter. Her ruler was a Lutheran, but a man not given to rash declarations, more particularly as he was one stage nearer Vienna, the Emperor's capital. Although by the summer of 1631, Gustavus had negotiated a treaty, the ink was scarcely dry on the document when Tilly invaded the country and occupied Leipzig. He had already arrested the Swedish advance by laying siege to Magdeburg, which commanded the Elbe and was a Protestant stronghold in the north. Gustavus, sadly for the city, made no serious attempt at relief, since his force was limited and he had as yet recruited no considerable contingents in Germany to help him in field service. Pappenheim, the hardest hitter among Catholic commanders, took the place by storm, the defenders robbing him of the fruits of victory by burning it to the ground, a disaster, terrible in toll of life, from which even the cathedral was with difficulty saved.

Gustavus had hoped that his capture of Frankfurt on der Oder would divert the Catholic forces, but he was disappointed, and the news from Magdeburg caused him first to retreat and then to take up a position at Werben, at the junction of the Elbe and the Havel. There, in July, he twice repulsed Tilly's forces, which lost 6,000 out of an available total of 21,000 men. Tilly was diverted to Saxony, thus throwing the Elector more firmly into Gustavus's arms.

The Swedes now advanced south, and on 7 September, at Breitenfeld, four miles north of Leipzig, Gustavus faced one of the towering captains of the age in a battle of manoeuvre. Tilly was strong in numbers and confident after years of unbroken success, while Gustavus was compelled to rely partly on a Saxon force of whose value he had no experience, and which, by his own standards, was ineffectively trained. It was the greatest battle of the war, and at noon, when issue was joined, only the boldest would have laid odds on the chances of the Swedes.

The King placed his own men on the right of his battle line, the Saxons on the left. Tilly attacked, but the speed with which Gustavus's light artillery was brought into play threw the Imperial infantry into disorder. Colonel Robert Monro, a Scot who was present and who wrote an account of the battle, said that Tilly, who "prided himself all his lifetime on his dexterity with his great cannon," was "cunningly overshot" by Gustavus, "and from a master turned into a prentice." He was also surprised by the power of the simultaneous three-files fire of the Swedish infantry, and by the fact that Gustavus "interlined" musketeers with his horse. Instead of massed columns, riding almost knee to knee, the Swedes were in small squares, each with room to skirmish, the musketeers being in independent groups. Tilly's officers saw before them a loosely extended chessboard in which cavalry and infantry alternated. For seven hours on end, through clouds of blinding dust, Tilly was to hear the unceasing sound of disciplined Swedish fire.

Although Tilly's left was foiled by Gustavus's right, the Saxons fled. After a promising stand they were unnerved by a charge of Croatian horse, red cloaks streaming in the wind, sabres flashing, uttering outlandish cries. Arnheim, the Saxon general, did his best to rally his men, but when the Elector himself spurred his horse out of battle, never drawing rein until he was well clear, he could hold them no longer. As they left the field, the Saxons fell on the Swedish baggage wagons, carrying off anything they could find.

The Elector's reverse exposed the wing of the Swedes, who now seemed to be at the mercy of an enemy preponderant on the field of battle. It was then that Gustavus showed his resilience and his battle sense, using his mobility to full advantage. Collecting his reserves and most of the cavalry of his successful right wing, he swept around Tilly's position, captured his guns, turned them upon the Imperialists and by a process of near encirclement won an outright victory before sunset. Twelve thousand were killed on the field or on the way back to Leipzig, 7,000 were made prisoner and promptly enlisted into Swedish service, and Tilly, hitherto invincible in set-piece warfare, could muster no more than a remnant of disciplined troops to cover a retreat in which he fought with valour, and in which he himself was thrice wounded.

The Baltic invader had struck terror into the heart of the empire. Vienna was "dumb with fright," and every city on the road thereto began to fortify and garrison. Richelieu and others urged Gustavus to advance at once towards the Imperial capital, but the King had other plans. He marched to the Rhine, made himself supreme in western Germany and then, these objects achieved, put his army into winter quarters between Mainz and Frankfurt. Then he held his court, being joined at Mainz by his Queen and Oxenstierna.

"Believe me," he said to those who tried to induce him to accept the advantageous offers which were soon made to him by the Emperor, "I love a comfortable life as well as any man, and I have no desire to die an early death. The Emperor would readily make a separate peace with me to get me to return to Sweden. But I dare not leave so many innocent people subject to his revenge. Were it not for this, I would soon get me gone."

Gustavus made many truer speeches. He had hitherto scorned the "comfortable life," though he was now enjoying splendour, together with the homage of rulers to whom he had hitherto been a stranger, and the praise of all Protestants. He had tested his abilities, and seeing that he had come so far, he did not mean to get him gone until he had achieved everything in his power to the advantage of Protestant Germany and of Sweden herself.

At the height of his power after Breitenfeld, Gustavus controlled seven armies and nearly 80,000 men within the empire. His forces were on the Rhine, in Franconia, in Hesse, Mecklenburg, Saxony, Saxe-Weimar and in many garrisons. He intended to raise another 100,000, of which a bare 9,000 were to come from Sweden, significant at once of his personal prestige and of what his own country could directly contribute.

Portraits made at this time show Gustavus with a serene and masterful face, far older than his years, his short hair receding. His light blue eyes, wide open and as observant as they could be, having regard to his well-known shortness of sight, were an arresting feature. So was his elegant pointed beard, of a style which in his case was aptly known as imperial. Italian soldiers of fortune called him *il re d'oro* from his tawny colouring, befitting the Lion of the North.

V

With the spring of 1632 and the renewal of campaigning weather, it was Tilly rather than Gustavus who took the offensive, gaining some early advantages. Gustavus went off in pursuit, coming up with his opponent on the banks of the Leck, below Augsburg, where Tilly believed himself to be in an impregnable position. To many generals it might have seemed so, but Gustavus's resource was equal to the occasion. Taking advantage of a favouring wind, his engineers built bridges under cover of smoke screens, in the use of which Gustavus was a pioneer. Then, after artillery bombardment during which the King himself laid sixty pieces, he forced the passage of the river and for a second time routed Tilly's host.

In the course of the encounter Tilly himself was wounded. He managed to leave the field, but died a fortnight later in the citadel of Ingolstadt. Legend took possession of him, and his remains were so well preserved that towards the end of the nineteenth century Lord Acton recalled that he had looked upon his austere features. Until the last few months of his life he had been the most formidable enemy of the Protestant cause, in spite of his having passed the Biblical span of life, and with his death there remained only Wallenstein upon whom the Emperor could call, and Wallenstein, like Achilles, was sulking in his tent.

Gustavus now found the way open to Munich, and he occupied the Bavarian capital. His move distressed many, among them Richelieu, whose firm political support of Maximilian, the Bavarian Elector, had brought upon French ambassadors more than one stinging outburst from Gustavus. Maximilian, Richelieu believed, was the staunchest among France's Catholic friends within the empire, and although the French statesman was deceived as to the worth of his ally, he now perceived that Gustavus would soon be utterly beyond his control.

When Ferdinand and the Catholic princes appealed to Wallenstein in their despair, they put themselves in the power of a man on whom they had inflicted an injury, one whose pride was such that he would not scruple to dictate his own conditions. Master of finance as well as of war, Wallenstein was living in splendour, apparently aloof from affairs, but actually administering his duchy with skill, and in secret negotiation not only with Gustavus for a joint expedition against Vienna, but with Arnheim, who had been one of his colonels. His army was his own, and when he decided to act on the Emperor's summons, it was with the reservation that he would obey when obedience suited his purpose, but no further. He would never allow himself to be dismissed a second time, and if he reappeared at the head of the Imperial forces, it would be as absolute chief. When the Emperor expressed a wish that his son the King of Hungary should

be associated with the general, Wallenstein replied with blasphe-
mous arrogance: "Never will I accept a divided command—no,
not even were God Himself to be my colleague in office. I must
command alone, or not at all."

Wallenstein's battalions duly assembled, and he took up a
fortified position near Nürnberg with some 60,000 men, many of
them experienced in war. Gustavus stood at the foot of the Alps,
and his adherents wondered, as they had wondered after Breitenfeld, whether he meant to cross them and to attack Catholicism
at its centre. Gustavus, conscious as ever of his long line of communications and of the limitations of his resources, decided that
it was better to face Wallenstein at once and defeat him in open
fight.

Wallenstein knew the King's strength and weakness. Gustavus
was peerless in battle, but he was in a critical position, five hundred miles from his base, and with an army dwindling from sickness and privation. Wallenstein refused a pitched battle, repulsed
six attacks against the heights of Alte Veste, and when Gustavus
moved towards the Danube, expecting to be followed, he refused
to be drawn. "The Snow King has blunted his horns," he declared
contemptuously. "He will soon be destroyed."

Gustavus then made a strategic misjudgement. If, after his repulse, he had done as Oxenstierna advised and advanced along
the valley of the Danube into Ferdinand's hereditary provinces,
the Imperialists must have followed him at a disadvantage, and
could not have reached Vienna before him if the King had decided to make Ferdinand's city his object. Instead, perhaps dis-
trusting his strength for such an enterprise, Gustavus turned
westward, towards Swabia, and Wallenstein disregarded his movements. Gathering his forces together, he threw them upon Saxony,
which had refused to give up the Swedish alliance. And when
Wallenstein made himself master of Leipzig, Gustavus contrived
one of his astonishing marches—two hundred miles in eighteen
days—to catch up with his opponent on the plain of Lützen, about
fifteen miles from the city.

If the Saxons had been truer to their treaty, or if an order to
rejoin at once which Wallenstein sent to Pappenheim had miscarried, Gustavus would have had the advantage of numbers,
and would have made that advantage felt. As it was, when the

fog lifted at about eleven o'clock on the morning of 6 November, 1632, and Gustavus gave signal for battle, he faced odds. They favoured an enemy of whom few had got the better.

On the right, where he was in personal command, Gustavus broke the Imperialists. Pappenheim was wounded in the lung, dying in his coach on the Leipzig road, staining Wallenstein's vital letter of recall with his blood. Then came news that the Swedish centre had been driven back, and that the left, under the Duke of Saxe-Weimar, had suffered a check. Gustavus moved across to restore his forces, riding towards his centre in company with the Duke of Lauenburg. A pistol shot broke his arm in a fierce melee. "It is nothing; follow me," he said, but then, his strength failing, he reined his horse, muttering to his companion: "Cousin, take me hence, for I am stricken."

As the King turned, an Austrian trooper shouted: "Art *thou* here? I have long sought for thee . . ." at the same time firing his carbine. Gustavus wore no armour, for an earlier wound had made the weight unbearable; instead he favoured a stout "polish coat," but it was now too little protection. The King fell from his horse with the cry: "My God!" and he was seen alive no more.

As his charger flew in terror along the line, wild with pain from a neck wound, the empty saddle telling the soldiers of the tragedy, word spread through the ranks that Gustavus was killed or a prisoner. Instead of breaking, the Swedes fought with the strength of despair until the fog returned, and nightfall brought the battle to a close. "Death had no terror for the lowly," wrote Schiller, "since it had stricken the anointed head." The men whom Gustavus had trained and led so superlatively held their ground, but even they could not secure an outright victory.

When fighting ended the King was discovered, a mass of wounds, his body trodden by the feet of horses, beneath a heap of dead. For a comparable moment in war it is necessary to recall a scene far later, when, as the ocean swell rose with approaching darkness, his fleet saw no light burning in Nelson's cabin. With the soldier as with the sailor, their inspiration long outlasted them. They lived to the limit, and they were granted the end they would have asked.

"The devil is very near at hand to those who are accountable to none but God for their actions," said the King one day to his chaplain, who had found him, as so often, reading his Bible. They were the words of a thoughtful and imperious man.

Gustavus died in his thirty-eighth year, many of his problems unsolved, some of his aims unformulated. Whatever account he rendered to his Maker, friend and enemy were in accord that he had shirked no task for the benefit of his country, that he had considered nothing beyond him and that he held true to his own standards. Seldom in history has there been a more majestic pattern.

3 . Struggle by land and sea

Just as the Swedes stood firm at Lützen, and though they lost their leader did not yield their ground, so did their efforts continue generally. They had staked much, and however long and complex the course of the war, they did not intend to withdraw from it without extracting every reasonable reward from friends and as much as possible from enemies.

The sustaining gifts of Oxenstierna as a statesman were such that, in spite of the death of his incomparable sovereign, and of the fact that, not being a crowned head, he could not deal on the same footing with princes, he maintained Sweden's high position with a skill unequalled by any northern statesman. This was never easy, and it was sometimes daunting, for the Swedes were rarely welcome in the lands where they fought; the drain on their manpower continued; and military reverses at last lost them their reputation for invincibility.

Oxenstierna continued to draw strength from France, but it was his own abilities and the sheer professional skill of Gustavus's soldiers, the "blue boys," with yellow and blue colours which grew so familiar and were often so dreaded in Germany, which maintained Sweden's prestige. And when peace was at last concluded, Oxenstierna brought her the reward of an important place in the councils of Europe, some stake in the affairs of the empire, and establishment on the southern shores of the Baltic. The gamble of 1630 paid off.

In the later phases of a war which settled nothing that could not have been arranged diplomatically, and which left most of Germany a stricken desert, Christian IV's ambitions for Denmark revived. He had succeeded to his throne at an even earlier age than Gustavus Adolphus, but while his fellow monarch became a legend in his lifetime, Christian's case was different. He was now old, and all he had achieved was the financial ruin of his country, the founding of a Norwegian capital which was long to bear his name, a large family of quarrelsome children, legitimate and otherwise, some enchanting building and the likelihood of physical and political encirclement by Sweden and her allies. Christian's principal remaining assets were enduring courage and a strong navy. It was his navy which saved him from ending his sixty-year reign in exile, though it could not shield him from humiliation.

As early as 1641, Christian succeeded in bringing about the adoption of preliminaries to a general peace within the empire. In the event, negotiations languished, and it was not unnatural that from the summer of the following year the King's jealous animosity against Sweden should begin to revive. If he could not be the chief agent in a pacification, Christian might perhaps essay, at long last, successful war. He assured the Emperor that if special consideration were given to Denmark's claims, Christian, despite his Protestantism, would espouse the Habsburg cause. Denmark's particular claims were the Archepiscopal See of Bremen, which Christian wished to be secured for one of his sons, and sovereignty over Hamburg, a free city which he was then preparing to blockade.

The King's designs, which were inimical to Sweden, became known to Oxenstierna, and in the name of the regency for Queen Christina, he sent secret orders to Torstensson to invade Danish territory. Torstensson was then campaigning in Moravia, and nothing suited him better than a march to the north and an attack on a hereditary foe. In December 1643, while Christian was unprepared except by sea and scoffing at the very idea of a sudden blow from Sweden, Torstensson moved into Holstein. Duke Frederick of Holstein-Gottorp bought neutrality by opening his gates, and Jutland lay almost defenceless.

Before the end of January 1644 the Swedes were masters of

the Danish mainland, and they waited only for the freezing over of the Little Belt to attack the island of Fyen. Their plan was to conquer Danish-held Scania and Jutland simultaneously, then, with Dutch help, to transport their victorious armies to the inter-mediate islands, including Zealand, on which lay Christian's capital of Copenhagen. But in February, Horn, in the east, was checked by the stubborn defence of Malmö, while Torstensson's bridge of ice to Fyen never materialized. The fate of Denmark now depended upon command of the sea.

At this crisis Christian, at the age of sixty-seven, saved his state, though narrowly. From the moment of Torstensson's ad-vance he had worked with the energy of younger days to save his islands. He even dared to take the offensive by attacking Göte-borg, though the plan was too bold. In May his fleet entered the North Sea; the King, sailing in person, encountered a Dutch armament which had been collected by Louis de Geer on behalf of Sweden, and compelled it to return. In the following month he faced a Swedish fleet under Klas Fleming and engaged in a series of running fights. The principal battle, fought on 1 July, was known as Kolberg Heath, after the bleak stretch of coast be-tween the island of Femern and Kiel Fjord. The contest was stubborn, and it ended in the Swedes' being pursued into the fjord, where Fleming was later mortally wounded by a shot from a shore battery.

In action as in preparation, Christian showed feverish zeal. At the Battle of Kolberg Heath, where he commanded a squadron, he suffered many wounds, from one of which he lost the sight of an eye. His flagship, the *Trefoldighed*, was attacked by four en-emy ships, but Christian, despite his wounds, never left the deck, and if he did not gain an outright victory, he saved the day and assured, on a longer term view, the security of his capital.

Sea fighting afterwards continued, the Dutch, alert as always to maintain what they considered to be a judicious balance of power in the Baltic, so vital to their trading interests, taking an active part on Sweden's behalf, and the naval rivalry was marked by at least one sad episode. This was the execution of the Danish admiral Galt for allowing a Swedish force to escape him. It was an act of injustice liable to happen with Christian at sea. The

King was not normally in supreme naval command, but he was able to interfere as and when he would, and he was in sore need of a scapegoat. Galt provided one.

On wider grounds, it was against the interest of Mazarin (who had succeeded Richelieu as the grey eminence of the Thirty Years' War) that Swedish forces should be embroiled away from Germany, the main theatre, and he now urged Oxenstierna to make peace with Denmark. There were many in Stockholm to argue the same course, and in August 1645 a treaty was signed at Brömsebro. It was highly advantageous to Sweden. Her ancient freedom from dues in the Sound and the Belts was confirmed, with certain reservations, and it was extended to the commerce of her possessions in the eastern Baltic and in Germany. Holland, on the eastern shore of the Sound, was ceded to her for thirty years, and she acquired the Norwegian provinces of Jämtland and Härjedalen, together with the islands of Goteland, once famous as a centre of Hanse trading, and Osel, commanding the Gulf of Riga. These were splendid gains. As for the Dutch, they had already humiliated Christian by sailing unchallenged through the Sound. By a separate agreement they were given concessions which reduced their payment of Baltic dues to an inconsiderable sum. Christian's second intervention in the affairs of Europe had cost him even more than his first.

The King is said to have flung the Brömsebro Treaty in the face of Korfits Ulfeldt, the royal son-in-law who conducted negotiations on the Danish side. It was an understandable gesture on the part of a sovereign who began his reign with dazzling hopes and who died, less than three years after he had made peace, with the knowledge that Denmark had lost primacy in the north.

II

The ending to the Danish war marked the peak of Oxenstierna's influence. Henceforward, for the remaining nine years of his life, he was in gradual decline, not by reason of his age, for he was younger than Christian IV, but because Queen Christina, a true Vasa in her imperious habits, would tolerate no preceptor, not even the man so regarded by her father. Oxenstierna was permitted to gather Sweden's harvest from the Thirty Years' War, but that was the limit of his achievement. Even in the negotiations for peace it was John Adler Salvius, a favourite of the Queen's, whose advice was preferred before that of the Chancellor's elder son, who, with Salvius, represented his country when terms were propounded.

When the Swedes first stated their demands, to which weight was given by the fact that their forces were in occupation of parts of the empire to which they could attach no reasonable claim, they were outrageous. They included Silesia, the whole of Pomerania, Mecklenburg, Wismar and the neighbouring island of Poel, the Archbishopric of Bremen, the Bishopric of Verden with certain other ecclesiastical lands, and "compensation" for the officers and soldiers of the Swedish Army. They asked for much which they did not expect to acquire, but as is so often the case with armed bargainers, they got a great deal, for they were backed by France.

The Silesian demand was soon dropped, as every plenipotentiary knew it must be. Pomerania, upon which Gustavus Adolphus had set his heart, was another matter. The Elector of Brandenburg had an indisputable right to the territory after the death of the last native duke, but Swedish insistence was such that it was agreed that an old division between eastern and western Pomerania should be revived. Brandenburg acquired the eastern part, Sweden the western, including the island of Rügen and the town of Stettin. Wismar and Poel also fell to their share, together with the secularized Archbishopric of Bremen and the adjoining See of Verden. By reason of her possessions, some of them held as fiefs of the empire, Sweden would henceforward have a seat and vote in the Imperial Diet. A contribution of seven million dollars was also levied—the original demand had been for twenty million—"in satisfaction of the Queen of Sweden's militia."

When added to her gains by the Treaty of Brömsebro, the accession of territory resulting in 1648 from the Peace of Westphalia made Sweden a considerable country. Her possessions, though scattered, included valuable footholds, two of them— Bremen and Verden—well within Germany, with a natural outlet not into the Baltic but into the North Sea. It was true that they would inevitably give rise to envy and dispute, that administration from Stockholm would call for uncommon skill and that in the event of renewed war some might be hard to defend. Moreover, Denmark had now been given thorough cause to fear encirclement.

Had Queen Christina been more stable, or had her successor been less ruthless and ambitious, Sweden's position in Europe, which held such great promise, and which reflected so brilliantly the guidance of Oxenstierna, could have brought rich rewards to a virile and expanding people. There was even a colony in the New World, on the banks of the Delaware River. But Christina, in many things perverse, lacked genius for statecraft and application for affairs. It was as if her father had bequeathed her, along with his kingdom, most gifts but that of judgement. "Thou hast made me so great," she once cried out to her Creator, "that if Thou gavest me the whole realm of earth, my heart were not content." Like Elizabeth I of England, Christina knew Greek, as well as Latin, French and German. Her classical reading could have shown her that the highest wisdom, even in princes, derives from realizing that humanity is limited. "Be modest in thine own conceit and in desire." The golden words, which echo through Greek tragedy, found no response in the Queen of Sweden.

Her extravagance was fantastic, and she was a stranger to self-discipline. She was urged continually to provide for the welfare of her country through marriage. Her cousin and playmate, Charles Gustavus of the Palatine, became her expectant lover and the choice of her people; but Christina regarded marriage as repulsive servitude, and she resolved never to endure it. Instead, she wrung from a reluctant Parliament, and from the Imperial Diet, an acknowledgement of Charles Gustavus not as her future Consort, but as her successor. A year later, in spite of Oxenstierna's protest, Charles's male descendants were placed in the line of succession.

The Queen's enthusiasms included Oliver Cromwell, the English soldier-statesman who had once so reverenced her father. "If blind fortune would one day let me look upon this face," she wrote after Cromwell had sent her his portrait, "I would think it one of the greatest graces she ever did," and she received his envoy, Whitelocke, with much courtesy, accepting a mastiff from him which she described as a "huge dogge." Whitelocke even tried to dissuade her from an act which she was openly beginning to consider—abdication. He made bold to tell her the story of the old man who determined to resign his properties to his son, but on the day of the ceremony, being asked to sit in the kitchen because of his inconvenient habits, revoked proceedings, "having resolved to spit in the parlour as long as he lived. So," concluded the fatherly Whitelocke, "I hope will a wise young lady."

Christina was, however, determined, and this was fortunate, for she left chaos behind her, and this must have intensified had she continued her reign. Within ten years she had doubled the number of noble families, and had endowed them with grants from royal estates so lavish that she had little left to offer. She alienated her peasants and emptied her treasury. She ended her reign by making known her conversion to the Catholic faith. There could no longer have been a place for Christina as head of a Lutheran state, though her character was such that even the Pope, despite unwearied patience and tact, found little satisfaction in his new spiritual subject. Christina intended to be a Catholic with a difference, and in this aim at least she succeeded for the rest of her life.

Charles X Gustavus, more generally known as Charles X, was in the line of Sweden's large-scale kings. Despite awkward bulk and a coarseness differing widely from them, he was a worthy nephew of Gustavus Adolphus and a befitting grandsire for Charles XII. A soldier who had learned his business in the German war, he crowded his short life with every kind of activity. His first resolve was to make a start upon repair of the damage wrought by his predecessor. Crown lands began to be resumed, in the interest both of the state and of economic husbandry, a process which made little headway at the time, but which was to be resumed on an effective scale by his successor. Charles then made a gesture which went straight to the nation's heart. Despite Axel Oxenstierna's opposition to the arrangements for the succession, the King knew him for the greatest living Swede. His conviction was as strong as that of any Englishman regarding Winston Churchill after the Second World War. With a magnanimous gesture, Charles turned to Oxenstierna for counsel—and when, in August 1654, the old man died, he appointed his son Erik in his place.

III

Wise as he proved in actions of domestic government, and assured as he was of the support of the greater part of his people, the last years of Charles's reign were those of warfare on an increasingly reckless scale. His schemes and ambitions at one time or another closely involved every country bordering the Baltic, and two sea powers, the Netherlands and Britain, whose territory lay beyond it. His problems, achievements and failures were both immediate and prophetic. From the events of his career could be deduced something of the pattern of his country's future.

The King's earlier steps were designed to secure his westerly foothold. His marriage in October 1654 to Hedwig Eleonora, the second daughter of the Duke of Holstein-Gottorp, was a move against future hostility by Denmark, particularly near the Elbe and Weser. This was all the more necessary since territories in Bremen were in revolt against Swedish mastership. The danger was overcome by coercive measures, the success of which enabled Charles to sweep into his ranks a body of mercenaries from northern Germany. His larger aim was against Poland.

There were excuses for the war other than the fact that war appeared to be Sweden's most lucrative industry. The Polish Vasa still refused to recognize their rivals as lawful sovereigns across the water. Poland, moreover, adhered to an earlier demand that the Swedes withdraw from Livonia and pay compensation for the throne which Sigismund had forfeited half a century before. To maintain this attitude was misguided at a time when Poles, Cossacks, Tartars and Russians were struggling in the Ukraine, when the Tsar, by marching into Lithuania, had secured many strongholds including what was then the border fortress of Smolensk, and when the Polish province of West Prussia appeared ripe for seizure.

If West Prussia was indeed the plum which attracted his closest attention, Charles's grander design, as developed by events, seems to have been to incorporate the whole southeastern littoral of the Baltic, and to buttress his empire with dependent principalities carved out of the interior of Poland.

In July 1655, after mustering a total force of nearly 50,000 troops for all theatres of war and garrisoning duties, Charles set out from his capital, which he never saw again. He was in high confidence. His country was recovering. His military experience was considerable, and the famous discipline of the Swedes seemed to have been restored.

Charles's immediate successes were sensational. Using Swedish Pomerania as his base, Arvid Wittenberg, followed by the King in person, hastened towards Warsaw. The Polish capital, with all its stores, surrendered unconditionally. John Casimir, the reigning monarch, who was Sigismund Vasa's second son, fled to Silesia, and the opportunity seemed now to have come for the move against East Prussia. Instead, Charles marched southward and reduced Cracow, the ancient Polish capital, after an eight-week siege. Many nobles, the future hero John Sobieski among them, did homage and received fiefs from Swedish hands.

Even Charles X could scarcely have expected that his moves would be viewed with indifference by powers outside Poland, and more especially by Frederick William of Brandenburg, known to his country as the Great Elector. Frederick William was already attempting to cross the Swedish plan by snatching West Prussia while Charles was engaged elsewhere. But he was cowed by the speed and energy of a king who marched from end to end of Poland, took Thorn and Ebling, and encircled his opponent in his Prussian capital. Early in 1656, Frederick William assented to the Treaty of Königsberg, which bound him to do homage to Sweden for East Prussia, hitherto under the Polish crown. He agreed, moreover, to surrender half its customs dues and to supply the Swedes with 1,500 auxiliaries. He received in return the Bishopric of Ermeland, which rounded off his duchy, and he preserved his army by this act of humiliation. Europe, as well as the Great Elector, now awoke to the fact that Sweden had found a successor to Gustavus Adolphus, and Charles, rejoicing in the birth of an heir, needed only to conquer Danzig, or so it seemed, to crown his triumph.

But the King had in fact succeeded too well too swiftly. Swedish discipline slackened. Polish spirit revived. The successful seventy-day defence of the monastery of Czestochowa by a handful of nobles, monks and soldiers against an army in array convinced devout patriots that God was on their side. John Casimir returned to Polish soil and solemnly consecrated his kingdom to the Blessed Virgin.

Charles strove to crush the rising by a march southward in the depth of winter. In February he won a costly victory at Golombo, far beyond Warsaw, and then prepared to besiege Lemberg; but his supplies were short, his losses had been crippling, the season was against him, as was the nature of the terrain, while he was far from his bases. As if all this were not enough, three separate forces were converging upon him, and it was only by stoic endurance, continued over many weeks, that he regained Warsaw. Although he sped from the capital to reduce Danzig, he thus allowed John Casimir to recapture his greatest city. Charles was faced with the fact that the winning of battles and temporary occupations were no substitute for true conquest. As so often in the past, Swedish resources were being stretched too far.

IV

At this stage crisis followed crisis. The Tsar began campaigning in the Baltic provinces, where Magnus de la Gardie, with a token force, strove to defend territory which his father had won for Sweden. Pope and Emperor were alike hostile, as were the Danes. The Dutch, determined at all costs to safeguard their mercantile interests in the Baltic, took the little colony on the Delaware as a warning of their distant striking power, and this was a loss which Sweden never made good. Dutch and Swedes combined well at sea. The Swedes fared badly when Holland changed sides.

One single ally might yet be purchased—the Elector of Brandenburg. Frederick William had much to fear from the return of John Casimir to Poland, whose allegiance he had renounced, and at least something to hope for from the Swedish conquests in Prussia. He signed a new treaty with Charles, the immediate effect of which was to increase the Brandenburg auxiliaries in the Swedish Army to 4,000 men.

Charles then led a force of 18,000 to the reconquest of Warsaw, which was defended by John Casimir and 50,000 Poles and Tartars. Overruling the Elector, the King insisted on battle, and after two days of manoeuvring he won an outright victory and entered the city. His feat raised Swedish prestige to new heights, and checked for a time the growth of a hostile coalition—yet it was not enough. The Elector refused to advance south of Warsaw; John Casimir would not come to terms; and Danzig, centre of the corn trade and a lucrative source of revenue to a mercantile nation, was relieved by a Dutch fleet.

With Poland still turbulent, Ingria and Livonia threatened, the Baltic itself in dispute and Sweden under some threat of invasion, Charles was forced to abandon his grand design. He had shown himself a notable tactician; a man of swift decision, ruthless energy and so open to military innovation that a primitive machine gun is among the surviving relics of his army; but his abilities were not matched by wisdom in his treatment of other states, though there were indications that even here he might learn from adversity. For in September 1656, Erik Oxenstierna negotiated the Treaty of Ebling with the Dutch, who were granted conditions as "most favoured nation" in Swedish-controlled sea trade. Two months later, after the sudden death of his Chancellor, Charles himself concluded the Treaty of Labau, by which Frederick William received full and perpetual sovereignty over East Prussia. Sweden thus consented that the Baltic coast from Memel to the eastern outlet of the Vistula should remain outside her sphere of influence, and she gained a breathing space.

Immediate business concluded, Charles, in league with George Rákóczy, Prince of Transylvania, turned once more upon Poland, and in a campaign which lasted through most of the year 1657, marched and countermarched against opponents with whom he could seldom close. He was soon engaged with an Austrian force which the Emperor advanced against him, and in the summer Frederick III of Denmark declared war. Charles had not, after all, used his precious time with profit.

The Danes, their nobles apart, were more united against

Charles than they had ever been under Christian IV, and at first their moves were promising. Marshal Anders Bilde took Bremen and Verden, while Frederick, confident in his fleet and in his friendship with Holland, lay in wait in the Baltic to cut Charles off at his first sign of a move homewards.

He misjudged his man. Charles, pressed as he was, had no thought of flight. Committing the defence of Sweden itself to Per Brahe and the peasants, leaving the Polish and Russian wars to smoulder on, he made a prodigious march from Brecz, in the heart of Poland, to Stettin, at the head of 6,000 picked men. There he was reinforced by Karl Gustav Wrangel, and within two months of the opening of the conflict, 13,000 Swedes had crossed the border of Holstein.

The Duke placed no obstacle in the way of his son-in-law, while Hamburg, a steadfast opponent of the Danish monarchy, supplied the invaders with every necessity. The Danes were driven from Bremen, and the achievement of Torstensson thirteen years earlier seemed about to be repeated. At this juncture Charles learned that the Brandenburg Elector (deserted, as he complained, by his Swedish ally) had sold his alliance to Poland, and Charles was now faced with the possibility that he might soon be imprisoned in the Jutland peninsula by a combined force of Poles, Brandenburgers and Austrians. Even if he cut his way through, he had no means of return to Sweden, for the Danish Navy thwarted every move by sea.

The peril was averted by a blend of daring, skill and good fortune. On the night of 24 October, 1647, Wrangel stormed Frederiksodde, on the shores of the Little Belt, where Bilde was mortally wounded, and 3,000 Danes laid down their arms. Three months later the Swedes astounded Europe by marching across the ice and conquering Funen in the face of a hostile force. It was a feat in the accomplishment of which two squadrons of horse and the carriages of the King and the French Ambassador were lost when, under pressure, the precarious bridge betrayed them.

The cold continued, and a pledge by his young quartermaster-general, Erik Dahlberg, that he could guide the army safely across the Great Belt determined Charles to seek Frederick in his Zealand capital. On 4 February the Swedes quitted Funen by

night, and in the course of a week passed from island to island
in southeasterly progress. Langeland, Lolland and Falster were
in turn conquered, and when Zealand itself was reached without serious check, Copenhagen became at the mercy of the invader. Danish commissioners were already on their way to treat
for peace, and neither the severity of Charles's demands nor his
choice of the traitor Korfits Ulfeld as negotiator warranted Frederick in breaking off discussion. Before the close of the month the
Treaty of Roskilde sealed Denmark's humiliation. Sweden had
broken the ring of her foes, and Charles had reached the height
of his achievement.

"Roskilde" is inscribed upon Charles's statue at Stockholm,
and with reason. By the terms of the treaty, Danish power was
excluded from the south of the Scandinavian peninsula. Scania,
Halland and Blekinge became Swedish. So did the island of Bornholm, the sole remaining Danish outpost towards the eastern
Baltic. Trondheim was acquired from Norway, together with the
maritime region of Baahus. Other clauses provided for the
transfer of troops to Swedish service, the renunciation of anti-
Swedish alliances, the closure of the Sound against fleets hostile
to Sweden and an indemnity for the Duke of Holstein-Gottorp.
In a three-day round of festivity which the sovereigns enjoyed
at Frederiksborg, Charles, between flagons, could have reflected
on the extraordinary ending to his Polish adventure. He had
marched far, he had put Europe into a fluster and he was now
reassured by the approval of Holland and England, maritime
powers who congratulated themselves upon the fact that as the
entrance to the Baltic lay between emulous crowns, they might
look for relief from extortion at the hands of a sole owner. In
England, General Lambert sagely remarked of the Sound: "It is
best in the hands that, it seems, are least able to keep it."

Charles's prospects had also grown brighter elsewhere in the
Baltic. The Great Elector was already penitent. The Tsar, meeting with repulse, was growing weary of his struggle for an outlet towards the west. The King of Sweden had only to abandon
Prussia, and the remnants of the forces against him would dis-
solve. His country could then enjoy that spell of peace which
was necessary for her to assimilate her new acquisitions and to
renew strength which even successful war had sapped. In Feb-

ruary concord in Scandinavia seemed assured. Less than six months later its foundations were shattered by the victorious hand, and the catastrophe of Charles's fierce brief reign had begun.

The treaty made at Roskilde had in fact given Charles too much, and he now dreamed of uniting the three ancient crowns of Scandinavia upon his own head. The details of the treaty negotiations were deliberately protracted, and when Charles demanded of the Danes that they help in closing the Sound to all foreign ships of war, he overreached himself, for Frederick, in the last resort, relied upon his Dutch alliance, and this was a provision which Holland could never endure.

On 7 July, at Gottorp, Charles secured the concurrence of his Parliament to renewal of war. Eleven days later he ordered Wrangel, who with his army had remained on Danish soil, to complete the operations of the last campaign by attacking, in turn, Copenhagen, Kronborg and Christiania, across the Skagerrak. By 7 August, when Charles himself rejoined the army, Copenhagen seemed a doomed city. It was saved by Frederick's personal courage, and by the spirit of the townspeople. Instead of the swift success upon which Charles had reckoned, he was faced with the prospect of a bloody siege, and by widespread revolt in districts he had already conquered.

Poles, Brandenburgers and Austrians were reuniting, and although the Swedes soon took Kronborg, and thus for a time held both shores of the Sound, the action had the effect of sharpening the existing anxiety in Holland and England about the continuance and efforts of the campaigns. The Dutch attitude toward Sweden was summarized in five words—"not a grain of Denmark." England was temporarily stunned by the death of Oliver Cromwell, and more inclined to Sweden than to Denmark. Such intervention as she continued was ineffective, and it was a Dutch fleet under Obdam which forced the issue. In one of the more decisive naval battles of northern Europe, fought on 29 October, 1658, Obdam sailed through the Sound, defeated the Swedes, eased the pressure off Copenhagen and frustrated Charles's ambitions, this time forever.

The act, which cost the lives of two Dutch flag officers, Witte de With and Pieter Floriszoon, was far more significant than

mere interference in the affairs of neighbouring states. Uninter-
rupted passage into the Baltic was vital to both England and
Holland, not only by reason of the carrier trade, in which the
Dutch had predominance, but because both countries relied
upon the region for essential naval supplies—timber, particularly for masts and spars, hemp, sailcloth, tar, pitch, tallow, resin,
oil, brimstone, iron. They were rivals, armed or in commerce, but
here their interests coincided. If Obdam, allied to Denmark, defeated the Swedes without the aid of single Danish vessel, it
was because Van Beuningen, the Dutch representative at Frederick's court, had boasted of his country's fleet: "The oaken keys
of the Sound lie in the docks of Amsterdam." Those keys had
been brought north to ensure that the vital door was kept open.

As for England, even Richard Cromwell, the ill-equipped successor to Oliver as Protector of the Realm, took such steps as his
resources allowed in preparation for naval intervention in the
Baltic, should this have proved necessary. Obdam forestalled
him, thus doing ultimate service to both countries. Charles X
might fight with Danes and Poles and Brandenburgers, but Europe's sea business must go on, and the Baltic must continue to
furnish the means for doing so. The matter was cardinal.

v

Much of the year 1659 was taken up with negotiations at the
so-called Concert of The Hague, at which Dutch, English
and French jointly attempted to force terms upon the Baltic
combatants. Their intention was to restore peace in the north on
the conditions laid down at Roskilde, which suited all three
powers.

This intervention, which in many ways was unwelcome even
to the Danes, who had long boasted their naval supremacy in
the Ostsee, was concurrent with Swedish reverses in the Danish
islands. At Nyborg, in Fyen, one of Charles's armies capitulated,
though the victors could not prevail upon de Ruyter, who commanded the Dutch armament in nearby waters, to convoy them
across the Great Belt to Zealand, where the Swedes could have
been faced with total defeat.

At this stage Charles sought earnestly, and at last genuinely, for peace. From the Poles he demanded only that John Casimir renounce his claim to Sweden and Livonia, and that in Prussia the state of affairs which obtained before 1654 be restored. In the west he asked that the powers of the Concert guarantee the conditions he aimed at, and that southern Norway, at least, should also remain his. To support his claims, he sent the aged field marshal Lars Kagg on a winter sortie up the eastern shore of the Kattegat. "Horsemen have frozen to death in the saddle and sentinels at their posts," wrote the doughty commander, "but not a man has been heard to murmur." But the effort failed, as did that of Charles's grandson later, before the walls of Hald, a border fortress upon which its sovereign conferred the style of Frederikshald. On the night of 12 February, 1660, without much warning, Charles himself succumbed to fever at Göteborg, being then little more than thirty-seven years old. The ambitious and capable successor of Gustavus Adolphus died at much the same age as his uncle. He left comparable problems behind him.

Two months later peace was made at Oliva with the Poles, by the regency acting for the the infant Charles XI. On behalf of his family, John Casimir renounced all claim to the throne of Sweden. West Prussia was confirmed in Poland's possession, and Livonia remained with Sweden. In East Prussia the Elector of Brandenburg was freed from the vassalage of any power, while Denmark, in a later treaty, recovered Trondheim and Bornholm, though in other respects the provisions of Roskilde were confirmed. The closure of the Baltic against foreign ships of war was abandoned.

A year later the Tsar of Russia consented to withdraw from his Baltic conquests, and for the first time in the seventeenth century long-enduring Sweden was at peace with everyone. She had trained superlative armies, with leaders worthy to use them, and she had held her place as a European power, though the prospect of large-scale disaster had faced her more than once, and she had shown little realization of the value and use of sea power. If politically her history had been checkered, and if many of her domestic problems—for instance, the proper balance of interest between her nobles, burgesses, clergy and peasants—had not been settled, she had maintained a tradition of warlike qualities, which she would continue and extend under other rulers.

VI

Among the greater sovereigns of Sweden, Charles XI has attracted the least attention, which accords with the secluded manner in which he spent much of his life. Nevertheless, it was his single-minded resolution which in the end enabled his country to return to what approached prosperity, after standing on the brink of ruin. Militarily, his achievement was to defend the provisions of his father's treaty of Roskilde, which the Danes, not unnaturally, did their utmost to reverse.

The reign began under a formidable-sounding regency in which the most important members were the aged Per Brahe, Gustaf Bonde, whose difficult business it was to stave off national bankruptcy, and Magnus Gabriel de la Gardie, who believed in taking subsidies from the French. The government in Paris continued to be prepared to support Sweden in the expectation of military services in the north which would help causes serving French interests. De la Gardie's idea was to do as little as possible to earn rewards, yet to keep just on the right side of his paymaster.

Louis XIV was not the man to be duped indefinitely by a Swedish chancellor, and after fourteen years' recuperation from the exploits of Charles X, the patient Swedes found themselves embroiled in an unpopular German war in French interests, with the Dutch hostile at sea and Denmark eager to avenge past humiliation. Wrangel, experienced general though he was, seemed no longer capable of working out a plan of operations, while his opponent, the Great Elector of Brandenburg, had by now a seasoned army at command. He won a victory at Fehrbellin which weakened Sweden's position in Germany still further, and temporarily shattered her military prestige.

In the hour of disaster Charles assumed full responsibility for the government of his country, and began to play the part of a dictator. At first nothing went right. Denmark, as was almost in-

SWEDISH TERRITORY
IN 1661

*Average limit of winter
pack-ice: in exceptional
seasons, such as 1657/8,
further areas are frozen*

0   50   100   150   200
MILES

N
O
R
W
A
Y

TRONDHEIM

Trondheim

JÄMTLAND

HERJEDALEN

L
A
P
L
A
N
D

FINMARK

Tornea

Uleaborg

Gulf of Bothnia

F I N L A N D

Wilmanstrand   Kexholm
Varala   Viborg
C
Nystad
Abo   St. Petersburg
Aland   Helsingfors
Is.   Sveaborg

Christiania

Filipstad   Upsala   Reval   Narva
Karlstad   ESTHONIA   INGRIA
Frederikshald   Skepperholm
Eskilstuna   Stockholm   Dago   Kardis
Uddevalla   Pernau
Norrköping Nyköping   Osel   LIVONIA
Linköping   Marienburg
Gullberg Jonköping   Wisby   Windau   Riga
Göteborg   Gothland   COURLAND
Elfsborg   Libau
Aalborg Halmstad   Wexio Oland
DENMARK   Knäred Calmar
JUTLAND   Helsingborg Vittsjö Bromsebro
Aarhus   Landskrona Karlskrona   Memel
Frederiksodde Copenhagen Karlshamm
Roskilde Malmo Kristianstad
Odense Korsor
Nyborg   Ystad Bornholm
Schleswig   Kolberg Königsberg Pillau
Gottorp   Treptow Oliva Wehlau
Itzehoe Rostock Stralsund Danzig Elbing EAST PRUSSIA
Altona Wismar Pomerania Cammin Marienburg
Bremen Lübeck MECKLENBURG Stettin Gottnow WEST
Hamburg   Garz Damm PRUSSIA
Verden
BRANDENBURG   Thorn
P O L A N D
Warsaw

B
A
L
T
I
C

S
E
A

evitable, declared war. Christian V, who had succeeded Frederick III, overwhelmed Sweden's ally, the Duke of Holstein-Gottorp, and took Wismar. The Elector, following up his victory, overran Bremen, Verden and Swedish Pomerania with local allies, while in a battle off Öland, fought on 1 June, 1676, a combined Danish-Dutch fleet overwhelmed the defenders, and the way was clear for a Danish invasion of the lost province of Scania.

Once more sea power had operated against Sweden, but as her opponents at Öland were Cornelius Tromp, who led the Dutch, and Niels Juel, who proved himself one of the ablest admirals the combined kingdoms of Denmark and Norway ever produced, the result was scarcely surprising. In the Battle of the Sound, eighteen years earlier, Danes and Dutch had combined to defeat Swedish aggression and to keep the Baltic open. The danger now was that the sea would be turned, for the time at least, into a Danish lake.

For two years the fate of Sweden seemed to hang upon the struggle in Scania, many of whose people were sympathetic to the invaders, since the province, not yet fully absorbed, had been mishandled under the regency. An army of 14,000 men crossed the Sound, Landskrona and Kristianstad fell, and Scania became the scene of bitter guerilla warfare, the peasants seizing the estates of Swedish nobles and officials.

After a spell of what seemed to be dazed helplessness, when he would speak to no one, Charles decided to lead an army in person to the rescue of Halland and West Gotland, and to try the effect of a pitched battle. Although without military experience, he believed that patriotism and imperious courage could make up for refinement in tactics as well as for numbers. In an engagement at Fyllebro, where he defeated a Danish detachment, it seemed that his notion might be right. Soon he found help and sometimes inspiration in Johan Gyllenstierna, who shared all his sovereign's ardour, and in Erik Dahlberg, the matured campaigner who had been the mainspring of Charles X's advance across the ice.

With the help of these two men, Charles XI gathered a national army, 15,000 strong, which he engaged in a winter campaign of manoeuvre. He was faced with a daunting task. Operating in a hostile country, the Swedes, mainly through disease, soon dwindled to some 8,000 men, but the King was determined not to quit Scania without a battle, and at last, on the night of 3 December, 1676, enemy vigilance relaxed, and they found themselves compelled to stand and fight near Lund.

The battle was desperate, as well it might have been with the sovereigns of Sweden and Denmark personally engaged. Charles and Helmfelt, one of his leading generals, crushed the Danish left under King Christian, but the troops rode so far in pursuit that the Swedish centre and left were brought to the edge of destruction. Gyllenstierna and Feuquières, the French Ambassador, actually rode away from what seemed to be a stricken field.

Their move, though circumspect, was premature. The common soldiers, stubborn as so often, held their ground. Charles cut his way back to them, and he then gained a complete victory. Nearly half of those actually engaged, 5,000 Danes and 3,000 Swedes, perished on the field, and Charles took 2,000 prisoners, together with the Danish camp and artillery. His ideas had been sound. Lund led to the recovery of Halsingbörg, Kristianopel and Karlshamm, and made him a hero to army and nation. Although there was almost everything still to do, the tide had turned, not so much in territorial recovery as in morale. The memory of Fehrbellin began to fade; a tradition of victory was rebuilding.

In May 1677, Christian, who had been helped by a successful incursion into Swedish territory undertaken by Gyldenlove from Norway, and who still held Landskrona and Kristianstad in strength, took the field with 12,000 men. Against this Charles could muster only some 6,000 as a field force. Meanwhile Niels Juel won victories at sea and the Danes continued dominant in central and southern Scania. On the other hand, Malmö remained obstinately Swedish. A great assault failed, and in June the Danes were forced to abandon a siege which had cost them 4,000 soldiers.

The summer's climax came on 14 July, when Charles gained a victory near Landskrona which was to seal the assurance of Fyllebro and Lund. After eight hours' fighting he drove the Danes from a field upon which they left 3,000 dead. Christian was thereupon compelled to stand on the defensive, and although Gyldenlove made dangerous incursions in the following year, the Swedish mainland had now been saved by her victorious sovereign.

In Swedish-held Germany the scene was darker. Stettin, wonderfully defended, fell at last to the forces of the Great Elector. Königsmark beat the Danes at Rügen, but nothing could prevent the bulk of Swedish possessions from falling into enemy hands. Restoration was at hand, but this was by the agency of France. Victories of Louis XIV in war and diplomacy atoned for the failure of his Baltic ally. In February 1679, Louis made up his quarrel with the empire, and it was French influence which ensured that when a general settlement was made, Sweden recovered all her German possessions except for a strip of Pomeranian territory on the right bank of the Oder. Denmark and Sweden made their own peace at Lund, and in 1680, Charles XI confirmed the unity by his marriage to Ulrika Eleonora, Christian's pious sister. Charles had seventeen years still to reign, and they could be devoted to the consolidation of a kingdom which had eluded dismemberment as much by the exertions and success of a powerful ally as by Charles's personal efforts. The King resented French assertion of that important say in Swedish policy which France had earned by her diplomatic and material help. Charles owed his own security to his ally: the fact was undeniable, but it was mortifying nonetheless.

VII

The remainder of Charles's life was given to consolidating the power of the monarchy, to the training of his son and heir, who was born in 1682, and to continuing the process of reassuming royal estates which had been alienated mainly, though not entirely, by Queen Christina.

The King's personal life was austere, almost that of a peasant. He was married on a remote manor, and his resources did not enable him to give his bride, to whom he became deeply attached, gifts worthy of her station. For months together, he dwelt remote from his capital, inaccessible to all save a few ministers and servants. Feuquières, who more than once stalked the royal quarry to his lair, got little profit from intrusion upon a prince who rivalled his own master, Louis XIV, in personal pride.

Charles delighted in feverish rides of from seventy to ninety miles in a single day, and in his wide and thinly populated realm these could be accomplished almost in solitude. On the parade ground, where few words were necessary, he was perfectly at home, but he detested the usages and pleasures of society, and to his people at large he remained mysterious.

Hating the ways of diplomacy, Charles entrusted others with the management of foreign affairs, but on strict condition that guiding principles should be carried out to his satisfaction, foremost among them being the integrity of Swedish possessions. Charles had scarcely any formal education, limited talents, an undistinguished appearance and a restricted outlook, yet his political success proved that a firm will, combined with honesty, courage and common sense, may give greatness to a king. His temperament and much of his outlook were inherited by his son. Had that son's activities been confined within his own kingdom, it is likely that he would have brought it to a state of unity and strength which would have been difficult to match in Europe. But Charles XII, when at the age of sixteen he succeeded the father he reverenced, was one whose destiny lay elsewhere. His life and career were made up of a series of shocks and ironies at which the world has marvelled ever since.

4. Peter the Great and Charles XII

Sweden had made her bid for empire, and to a limited extent she had succeeded. Of her rivals, the most dynamic was Brandenburg, but the most massive was Russia, and it was the awakening of Russia at the hands of a single man, Peter the Great, which marked the next great stage in the struggle for power in the north of Europe, and in particular on the Baltic shore. The autocrat who thrust Russia into the turmoil of European politics was a character in whom the practical, the superstitious and the sinister were mixed in strange fashion. He was huge in frame, tumultuous in disposition; everything about him befitted his destiny.

Three strands may be discerned which gave unity to his career, and they were linked. From his boyhood he was enthralled by ships and the sea, which was an odd craze in a prince whose realm was virtually land-bound. By way of the sea he found means to extend knowledge among his subjects, much against popular inclination. And his most cherished project, the building of a new capital at St. Petersburg—his "window upon the west," with the splendour of its Admiralty building out of all proportion to its nominal function—was undertaken first in defiance of and then at the expense of a sea power, if Sweden, at least by comparison with Muscovy, be considered of that status.

Peter's life was never less than extraordinary. What gave him impetus was that he lived for an idea. It was one which could be realized within a single reign of reasonable length—and in the event, Peter was granted the necessary time. Only a handful of people have affected the course of history so much, or left so deep an impression upon their people. Sooner or later Russia must have looked to the west, but it could have been later, and in that case the possible consequence defies speculation.

Peter happened to live contemporaneously with Charles XII. Had this not been so, the destinies of Sweden and Russia must have been more peaceful, and the tragedy of a Swedish king rivalled only by Gustavus Adolphus in the legends of his country could not have affected Europe in the way it did. For it is not only lovers and friends who sometimes seem made for each other. At times enemies and rivals appear to have the same matching quality.

If theorists are right, and it is the climate of thought, movements and economic needs rather than individuals, however powerful, which determines history, then movements and needs have a way of producing instruments for their ends in a succession of outsize people. Certainly this was so in the opening years of the eighteenth century, and so, to a high degree, it has continued.

While Charles of Sweden was being trained in verities and austerities by his father, showing an aptitude for things military, for languages and for mathematical calculation which was widely remarked, Peter's early years were in great contrast. He was ten years older than Charles, and nearly as precocious: less intellectual, but of tempestuous energy and tireless purpose. Neither man did anything by halves. Neither flagged, once he was master of his own: but of the two, Peter, though in some ways the lesser man, was the longer stayer, and while his ultimate resources defied calculation, Charles, for years at a stretch, worked with an empty treasury, and made reputation serve in place of matériel.

At least two earlier Tsars had shown interest in progress. They were Peter's amiable father, Alexis, and his own immediate predecessor, his half-brother Theodore III, who was an invalid. But when Theodore died in 1682, and the Tsarevna Sophia became Regent for her young brother Ivan and her half brother Peter, a tragedy occurred which was never erased from Peter's memory. The occasion was a revolt among the ultraconservative Strieltzy, a body of musketeers who formed a privileged infantry militia.

At Sophia's instigation the government, six years earlier, had dismissed Artemon Matveyev, an advocate of Western culture, for proposing the election to the Tsardom of the healthy-seeming Peter, then in his fourth year, instead of the sickly Theodore. Summoned back after Theodore's death, Matveyev found that although his hopes had been fulfilled, and that Peter had been declared Tsar by his mother's family, dangerous movements threatened the young sovereign. The mainspring was Sophia, and the anti-Western personalities in church and state who had already caused Matveyev disgrace. They had things their own way to the extent that Ivan was made joint Tsar with Peter, in spite of the fact that he was as much an invalid as Theodore.

In bravely trying to quell trouble in Moscow, Matveyev was hacked to pieces by the Strieltzy as he vainly clutched at Peter's sleeve for protection. Peter would have saved him, but though the person of a Tsar was sacred, it was not so with his friend, and the soldiers made nothing of murder before the royal child, to whose plea they did not listen. Matveyev was the apostle of change, and he opposed the Strieltzy. It was against their wishes that he had returned to the capital. Interference doomed him. He had sinned against what Conrad once termed the "sacred inertia" of Russia.

For another six years, until the death of Ivan, Peter had to bide his time, but he did not forget. His mother, the Tsaritsa Natalia, had been a favourite pupil of Matveyev's, but she had been excluded from any share in politics, and during Sophia's regency she lived most of the year at Preobrazhenskoe, on the outskirts of the capital, where Peter learned to drill soldiers and to storm miniature forts, and where he absorbed the elements of geometry from a Dutchman, Franz Timmerman.

In his fourteenth year, as a result of finding an English craft, or what was left of it, within the precincts of his estate, Peter began his interest in things which float. After some experiments with small vessels, he practiced sailing on a larger scale on the lake at Pereyaslavl, eighty miles from Preobrazhenskoe, where a German shipwright encouraged his enthusiasm. Neither Sophia nor his mother approved of Peter's amusements, and in 1689, while he was still a stripling, Natalia induced him to marry Eudoxia Lopukhina, a girl of piety and beauty, but without appeal for her bridegroom. Three months after the wedding Peter, finding domesticity intolerable, returned to his marine activities. Meanwhile a palace revolution took the government out of the hands of Sophia, and Peter found a friend in a Swiss, François Lefort, a good-natured soldier of fortune who persuaded him to take his sailoring still more seriously—he had already visited the White Sea, but as it was icebound for most of the year it gave him little satisfaction—and later to complete his education abroad.

Peter's first campaign, aimed at a sea fortress, was against the Turks at Azov, a stronghold which could be approached from Russia by river. It was a complete failure, but Peter could learn from experience, and less than a year later, after great exertion, he mustered fresh flotillas and began a new assault. This time he was successful. Azov surrendered, and the victory, the first won by Muscovy as a sovereign power against the Turk, appealed to the popular imagination, and was a step towards a share in control of the Black Sea. Peter returned to his capital a hero, marching behind his admiral, Lefort, and his general, Shein, with a pike across his shoulder.

Azov had been won largely with the help of foreign technicians, and a galley, ordered from Holland, had served as a builder's model. Flushed with his triumph, and more than ever assured that only with outside help could Russia take her place among the more advanced nations, Peter next decided to send a grand embassy to the principal Western powers, to extend his knowledge and perhaps gain help in further warfare against the Turk. He would accompany it in person, and would be the first Prince of Moscow to travel abroad after his accession, his eyes, ears and hands ready for enlightenment.

A few days before he set out, there was a conspiracy against the young Tsar's life. It was repressed with a ferocity to which Peter was liable, and six of the ringleaders were executed. Under torture, they revealed that the Tsar's uncle, Ivan Malaslovski, had counselled Sophia to do away with Peter. Ivan was beyond Peter's vengeance, for he was dead; but his corpse was dug up, dragged by swine to the foot of the block at Preobrazhenskoe and defiled by the blood of the beheaded traitors.

In March 1697 the embassy set out. It was led by Lefort and

Theodore Golovin, Peter attaching himself as a volunteer sailor, "Peter Mikhailoff," so as to have greater chances to explore the mysteries of shipbuilding and other practicalities—tooth extraction included—about which he was curious than would have been the case had he gone in state. The enterprise attracted wide attention, for the Russians were an unknown quantity in Europe, and the contrast in their great men between their observance of punctilio and their private habits, which were at best crude and at worst bestial, was a cause of astonishment.

Peter thought highly of the Dutch, for they were masters in the arts, in seafaring, trade and politics. He was able to learn much in the dockyards of Saardam and in an England which then had a Dutch king, William of Orange. His ways were disconcerting even in a hard-drinking age: for instance, his potations of brandy and pepper. He had a pint of this mixture, together with a bottle of Spanish wine, for his morning draught, while his appetite was prodigious. His disregard of property, as when he drove a wheelbarrow through John Evelyn's cherished hedge for the sake of exercise, was entire. Even William himself, who by request received him privately, was vexed by the attentions of Peter's pet monkey when he paid his guest a return visit.

Peter noted military organization in Austria, fashions in France, tailoring in England, administration in Germany and shipbuilding methods everywhere he could. When he returned, he brought back in his train engineers, metal founders, pilots, surgeons, gunners, woodworkers and road builders, smiths, artificers of every kind— seven hundred were drawn from England alone.

If in a practical way the mission succeeded, politically it was fruitless, for none of the powers were eager to be drawn into a remote war with Turkey at the behest of Russia when greater problems were nearer at hand. When Peter was about to go to Venice, to learn something of her famous Arsenal and to plead with the seigniory to revive their old ardour against the Turk, and to join him in future adventures, he was suddenly recalled to Russia by news of fresh trouble with the Strieltzy.

Although Sophia, who had been sent to the monastery of Dyevichesky, was said to have been behind the mischief, the jealous and monopolistic Strieltzy were in fact restless at the employment of foreigners such as Patrick Gordon in the higher ranks of the armed services, and at the settlements of Germans which Peter had established. Their movement was also the protest of indolent, incapable, ultra-orthodox and pampered troops against a system which asked of them more work and greater efficiency.

A few volleys from Peter's foreign mercenaries settled the trouble. After an hour's engagement 2,200 rebels were captive in Peter's hands. The clash took place on the banks of the Iskar in June 1698, and it was after rather than during the battle that carnage occurred. Not less than a thousand Strieltzy were done to death with every refinement of cruelty, spread over weeks of elaboration. Matveyev was avenged in a big way.

Sophia, though she was innocent of anything more than a wish for the return of older customs, was shorn as a nun, and Peter also took the opportunity to get rid of his Tsaritsa, who disappeared from the world, most unwillingly, beneath the hood of "Sister Elena." In the midst of his brutal frenzy against the Strieltzy, Peter turned his wrath upon the long beards and Oriental robes which symbolized the archconservatism of Holy Russia. At Preobrazhenskoe he clipped the beards of many of his chief boyars with his own hands, and then prudently condescending to a lucrative compromise, he decreed that although the immemorial beard might still be worn, it was to be the object of a graduated tax.

At this very time, when Peter was alternating bouts of debauchery with protracted cruelty and humiliations, he was preparing to cross swords with Charles XII, a young monarch who had already decided against methods of torture in the administration of justice, since, in his own words, "Confessions so extorted give no sure criteria for forming a judgment." The training of the heir of the royal house of Sweden had been designed to lead to objectivity and self-control, to which Peter was a stranger. And as it was Sweden which stood between Peter and full access to the Baltic, the sea through access to which he must realize his plan of a modernized Russia, it was against Sweden rather than Turkey that he plotted.

II

Even before his return home to deal with the Strieltzy, Peter had found a likely confederate. At Rawa he had encountered the lately elected King of Poland, Augustus II, Elector of Saxony, and had found him much to his taste. The young Tsar had been enchanted by the worldly wisdom and exuberant jollity of a facile and self-indulgent monarch whose appetites matched his own. The question of the Baltic, where both men stood to gain from Sweden, seems to have been discussed over their wine, but no immediate agreement was come to. Peter could not embark on a new war until he had settled, for the time at least, with the Porte. All the same, if Baltic provinces were to be filched, now if ever was the chance, with their legal sovereign an untried youth of sixteen. With affairs in Russia re-established, Peter set about winning Augustus as an active ally. The Tsar had proved himself at his second attempt at Azov. Matters might go easier in the north, for Augustus met him more than half way.

Nothing better illustrates the truth of the cynical phrase that in the hands of ruthless statesmen solemn treaties and engagements are scraps of paper than the way in which interested parties behaved when aiming to attack Caroline Sweden. Charles XII inherited his sire's dislike of the ways of diplomacy. His own early experiences, after he had been requested by his Estates, young as he was, to assume supreme responsibility for government, served to confirm his opinion. His father and mother had enjoined him to become a man of honour. Their precepts had been taken so much to heart that however long Charles had lived, he would never have been capable of shuffling, and scarcely of compromise. He was a born intransigent.

Early moves in what became known as the Great Northern War took place after Johan Reinhold Patkul, a Livonian squire subject to the King of Sweden, had fallen foul of Charles XI and his methods of land recovery. To save himself from the penalties of high treason, Patkul left the country and lived a vagabond life, being condemned in his absence to lose his right hand and his head. In 1698, as the new King refused him pardon, Patkul entered the service of Augustus II, and at Dresden he importuned his master with proposals for the partition of Sweden. Denmark, Saxony and if possible Brandenburg were to be comprised in the alliance. When Brandenburg failed, Russia was admitted into the scheme, though Patkul insisted that the Muscovites "were not to practice their usual barbarities," a stipulation significant of the opinion then held of Patkul's soldiery and an attempt at insurance against the devastation of Patkul's own acreage. Denmark was to draw off the Swedish forces to protect their western provinces, while Peter and Augustus attacked simultaneously in the east.

One of the earliest measures of Frederick IV, on his accession to the throne of Denmark in 1699, was to conclude an offensive alliance with Augustus II, the step being accelerated by the marriage of Charles XII's favourite elder sister, Hedwig Sophia, to the Duke of Gottorp, a thorn in Denmark's side, for whom Charles soon conceived strong affection. The treaty was, however, to be binding only if Russia acceded to it within three or four months.

Patkul, completely in Augustus's confidence, arrived in Moscow in September 1699, to find that he had been forestalled by a Swedish embassy sent by Charles to confirm the Treaty of Kardis, which had been made by a Swedish regency nearly thirty years before. Although he was superstitious enough to avoid kissing the cross at the renewal ceremony, Peter solemnly assured the Swedes that he would observe his obligations—yet at a secret conference, held at Preobrazhenskoe with Saxon and Danish envoys, he agreed on details of a Swedish partition. He was to receive Ingria and Estonia, Augustus was to receive Livonia, while Denmark was to seize what she could of Swedish territory in Scandinavia and elsewhere.

Charles, although suspicious of Russian intentions, saw greater danger from Denmark, where he heard that his cousin Frederick was mobilizing an army. Believing the best defence to be attack, he planned to re-equip his fleet, and to penetrate Holstein, using Pomerania and Wismar as his bases. At this juncture, early in 1700, Europe was startled by news that the Saxons had invaded Livonia. In May they were driven from the outskirts of Riga by the experienced Dahlberg; they were defeated at Jungfernhof and driven over the Dvina. The Livonian gentry showed no disposition to follow Patkul's example of repudiating Sweden, and Augustus, now in serious difficulties, urged Peter to advance into Ingria. Peter did so, with a force of about 40,000 men under the command of Theodore Golovin. Peter himself, as was his custom, rode with the army, but in a subordinate position. He reached the neighbourhood of Narva in October, where the Swedish commander rejected every summons to surrender.

At the end of November, by which time their siege artillery had reached them, the Russians were disconcerted by the rumour that the young King of Sweden, who was supposed to be inextricably involved with Denmark, was marching north at the head of a substantial army. Rumour did not lie. The pressure of an Anglo-Dutch naval force which had been sent into the Baltic to localize the war added to the vigour with which Charles acted by land and sea, and compelled Frederick to sign a treaty before he had even begun his offensive. Charles won a first and almost bloodless success. He was now able to give his whole mind to the relief of his eastern territories, and he acted with the speed which had characterized his father and grandfather.

By early October he reached Pernau, with the intention of relieving Riga. There, hearing that Narva was in straits, he decided to march to the far north. This decision was made against the advice of his generals, who feared the effect on untried troops of a wasted land, boggy roads, three formidable passes and the onset of winter.

All went well. The first two passes were undefended, and the third, at Pyhäjoggi, was forced by Charles at the head of a picked body. On 19 November his little army reached Lagena, about nine miles from Narva, and early on the following morning it advanced in battle array.

Peter did not wait for his antagonist. He distrusted the quality of his levies, which he would never have brought to Narva at all had he conceived the appearance of Charles to be a remote possibility. He retired, with Golovin, to Novgorod, leaving his forces in charge of Carl Eugen de Croie, an officer with experience in the Austrian and Danish armies.

On 20 November, Charles, at the head of 8,000 men, attacked the Russians behind entrenchments in the midst of a snowstorm. Within an hour the Muscovite left was broken, while their cavalry, which might at one crucial moment have turned the Swedish flank, fled in panic. Only on the right did the Russian Guard, Peter's best troops, defend themselves obstinately behind their wagons until the end of the short winter's day. De Croie surrendered to escape being murdered by his own men, and most of the foreign officers followed his example.

Upon Europe in general, the effect of the victory was prodigious: remote as it was, it caught the popular imagination. Here was a man of eighteen, head of a nation already renowned in war, who had defeated a force five times his number. It was before the complex battles of the War of the Spanish Succession had begun to afford new standards of comparison, but such a feat of arms would have been memorable in any age. Charles seemed to have inherited the mantle of his own hero, Gustavus Adolphus. Though severe and remote in his person, he became the darling of every salon, and the fame of his Blue Boys spread. But to win battles is one thing, to exploit them is another; and Charles, like Gustavus before him, continued to be faced with problems of strategy which could be resolved only by success or failure on a large scale.

The completeness of the victory at Narva was, in the long run, injurious to the victor. The King's best counsellors urged him to turn his forces upon the fugitives, establish winter quarters in Russia and take advantage of Peter's defeat to render him harmless for the future. Charles thought otherwise, and to his countrymen his word was law. He saw Augustus as his principal enemy, and decided to postpone settlement of the Russian quarrel until Augustus had been summarily chastised. "There is no glory in winning victories over the Muscovites," he said, rashly adding, "they can be beaten at any time."

With the advantage of hindsight, it is easy to say that Charles was wrong. In fact, his reasoning seemed sound. He believed the Saxons to be more formidable than the Russians, and they were in his rear: moreover, he had cause for hating Augustus more than his other foes. The hostility of Denmark was intelligible; so was that of Russia, so long as Sweden barred her from the Baltic. There was no excuse for the Elector of Saxony, who had deceived him until the last moment with false assurances of friendship, yet had been the prime mover in the league of partition.

Charles settled that his next task must be to place a nominee of his own on the Polish throne. On the face of it this was a decision not of overreaching ambition, but of prudent self-defence.

Unfortunately, Charles knew too little of the character of Peter, and he misjudged his energy and resource. Had Charles realized his adversary's nature, the strength of his determination and his eagerness after every setback to try again, it is possible, though not certain, that he would have acted otherwise than he did. As it was, he saved his enemy. Peter, mindful of the lesson of Azov, raised fresh levies, ordered churches and monasteries to send him their bells to be cast into guns to supply the place of those lost at Narva, gave Augustus a handsome subsidy and at a conference at Birse, in Samogitia, at which the Elector-King and Patkul were both present, it was resolved that neither Saxony nor Russia would make a separate peace with Sweden.

III

In the same month that Charles won his northern victory, Charles II of Spain died, bequeathing his monarchy to Philip of Anjou, grandson of Louis XIV. The French King had already agreed with the maritime powers of Holland and England that such a legacy, if offered, would not be taken up, and that Spain and her Netherland territories should fall to the Austrian Archduke Charles. Louis now repudiated his agreement, and war on a large scale became inevitable. Both sides competed for the help of the redoubtable Swedes—French and Imperial ambassadors in the camp of war, Dutch and English at Stockholm.

Percipient Swedes saw a golden chance to end the existing struggle, and to make Charles XII the arbiter of Europe, as Gustavus had been at Mainz, but the occasion was missed. When at last the King consented to give reply to increasingly pressing invitations he said: "It would put our glory to shame if we lent ourselves to the slightest treaty accommodation with one [Augustus] who has so vilely prostituted his honour."

The answer showed that Charles was a man with room for only one matter at a time; that he was not interested in opportunities of the wayside, however golden—and therefore that the Northern

War, which increasingly exasperated the rest of Europe, must continue. From this decision, this wish that justice overtake Augustus, stemmed years of misery. Charles continued to astonish friends, enemies and neutrals by his military prowess; if only, so the powers agreed, it had been in a more satisfactory cause! Both sides had claims upon him—the French through traditional friendship; the empire because he himself, through his German possessions, had an active link with Vienna. As it was, he went ahead with his own plans, blind to all diversions.

In July 1701, Charles transported his army across the Dvina in the face of 30,000 Russians and Saxons entrenched on the opposite shore at Dünamünde, routed them in a two-hour engagement, and followed up his success by occupying Courland, which was a Polish fief. Having cleared Saxons and Russians out of the entire country, he established winter quarters at Würgen, preparatory to a move into Poland proper.

As his demand that Augustus be deposed from the Polish throne was refused, Charles set out for Warsaw, which he entered in May 1702. Early in July, though greatly outnumbered, he beat a Polish-Saxon army at Klissow, the battle costing the life of his brother-in-law, the Duke of Holstein-Gottorp, who was killed at his side. Three weeks later Cracow was in his hands.

All was now ready for the formal supersession of Augustus, but the crafty Prince had complicated matters by seizing the Sobieskis, the most acceptable Polish candidates, and had locked them up in the fortress of Pleissenberg. Charles himself then picked upon the Palatine of Posen, one Stanislaus Leszczyński, a man of respectable talents but without the force of character or political influence to keep his throne without continual help. Stanislaus was elected in 1704 and crowned, with great splendour, in the following year, Charles providing a new crown and sceptre. The first act of the new King was to conclude an alliance between Sweden and the Polish Republic, on the basis of the Peace of Oliva. Poland was to assist Sweden against the Tsar.

Swedish successes continued throughout 1705 and the year following, when Charles was at last able to exact penalty from Augustus. In October 1706 the Saxon Elector formally recognized Stanislaus as King of Poland, renounced his anti-Swedish alliances, undertook to support Charles's army during the winter in

Saxony itself and promised to deliver up Patkul. The Livonian was broken on the wheel and then beheaded, a fate which Charles justified on the ground that, if only for example's sake, such a mischievous traitor should be punished to the full.

Meanwhile Augustus twisted. He begged Charles, on account of his personal safety, not to publish the terms of the treaty, at the same time assuring Peter of his unalienable devotion, and enquiring in Denmark about the chances of a new anti-Swedish league. Charles showed up his falsehood by publishing the document, and by making Augustus ratify it afresh. At this stage, seeing the inflexible nature of his enemy, Peter seriously attempted to come to terms. He could hope to do this only by seeking the good offices of other powers, for Charles refused to have any direct communication with Moscow. The quest was vain, for now that Augustus was humiliated, and confined, temporarily at least, within his German electorate, Charles was free to embark on a greater task. This was to secure, once and for all, the territories of the Gulf of Finland.

IV

As early as May 1703, Peter had felt strong enough in the north to begin projects dear to him: the founding of a capital at the mouth of the Neva and the building of seagoing ships for use in the Baltic.

The troops which Charles had left, after Narva, to defend his Baltic provinces amounted to a mere 15,000 men. In the most favourable circumstances they could not hope to hold, against enormous numerical odds, country extending from Lake Ladoga to Lake Peipus, from Lake Peipus to the Dvina and from the Dvina to the Gulf of Riga. Not only did the King take away his best officers and men for service elsewhere, but he forbade the Senate, who looked after matters at home in his absence, to send reinforcements to the provinces so long as more important operations lasted. He was always hungry for men, and he argued that Peter could be held in check with token forces. It was one of his worst miscalculations. It underlined his error in giving far too much attention to Augustus and far too little to Peter, who was an antagonist not only worthy of Charles's mettle, but one with whom essential interests of Sweden clashed in both the long- and the short-term view.

During 1701 and 1702 the Russians made frequent incursions into Ingria and Livonia, and in January 1702 they defeated the Swedes at Errestfer, where Schlippenbach lost 3,000 killed and wounded, and 350 prisoners. Peter was in ecstasies. "Narva is avenged!" he cried, and gave his successful commander, Shere-metieff, a marshal's baton. Urged on by his sovereign, Sheremetieff made another attack six months later at the head of 30,000 men, the Swedes losing more than half their total force engaged. The Russians then proceeded to devastate everything between Per-nau and Reval, and thence around the coast to Riga.

Operations were also conducted on Lake Ladoga, and early in 1702 the Russians took Nyenskans, the Swedish fortress at the mouth of the Neva, thus regaining access to the Baltic. In September, Peter went north in person in order to superintend the final conquest of Ingria. The small fortress of Nöteborg was taken by assault after a heroic defence by a garrison of 400 against an army of 10,000, and in the autumn Peter, taking thought for the future defence of his projected city, began to fortify the island of Kronstadt. He also established shipyards both on the shore of Lake Ladoga and the banks of the Neva. Attempts by the Swedes to interrupt the work were so little successful that they became a nuisance rather than a threat.

In the spring of 1704, Peter's army, having reduced the open towns of Ingria to ashes, began to invest the fortresses of Dorpat and Narva. Dorpat surrendered to Sheremetieff after a month's siege. Narva was taken by Ogilvie, a Scot who had succeeded Gordon in Peter's service. It fell to an assault on 20 August, and became the scene of massacre, in which neither women nor children were spared. Peter arrived two hours after the surrender, and stopped the carnage by cutting down a dozen marauders with his own hand. This action was not inconsistent with earlier cruelties. He understood the usages of so-called civilized warfare. He also knew the reputation of his soldiers, and intended to raise it, so far as he was able. Russians had not been accustomed to taking prisoners. Peter found a use for able-bodied Swedish labour in the building of St. Petersburg, which was excessively costly in human life, raised as it was under war conditions in a swampy, fever-haunted region where only a ruler with prodigious reserves of men and materials could have turned dream into reality.

Peter now had all that he really wanted, and would have come to terms on condition that he could keep his rising city. But he required time to consolidate his position, and the longer he could employ Charles "sticking in the Polish bog," as he described it, the better for himself. As it seemed possible that Charles would continue to oblige him, it caused Peter at one stage to say: "Am I not right in always drinking to the health of this enterprising hero? Why, he gives us for nothing what we could never buy at any price!"

Peter's bids for peace failed in Holland; in London—where he offered a staggering bribe to Marlborough—and in Paris. Charles insisted that the line of the Neva was vital to Swedish interests, while his ambassadors at Vienna, The Hague and elsewhere argued that if Russian power were allowed to increase, all Europe would be exposed to the peril of a new barbarian invasion—and men were inclined to believe them. The Emperor at Vienna recognized Stanislaus as King of Poland, and Prussia, despite an offer of 100,000 thalers, refused the task of mediation. Charles had yet to be beaten in a pitched battle, and when he decided, as he did in 1707, to advance against Peter from Saxony, the Tsar's chances of keeping his new city were rated low, while there were even those who said he was unlikely to keep his throne.

The process by which Charles lost his Baltic possessions through his invasion of Russia is a story as sad and fantastic as that of his grandfather. By this time he seemed utterly dominated by the idea of war, in which he appeared invincible. No scheme could be too grandiose by which to achieve his ends.

Charles was delayed at the outset by the tardy arrival of reinforcements from Pomerania, and was unable to take the field against Peter until the summer, 1707, when he had with him an army of 24,000 horse and 20,000 foot, the greater part of whom were veterans. Peter decided not to oppose his enemy in the open, but to retire before him, devastating the country as he went, harassing his line of march wherever possible and disputing passage of the principal rivers. It was as sound a plan as he could have contrived, for a Tsar alone could afford to trade space for time, and to go on trading it.

On Christmas Day, Charles reached the Vistula, which he crossed a week later, though the ice was in a dangerous state. On 26 January, 1708, he reached Grodno, only two hours after Peter's departure, and by the middle of February he was encamped at Smorgonie on the Viliya, one of the tributaries of the Niemen.

Two courses lay before him. Either he might recover the lost Baltic provinces at once, and so attain his principal object, or he might pursue Peter into the heart of his Tsardom and dictate his own terms of peace after destroying his army, as he had already done in the case of Saxony. Many of his ablest officers advised the first course as being both "cheap and reasonable," but the more spectacular approach appealed to Charles's love of adventure, tempting him by presenting difficulties which would have daunted anyone else.

His idea seems to have been first to cross the Dnieper, and to unite with a force which Lewenhaupt was bringing from Riga. Then he would winter in the Ukraine, whose fortresses would be held at his disposal by the Cossack chief Mazepa, who had decided that the Swedes were a safer bet than Peter. Simultaneously an army under Lybecker from Finland, with the help of the Swedish Navy, was to take St. Petersburg and recapture Ingria. Meanwhile Stanislaus, aided by a Swedish force, was to quell all disaffection in Poland.

In the summer of 1709 the Swedish armies, reinforced by Poles, Cossacks and Crimean Tartars, would attack Peter from three directions and between them crush him or force him to remotenesses beyond Moscow. Such was the sanguine scheme— but the dispositions and campaigns of 1708 had first to go well, for it was upon them that final success would turn.

As is usual in war, nothing went according to expectation, Charles was able to cross the Berezina River and the Drucz without difficulty, but on reaching the Wabis, he found the Russians posted on the other side, near the little town of Holowczyn. They were in an apparently impregnable position, and were bent on barring his passage. But the King's experienced eye instantly detected the one vulnerable point in the Russian line, and on 4

July he hurled all his strength against it. After an engagement which lasted from daybreak to sundown, the Russians were forced back with the loss of 3,000 men. It was the last pitched battle won by Charles, and it opened the way to the Dnieper. Four days later he reached Mohileff, where he stayed until 6 August, waiting for Lewenhaupt. He had exhausted a large part of his munitions, and his men were glad of the respite.

Then fortune began to turn in Peter's favour, and he was quick to take advantage of it. His policy of charred earth had had a cumulatively depressing effect on the Swedes, and the Russians, failing in planned operations, became bolder and more successful in forays and surprises. And when Lewenhaupt joined his master in October, it was only with the remains of an army. On his way he had fought a two-day battle against odds in which he suffered 8,000 casualties, and lost 16 guns, 42 standards, and 2,000 wagon-loads of provisions. Far from affording Charles relief, Lewenhaupt himself needed it. Moreover when Mazepa joined his ally at the Severian town of Horki, it was as a fugitive.

Mazepa had got away with a bodyguard, after arousing Peter's suspicious wrath, but when at last the Swedes reached Baturin, the Cossack capital, it was to find a heap of smouldering houses, scattered bodies and nothing alive within miles.

Then came winter, the severest for a century. In the vast open steppes of the Ukraine the Swedes felt the full vigour of the Scythian blast. By the time the army arrived at the little fortress of Hadjaetch, which was taken by assault in January 1709, wine and spirits froze into solid blocks of ice, birds on the wing fell dead, saliva congealed in its passage from the mouth to the ground. Never had the King seemed more superhuman than during those awful days. "Though earth and sky were against us," said an eyewitness, "his orders had to be obeyed, the daily march accomplished."

The frost broke at the end of February, and spring floods put an end to active operations for some months. Charles made his camp at Rudiszcze, between the Orel and the Vorskla, tributaries of the Don. His army had by this time dwindled to 20,000 able-bodied men, and he had found no means of replenishing his supplies. Yet he remained full of confidence. He hoped, with help from the Tartars, at least to hold his own until Stanislaus joined him with his Poles, and with Krassow's supporting army corps.

On 11 May he began the siege of Poltava, a small fortress on the western bank of the Vorskla, and a centre of the Ukraine trade, but most of the Swedish powder had been spoiled during the severe weather, and the report of their guns, usually so formidable, sounded no louder than the clapping of gloved hands. Then the main Russian army arrived, and extended itself on the opposite bank of the river. Peter himself joined it on 15 June, but at first would not run the risk of a clash. Charles had never yet been beaten in anything approaching a full-scale battle, and weakened though his enemy was, Peter did not yet feel himself to be his equal.

Two events changed the Tsar's mind. The Poltava garrison managed to get a message through to say that their powder had given out, and that sappers were burrowing beneath their palisades. If the place were to be saved, help must come at once. On the same day that Peter disposed his troops to relieve the town, calamity overtook Charles. While reconnoitring the enemy camp, he was hit in the foot by a bullet, and was unable to ride or walk. Yet he was still ready enough to fight, and at a council of war held on 26 June he appointed Rehnsköld commander in chief, ordering him to attack the Russians next day.

The Swedes, who joyfully accepted the chances of battle instead of the miseries of slow starvation, advanced with their traditional élan, and were at first successful on both wings. Then tactical blunders were made, none of which could be redeemed, as had always been the case before, by the personal intervention of the King. Peter took courage, drew all his men from their trenches and enveloped the foe in a vast semicircle. His guns, designed by a French engineer in Russian service, Le Mètre, firing five times to the Swedes' once, annihilated Charles's infantry. Peter followed up his success by putting the cavalry to flight. "Constant success for ten years—two hours' mismanagement." Such was Marlborough's pithy comment on the King of Sweden's disaster.

Charles himself, semi-conscious with pain, took refuge with Mazepa in Turkish territory, but the bulk of his army, horse and foot, were forced to surrender. "The enemy's army has had the fate of Phaeton," wrote Peter. "As for the King, we know not whether he is with us or with our fathers. Now, by God's help, are the foundations of Petersburg laid for all time." The utterance was characteristic. The Tsar knew exactly what was at stake, and the results which could flow from one successful encounter. He had told his men before the battle that they were fighting for Russia, not for him, and by Russia he meant the country he was remaking to his own conception.

At the end of the year he laid the foundation stone of a church dedicated to St. Sampson. It was to commemorate the victory of a patient man who had at last vanquished his masters in the art of war.

v

With Charles out of the way, enemies got busy. First, and inevitably, the hostile league against Sweden revived. In October, Peter and Augustus met on a bridge of boats on the Vistula, where they arranged a new treaty, Peter guaranteeing to aid his friend to regain the Polish throne. Augustus had already concluded an alliance with Frederick IV of Denmark, designed "to restore the equilibrium of the north, and to keep Sweden within her proper limits."

The Danes were quick to act against the neighbours with whom they had so often been at odds. In November, 15,000 landed in Scania, and at first it seemed as if the lifework of Charles XI might have to be done again. But although Rehnsköld and Lewenhaupt were prisoners in Russia, the Swedes had a fine general in Count Magnus Stenbock. In March 1710 he routed the enemy at Halsingborg, and drove them from the home country. Never again were Danes to accomplish a large-scale invasion of Sweden: one cloud, at least, had been lifted forever. They would raid and harry, sometimes with success, but that would be the extent of their inroad.

Failure though it was, the brief campaign in Scania had helped Peter. It enabled him to take Riga, into which he personally fired the first bomb, and he became master of Pernau and Reval. The acquisition of these Baltic cities pressed hard on the Swedes, for the Russians had already driven far into Finland, on the opposite shore of the gulf, and had captured the fortress of Viborg.

Checked at war, Charles was now forced to employ the diplomacy he so despised, and his pen proved almost as formidable as his sword. Immediately after Poltava, Peter had demanded the extradition of Charles and Mazepa, offering the Grand Mufti 300,000 ducats and 1,000 sables if he would hand over the fugitives. This proved to be a blunder, the Mufti replying with great dignity that such a breach of hospitality would be contrary to the religion of Islam. In the case of Mazepa, the request was in fact irrelevant, for the Cossack hetman survived Poltava little more than a month.

Charles's approach was very different. He pointed out that the fortification of Azov and the building of a Russian Black Sea fleet had long made Peter's designs apparent, and that a Turkish-Swedish alliance was the best counter to so obvious a danger to the Ottoman Porte. "Reinforce me with your valiant cavalry," he pleaded, "and I will return to Poland, re-establish my affairs and again attack the heart of Muscovy." It was not until 1711 that his wish for Turkish help was implemented, the first result of the war being the near annihilation of Peter and his army and the loss of Azov.

Although it seemed at one time as if Peter might forfeit in the south much of what he was gaining in the north, Turkish ineptitude in three separate campaigns drove Charles to despair. He himself, buoyed up at one moment by motions of good will and at the next cast down by the failure of schemes and combinations, was forced to remain at best an honoured pensioner, at worst a prisoner, since his safe-conduct home could not be satisfactorily arranged. At one stage, indeed, in an episode worthy of a storybook, he defended his house at Bender against an innumerable host. He slew several Janissaries with his own hand, and submitted only when the building was burning above his head. It was perhaps not surprising that successive Grand Muftis knew few moments of ease while Charles remained their guest, and it was with relief that in 1714 the ruler saw him depart. Charles rode, disguised, in advance of a little force, across the heart of Europe, being careful to avoid Saxon territory. He reached Swedish ground at Stralsund at midnight on 11 November, taking his subjects by surprise. Wismar apart, this was the only place left to him on

German soil, and as he surveyed the remant of his empire and heard the reports of his devoted but weary subjects, his reflections cannot have been rosy. It was over fourteen years since he had set out from Stockholm, which indeed he never saw again.

During his enforced stay in Turkey, Charles made a lasting impression. It was that of a man whose strength only God could break. His hosts called him *Demir-bachi:* Iron Head. There was wit as well as truth in their characterization.

VI

During Charles's absence Baltic affairs had complicated. As early as 1710 the Swedish Senate, doing their best in the absence of their sovereign, had concluded a neutrality compact with the Emperor, Prussia, Hanover, Britain and Holland, whereby Swedish possessions in northern Germany were guaranteed against attack, on condition that the army in Swedish Pomerania was not used with hostile intent in the empire, Poland or Jutland. Charles, when he heard of the arrangement, promptly rejected it as interfering with his military plans, thereby irritating the two maritime powers, who were already annoyed by the activities of Swedish privateers in the Baltic.

Two years later the King reaped the fruit of his unwisdom, for not only did Peter and Augustus decide to act against him in Germany as well as in the Baltic provinces, but they induced Frederick IV of Denmark to join them. Frederick was to march upon Stade, the chief fortress in the Bremen-Verden territory; Russians, Danes and Saxons were to besiege Stralsund. The Danes were successful on their own, but the sole result of the Stralsund campaign was a violent quarrel between Frederick and Augustus, which Russian envoys had difficulty in composing. The siege was abandoned.

It was Magnus Stenbock who made the next active moves. He transported an army from Sweden to Rügen in the face of a hostile fleet, and after reinforcing himself from the Stralsund garrison, marched westward into Mecklenburg, reached Wismar in safety and proceeded to live off the land. But he could not live in safety, for the Danes were advancing upon him from the southeast, Russians and Saxons from the southwest. To prevent their junction, Stenbock decided to attack the Danes first. After a series of forced marches he met them at Gadesbuch, and on 20 December, 1712, won a victory which drew the applause of Marlborough, though it was ultimately of little service to Sweden.

Hoping to crush Denmark, as Torstensson had done before him, by occupying Jutland, Stenbock marched northwards through Holstein, hotly pursued by Saxons and Russians. Faced in Jutland by an undefeated Danish army and in the end surrounded, Stenbock finally took refuge in Tönning, the chief fortress of Holstein-Gottorp, Sweden's sole ally. Three months later, after an unsuccessful attempt to break the siege, he capitulated. He obtained honourable terms of surrender for his army, thanks to the good offices of the Holstein minister Görtz, who from now until his death played an increasing, though not always so useful, part in Swedish affairs.

Unsatisfied with the result of his new coalition, Peter began to seek fresh allies, but met with little success. The maritime powers, apprehensive of the effect on their trade of a new element in the Baltic, would not listen to his schemes, nor would Brandenburg, whose Elector had recently acquired the title of King of Prussia. The Tsar thereupon fell back upon a scheme of conquering the whole of Finland, "to break the stiff neck of the Swedes," as he described it, and to have something even more substantial with which to bargain when the time at last came for a peace settlement. Despite the personal heroism of Karl Gustaf Armfelt, the Swedish defender could do little with the inadequate forces at his disposal. His own fate, and that of Finland, was settled in March 1714 at the bloody battle of the Storkyro, where Armfelt stood at bay with untrained troops against threefold odds and was annihilated. Five months later Peter won a victory at Gangut in the Hangö gulf, which Russians count as one of their greatest feats at sea.

Matters had already gone as badly for Sweden in Stettin as in the north. The town was besieged by Russians and Saxons throughout the summer of 1713, and was forced to capitulate in September. It was occupied by Prussian and Holstein troops on the understanding that it would be restored to Sweden at the conclusion of a general peace. The Sequestration, as it was called, was largely the work of Görtz, who hoped to tempt Prussia over to Sweden's side, and indeed the court of Berlin actually agreed to drive the Danes out of Holstein and to guarantee the neutrality of Charles's German possessions in the hope of later compensation. But Görtz had reckoned without Charles, who at once denounced the arrangement, refusing to recognize the right of Prussia, a neutral power, to occupy one of his fortresses under any circumstances whatsoever.

VII

At this stage a character fresh to the scene began to play an increasingly important role in Baltic politics. It was George Louis, the experienced but unattractive Elector of Hanover. Hitherto he had been a land animal. A turn of fortune was to make him amphibious.

Greed made George Louis eager to make what he could from Swedish partition, but he shared the long-standing German fear of the results of large-scale Russian incursion into western Europe, he was apprehensive about the designs of Denmark and he knew that he must move with caution. The Elector commanded respectable forces. He himself had served with John Sobieski at the relief of Vienna, had taken part in the War of the Spanish Succession and had already joined Sweden's enemies to the extent that it was Hanoverian troops which with Danish consent were occupying Verden, a place he coveted for his electorate. By 1714 only one life stood between him and the throne of Great Britain—that of the childless Queen Anne. When George succeeded to his kinswoman's throne, he might expect the use of a navy considerable in size, skilful in war, and feared throughout Europe.

In April 1714, only four months before Anne's death and his own elevation, George Louis put forward the proposal that since Sweden appeared to be on the verge of collapse, it was not too soon to divide her property. His suggestion was that Prussia should keep Stettin, that Hanover should be given Bremen, which would afford the electorate a useful seaport, and of course Verden, and that Denmark should absorb Schleswig-Holstein. The

Hanoverians would occupy Wismar, which was to be transferred to Mecklenburg. Peter naturally welcomed this fresh turn of events, which did not affect Russian interests, and which added to Sweden's embarrassments. The plans foundered on the hostility of Denmark. Frederick refused to part with Bremen, of which he already had possession.

Charles XII had returned to find a fresh coalition ranging forces against him, the mainspring of which was not Peter but the new King George of England. George soon managed to suborn the King of Prussia, while Denmark's participation could be taken for granted. Hitherto the government in London had exercised restraint against Sweden: now, though not without regret, ministers agreed that the first use to which their sovereign should put his fleet was to send it to the Baltic, there to operate with Danes and Russians.

Such a move was against the long-standing principle of a balance of naval power, and the sympathy of every statesman not bemused by narrow ideas for his own aggrandizement was by this time with the unfortunate Charles. Beleaguered at Stralsund, he was to be at open war with Britain, Hanover, Prussia, Russia, Saxony and Denmark, while the Dutch agreed to support the overwhelming combination in order to sustain their interests at sea. Although his inflexibility had done much to bring him to this pass, Charles's fate seemed unreasonably secure, his collapse inevitable, despite an alliance made with Sweden's traditional friends in Paris. The result could only give rise to further problems, further scrambles for the remnant of his property, further combinations.

Charles's defence of Stralsund was as remarkable as anything in his career. For almost twelve months, at the head of his Blue Boys, he kept his enemies out of his fortress. At length, when the place itself was little more than a heap of stones, he himself embarked in a small boat and cut his way through the ice to the galley *Hvalfisken*, which lay some distance out to sea. He boarded her by night, transhipped to a larger vessel and in the early morning of 13 December, 1715, landed at Trelleborg, setting foot on the Swedish home soil for the first time in fifteen years. The day he did so, Stralsund surrendered, and the joy of the Kings of

Denmark and Prussia knew no bounds. They could now boast, equally with Peter, that they had vanquished Charles XII, though not, as Peter had done, in open battle.

It had become evident to all members of the anti-Swedish league that until Charles had been defeated in the heart of his realm, the war might drag on indefinitely. Yet when it came to a plan of invasion, difficulties mounted. Saxony and Hanover were jealous of Denmark. All three allies were suspicious of the Tsar.

Peter's actions justified them. Early in 1716 he punished the independent city of Danzig for trading with Sweden, and seized all Swedish vessels in the harbour, later compelling the Danzigers to build him privateers. In May he made a separate treaty, named after the city, on the occasion of the marriage of his niece Catherine Ivanova to Duke Charles Leopold of Mecklenburg-Schwerin, a notorious character who possessed a legal wife already. By this treaty Peter guaranteed Wismar to the Duke, an action which infuriated George of England and Frederick of Denmark.

The opportunity for the kings to show their feelings came when Peter sent an army to join the Danes and Hanoverians before Wismar. The Russian general was informed that his services were not required, and when the fortress capitulated, Peter's contingent was refused admission. The Tsar was furious, but his necessities compelled him to dissemble his feelings, and at a meeting with Frederick at Altona, he agreed to a new attempt upon Scania.

The threat to Charles could have been daunting, for 30,000 Russians and 20,000 Danes began to assemble in Zealand. They were to descend upon Sweden under cover of English, Danish, and Russian ships. In August 1716, Peter himself made a cruise off the Scanian coast to examine the lay of the land and the strength of the Swedish dispositions. He did not like what he saw, and he reasoned that since he had beaten Charles once, it was tempting Providence to assault so formidable a general in his own country. He was also as suspicious of his allies as they were of him, and after long debate in two councils of war, he decided to abandon the project, much to the dismay of his partners in the enterprise. Relations were made still worse by the fact that George I refused to have any personal dealings with Peter until all Russian troops had been withdrawn from Mecklenburg.

At this stage Peter visited Paris, the result being a treaty by the terms of which France, Russia and the Netherlands guaranteed each other's possessions. This meant little so long as Sweden remained unconquered, and at this stage, hoping, as he confessed it, "to bring the King to reason," Peter resolved once again to try to treat directly with him.

Hitherto Charles himself had rendered this impossible, but the King had fallen under the spell of the specious Görtz at least to some extent, principally because Görtz was the only one of his advisers who believed, or appeared to believe, that Sweden's strength was not exhausted, or at any rate that she had sufficient reserves to give weight to diplomacy. This was Charles's view, and he was now willing to consider relinquishing part of the territories of Bremen and Verden in exchange for a commensurate part of Norway. He had, in fact, already engaged in invasions of Norway which were due not to wanton aggression, but to Peter's principle of gaining territory to secure better terms of peace.

Görtz had at one time lent his hand to a scheme for aiding the Jacobite Pretender to the English throne, but Charles had rejected it as offending his code of honour. When Görtz sounded the government of George I about Charles's proposed concession, he found it indifferent, whereupon he turned to Russia. Formal negotiations were opened at Lovö, one of the Aland Islands, in May 1718, Görtz being the Swedish and Ostermann the Russian representative.

In view of the instability of the league, Peter was as willing as at any time in his life to come to terms—but he was resolved to keep the major part of his conquests. Finland as a whole he would retrocede, but Ingria, Livonia, Estonia, Karelia and the district of Viborg must be surrendered. If Charles would agree, Peter would aid him elsewhere, for it was not merely peace but an alliance he was seeking. "When all ancient grudges and sorenesses are over between us," he wrote, "we two between us will preserve the balance of Europe."

Ostermann soon saw that Görtz was hiding the Russian conditions from his master, and that Swedish feeling was altogether opposed to the negotiations, rightly judging that nothing obtainable elsewhere could compensate for the loss of the Baltic provinces. Twice the talks were broken off, so that Görtz and Ostermann could consult their principals. In October, Ostermann, in a private report to Peter, accurately summed up the situation. The talks were Görtz's idea entirely, he reported. He had been inspired by the bribe of 100,000 rubles which had been offered him by the Tsar if peace were concluded. Sweden, so Ostermann argued, was really at breaking point. Every artisan, and one out of every two peasants, had been conscripted. The treasury was empty, and Görtz's expedient of issuing paper money instead of the heavy and sometimes grotesque copper plate current in Sweden since the time of Christina found no general favour. The people, who had already suffered so much for their King, longed only for peace. A devastating raid on Swedish soil might end everything in Russia's favour; or Charles, on one of his adventures, might break his neck. "Such an ending," said Ostermann, "would relieve us from all our obligations," and indeed, Charles's war mania had reached such a point that he could now describe a foray in which three hundred lives were lost as "a merry prank."

On 30 November, 1718, part of Ostermann's anticipations were realized in an extraordinary way. Charles XII was shot through the head in the trenches before Frederikshald in Norway, a place he was then besieging. A French officer standing nearby described the event as being "like a stone falling into mud." The King had said, when visiting the field of Lützen years before, that he had always tried to live like Gustavus Adolphus. "May God give me grace," he added, "to die as he did." At another time he had remarked that occasion and place of death were unimportant, and that the only peace that mattered was peace of mind. By some unique alchemy he had enjoyed it, even in extreme misfortune. He had inherited his father's sense of doing right, and his pattern of behaviour never varied. His was, in Johnson's words:

> A frame of adamant, a soul of fire,
> No dangers fright him, and no labours tire;
> O'er love, o'er fear extends his wide domain,
> Unconquer'd lord of pleasure and of pain.

Samuel Bentham once wrote: "Fighting once in a while is well enough, but it is an abominable trade to follow." Although it is easy to agree with him, yet Johnson, most unmilitary of sages, echoed a deep feeling in the masculine nature when, in discussing Charles with Boswell, he remarked: "Were Socrates and Charles XII both present in any company, and Socrates to say, 'Follow me and hear a lecture in Philosophy'; and Charles, laying his hand on his sword, to say, 'Follow me and dethrone the Czar,' a man would be ashamed to follow Socrates. Sir, the impression is universal; yet it is strange."

Far from rejoicing at the death of his enemy, Peter never allowed anyone to speak otherwise than well of the Swedish King. When the wars were over, the Tsar invited some surviving Swedish officers who had been his prisoners to dine with him. "I believe," he said, "that not since the world began was there ever so perfect a man and hero as brother Charles; yet he was not more fortunate on that account, because he was too great to rule over men . . . When he made a promise he kept it, though it had cost him crown, kingdom and life; but so did not always his neighbours in return. Therefore that man comes off best in ruling over men who is aware of human weaknesses in himself."

This was a wise assessment, and the fascination exercised upon Peter by Charles's personality has been felt by many. The King's personal attire, his plain blue uniform coat, black stock, tricorne hat, field boots and sword are preserved by his countrymen, and commemoration has continued. Voltaire wrote his life, and Samuel Johnson ended thirty superlative lines in *The Vanity of Human Wishes* with the couplet:

He left the name at which the world grew pale,
To point a moral, or adorn a tale.

VIII

Even with Charles dead, all was not over. Görtz, who had made himself disliked by all classes in Sweden, was promptly arrested for high treason, and within a few weeks he was executed. In March 1719, Charles's sole surviving sister, Ulrika Eleonora,

PETER THE GREAT AND CHARLES XII

was elected Queen of Sweden, and negotiations with Russia were resumed. But the Swedes did not come as suppliants, and declared that they would rather continue the war than cede the Baltic provinces.

Peter, on Ostermann's advice, mounted a raid on the country which did enormous damage, won his first deep-sea victory and showed personal skill in the conduct of naval operations. The Swedish Government, far from being intimidated, promptly broke off negotiations, turning instead to England, Prussia and Denmark. Surely, so her statesmen argued, western Europe would not allow the country to go down before the barbarian?

They reckoned without George of England, Elector of Hanover. His moment had come. By the terms of treaties signed at Stockholm in November 1719 and the following January, he acquired Bremen and Verden for his electorate, and Stettin for Prussia, a rueful Denmark being compensated by a money payment and territory in Schleswig. Sweden agreed to the loss of these German territories on the understanding that the English fleet would be used to coerce Russia and prevent her continuing raids. She trusted too much. George, having got what he wanted, in the end left Sweden to make what terms she could with the Tsar, and although an English fleet was indeed sent to the Baltic, her commander could not put an end to Russian depredations.

Isolated and abandoned, Sweden had no choice but to reach an agreement with her last foe. She had no true friends, and her miseries were bearable no longer. In August 1721, at the Peace of Nystad, she yielded all that Peter wanted. For the first time in history, Russia was supreme by land and sea in the eastern Baltic. For the first time, she had a navy.

On 14 September a courier, with a sealed packet containing the treaty, overtook Peter on his way to Viborg. On reading it, the Tsar remarked with justice that it heralded the most profitable peace Russia had ever made. "Most apprentices," he said, "serve for seven years, but in our school the term has been thrice as long. Yet, God be praised, things could not have turned out better for us than they have done!"

Peter spoke the truth. He had been the architect of his own victory. By his will and direction Russia had been transformed into a country whose say in world affairs could never again be

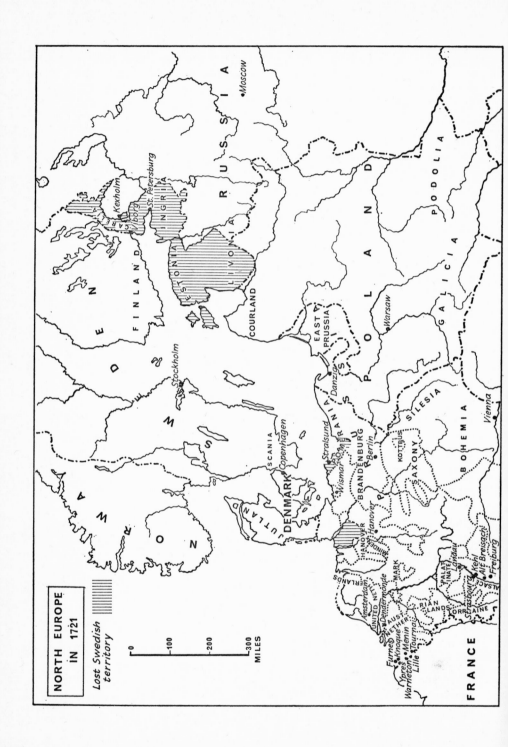

NORTH EUROPE IN 1721

Lost Swedish territory

0   100   200   300
MILES

disregarded. Sweden had lost her hope of remaining a great power. Her hour had been brief, but it had been memorable, and she had gone down before a striking antagonist; for the more Peter's character and career are studied, the more rewarding they become. The Tsar even impressed Paris—a fact which, considering that this was the age of Louis XIV and his afterglow, was itself an achievement.

The Duc de Saint-Simon, in his *Mémoires,* gives the most finished portrait of the victor as he appeared in his mature years on a visit to the court of France. He speaks of Peter as "a prince so great, so illustrious, comparable only to the greatest men of antiquity. . . . The monarch excited wonder by his extreme curiosity, which always related to his ideas of government, commerce, education, police; and this curiosity looked into everything and despised nothing, however slight, that had consistent, evident and wise utility; he esteemed only that which deserved esteem; in which he showed the intelligence, discrimination and quick apprehension of his mind. . . . He allied, in a manner altogether surprising, the loftiest, proudest, most sensitive, sustained and at the same time least embarrassing majesty with a politeness that made itself felt at all times, though still as a master. He had a sort of familiarity which came from liberty; but he was not exempt from a strong tincture of the ancient barbarism of his country, which made his manners quick, even precipitate, his whims uncertain and himself incapable of enduring restraint or contradiction to any of them." Saint-Simon describes the still prodigious eating and drinking and the wild habits of his entourage.

"He was a very tall man," he continued, "very well made, rather thin, the face somewhat round . . . very fine black eyes, large, vivid, piercing, and well shaped; his glance majestic, and gracious when he meant it to be so, otherwise stern and fierce; and with all this a tic, which was not frequent but convulsed his eyes and his whole face and was very alarming. It lasted a moment, with a wandering, terrible look, and then he recovered immediately. His whole air showed his mind, his reflection, his grandeur, and was not without a certain grace. He never wore any but a linen collar, a round brown wig, without powder, which did not touch his shoulders, a brown coat tight to the body, plain, with gold buttons, waistcoat, breeches and stockings, no gloves and no cuffs; the star of his order on his coat and the ribbon across it, the coat itself often unbuttoned; his hat on a table, never on his head, even out of doors. In this simplicity, however ill attended or ill vehicled he might be, it was impossible to mistake the air of grandeur that was natural to him."

5 . Prussia, Danzig and the struggle for Finland

Hitherto, with the exception of Poland, Baltic powers had been naval as well as military, and Russia would continue so to be under Peter's successors. Denmark, Sweden and Norway had age-old maritime skills, though so far as warfare was concerned, the Baltic favoured raids, assaults and small-scale actions rather than those broad strategic movements by means of which ocean powers conducted their affairs. Oared galleys, which had long been proved useless to the navies of oceanic powers, not only survived but flourished in such confined waters.

In the Baltic, as in the Mediterranean and the Black Sea, local superiority was quickly won and lost. Coastal configurations favoured surprise, while the natural resources of all bordering countries were such that flotillas, full-rigged ships and squadrons could be built or rebuilt rapidly, by shipwrights as familiar with war as with fishing and trade, and possessed of supplies of high-grade iron ore and charcoal necessary to the manufacture of ordnance. If the Baltic was the source of most of Europe's best naval stores, her countries had use for them at home. Chroniclers of the sea wars in northern latitudes have an overwhelming mass of material upon which to work, much of it disregarded in general history.

After the ending of the Great Northern War, Brandenburg-Prussia could make her voice heard to effect in any matter touching the southern Baltic, though it was not for more than a century and a half that she built a regular navy, and then mainly for use elsewhere. Prussia was not a giant, like Russia. In Acton's phrase, she was an athlete; one with possibilities of strong and continuous growth. As had been the case with Sweden, her rise depended upon a succession of rulers who aimed at enlargement. With her acquisition of Stettin, she had a Baltic port to serve the growing capital at Berlin.

Prussia took her use of the Baltic for granted, on the assumption that the maritime powers would never allow themselves and other interested nations to be held to ransom by a predominant northern navy for more than a limited period. On the whole, and in spite of the conduct of George I, her reasoning was sound, though there were times, even after the wars of Peter and Charles had ended, when it seemed as if the balance might be disturbed. Had this come about, Prussia, through the strength of her armies, would probably have been able to get her way in Baltic matters, since her interests were cricumscribed. While she was building up her strength, the attention of her rulers was focussed upon territories. Little could be had by sea which could not be achieved better by land. Soldiers were Prussia's coinage.

It was the Great Elector Frederick William who founded the Prussian Army, but he was a man of wide enough interests to encourage the building of privateers, and even to employ ships and capital in the Africa trade. Such activities lapsed during the electorate of his son. Born at Königsberg, Frederick I was determined to gain a crown, his dream being realized in 1701, when, at a ceremony of great splendour in the city of his birth, he became the first in a succession of Prussian kings. Frederick died during the course of the Northern War, his territory in Brandenburg and Prussia separated by enclaves in other hands, and with no military achievements to his credit. It was enough that he had become a king, and that he had encouraged the tide of immigration begun by his father, particularly from Holland and France, which so enriched agriculture, industries and professional skills in his country.

Immigration has become so associated with virgin lands that its importance in an earlier, more thinly populated Europe is in some danger of being forgotten. It was a fructifying movement whose consequences, if hard to assess, were certainly enormous. For one example, the Dutch revolutionized Prussian farming.

They drained marshes, encouraged cattle breeding, cultivated the potato, while to them was also due the cutting of the Frederick William canal, which with the aid of the waters of the Spree and Havel connected the Oder and the Elbe, so that Berlin traffic could be water-borne to Hamburg or to Stettin. At the close of a century (1670-1770) not less than 600,000 people, a sixth of the population of the Prussian monarchy, were immigrants or the descendants of such. In the case of the French, they were mainly exiled Protestants. Even as early as the time of the death of the Great Elector, there were 20,000 French settled within his territory, including the personnel of five infantry regiments and skilled artillerymen. There was even cross-fertilization, for Russia loaned Prussia a breed of giant grenadiers, while German technicians strengthened Russia's military resources. The Great Elector and his successors owed this human wealth in large part to their religious toleration. Provided they served the state (a requirement which was absolute, unsparing and general), Prussian subjects could worship God in what manner they preferred.

Just as there is said to be an anarchist lurking within every Russian, so there came to be a machine embedded in every Prussian. Soil, climate, the nature of the government, a general atmosphere of active obedience, all combined to produce a character which proved formidable in war and peace. Fortitude, efficiency, submission to control—these were the main attributes of a nation occupying a central place in Europe, and of increasing consequence in the Baltic. When Brandenburg and Prussia were linked by land, she would indeed become the dominant force on the southern shore, for it would mean that the claim of Poland to maritime significance had been eliminated altogether.

Meanwhile there occurred, in the earlier half of the eighteenth century, two episodes indicative of the future: the first was the final adventures of Charles XII's candidate for the Polish throne, the second the continuing struggle by Sweden to prevent Russia from gaining an even firmer hold on Finland. One was trifling in relation to broader events; the other was the effort of an impoverished country not to lose the claim to paramountcy in the Gulf of Bothnia.

II

Augustus II of Poland and Saxony has gone down in German history as "the Strong." Charles XII would have employed another adjective, and Augustus's exploits were indeed more considerable in the chase, at the table and above all in the bedchamber than in the camp of war. The Elector-King, who died in 1733, did, however, leave a legitimate son, and nations of Europe other than Saxony, in particular Austria and Russia, expected him to receive sovereignty of Poland.

Stanislaus Leszczyński chose the time of the impending election to reappear upon the active scene—having travelled half across Europe disguised as a coachman—and as he was at that time father-in-law to Louis XV, King of France, his chances of regaining the throne upon which he had at one time been placed by Swedish arms might have seemed as reasonable as that of the younger Augustus. They were improved when Theodore Potocki, the Polish Primate, who had long been one of Stanislaus's adherents, solemnly pronounced him chosen.

Unfortunately, Stanislaus, though he had adherents in Poland, had no force to sustain him, and when it was known that both Austrians and Russians were prepared to back Augustus with field armies, Stanislaus, the Primate, the French and Swedish envoys and the King's closest supporters shut themselves up in Danzig, while a phantom Diet declared the succession to have fallen to Augustus III.

From his experiences a quarter of a century earlier, Stanislaus knew that his chief hope of retaining any hold on Poland was for France to invade Augustus's electorate, as Charles XII had once done to such purpose. "I shall be compelled to return to France if the King does not occupy Saxony," he wrote to his daughter, and he wrote the truth. France would have been glad enough to have had a king in Poland allied to her royal house and tied to her by political interest, and she could bring help to Danzig by sea.

French intervention in Baltic affairs could never be regarded lightly by Russia, and her principal general, Count Lacy, who had served Peter the Great with distinction, was ordered to invest and reduce the city. The siege began in the winter of 1733, at first with so little success that Lacy was relieved by Marshal Münich, who brought considerable reinforcements to an army reduced by disease, cold and fruitless assaults. Danzig was well supplied with artillery, and until its effect could be countered, events were likely to favour the defence. At one time both Louis and Stanislaus looked to help from Sweden, and had Charles XII been alive they would not have done so in vain. His sister's successor, Frederick of Hesse, was of another temper, and his country chose neutrality.

Louis XV had made attempts to sail a fleet into the Baltic as early as the summer before the siege, but his ships had returned to Brest, and it was not until May 1734 that the *Achille* and *Gloire* were able to land a force of 1,800 men, under cover of their guns, at Weichselmünde, at the mouth of the Vistula. This was not enough. Münich, who had suffered from the refusal of the King of Prussia to allow siege pieces to cross his territory, had by this time secured mortars from Saxony, which enabled him to bombard and capture Fort Sommerschanz, cutting off Danzig from Weichselmünde. La Motte Pérouse, the French general, decided that his position was untenable, and re-embarked.

Louis had an active ambassador at Copenhagen, Plelo, who persuaded the French commander to make a further attempt, since more ships had become available. Pérouse made a new landing on 20 May with 2,400 men, but three days later Plelo himself was killed, whereupon the heavier ships withdrew, leaving the soldiers ashore. A week later Pérouse made a gallant attempt on the Russian entrenchments, but he was repulsed, and forced to take refuge under the guns of Weichselmünde. It was memorable as being the first occasion on which French and Russians crossed swords.

The Russian fleet now had the chance to prove itself. For ten days vessels of shallow draught kept up a continuous bombardment of Weichselmünde; Pérouse was forced to surrender; and on the arrival of big ships, he and his men were taken by sea to St. Petersburg. French ill success was a prelude to the fall of Danzig, which surrendered unconditionally on 30 June. The city had endured a siege of 135 days, and had cost the Russians 8,000 men. The decisive factor was the advent of heavy artillery, and the strength of the fleet which Peter had assembled, and which had been kept in readiness by his successors.

The Primate and other eminent Poles were now arrested, but Stanislaus, a master of disguise if not of war, contrived to escape in the habit of a peasant. On the advice of Louis, he abandoned his claim to the Polish throne, and ended his career as Duke of Lorraine, with the nominal title of King. Austria agreed that on his death Lorraine, formerly a part of the empire, should pass to France.

The French expedition had proved that an army could be landed successfully, far from the home country, under cover of men-of-war, but that such a sortie was worse than useless if not made in sufficient strength, or in an area where superior sea power could be brought to bear. The Russian ships, though they had not been able to prevent French disembarkation, were well handled under command of an Englishman, one of the many in Muscovite service. They had shown that they were capable of success beyond the limits which Peter had originally proposed.

III

Wise as she had been in deciding not to take part in the affairs of Danzig, Sweden did not long profit from her restraint. Heretofore her wars and sufferings had been due to her kings. Since the death of Charles XII, royal authority had been decisively weakened, but with the passing of the years tales of former glory were eagerly listened to, dreams of recovery in the eastern Baltic revived. So much was this true that the Chancellor, Count Arvid Horn, now an aged man, began to be ridiculed for his seeming perpetuation of an "inglorious peace." He and his followers were nicknamed "the Night Caps," a term later softened and shortened into Caps. Men of a more active temper such as Carl Gyllenborg and Tessin, the latter the son of a famous architect of Charles XI, looked to the tricorne, worn by officers, and styled themselves "the Hats." The names lasted a long time, though the policies and personalities of Hats and Caps were capable of modifications and contradictions such as characterized Britain's Whigs and Tories.

The foreign policy of the Hats, who quickly won majorities in the Riksdag, signified a return to the historical alliance with France, from which Sweden had once benefited so much. The Hats aimed at restoring Sweden's former position in Europe, and nothing suited France better. She regarded with the warmest approval the rise of a party content to be her armour-bearer in the north, and soon a golden stream of bribes and subsidies began to flow from Paris. It represented millions thrown away, though it was some time before France perceived it.

The first blunder of the progressive party was a hasty and ill-advised war with Russia. The complications resulting from the almost simultaneous deaths of the Emperor Charles VI at Vienna and the Russian Empress Anne seemed to favour adventurous schemes; and despite the frantic protest of the Caps, a project for the reconquest of the Baltic provinces was rushed through the Riksdag. In the summer of 1741 war was formally declared.

The aim seems to have been to concentrate force in Finland, at least during the early stages, and to make a thrust in the direction of St. Petersburg. Carl Emil Lewenhaupt set off to take command of the army, while the navy, twenty-three ships of the line, with supporting galleys, was placed on an operational footing. So confident were the Hats at the outset that they declared in Stockholm that peace terms would be dictated at the gates of St. Petersburg within six months. This time, so it was argued, there would be no need to undertake such a perilous adventure as Charles's reckless drive into the Russian interior. The enemy could be defeated nearer home.

As it does so often in the opening stages of a war, enthusiasm outran sense. No blow was struck for a full six months, and when it came it was delivered by the Russians. They routed the Swedes at Villmanstrand and destroyed the frontier fortress. Sickness was meanwhile raging in the fleet, carrying off seven hundred men and the admiral, Rajalin. The loss in manpower was made good from the ranks of the army, but nothing was achieved.

In 1742, Lewenhaupt made a "tacit truce" with the Russians through the mediation of the French Minister at St. Petersburg, but by the time it came to an end, the Swedish forces by land

and sea were so demoralized that the mere rumour of a Russian attack made the army abandon everything and retire to Helsingfors. The politicians, though they had clipped the wings of sovereignty, had put nothing effective in its place. The soldiers and sailors were as good material as ever: what they looked for was leadership, and they did not find it. A more futile campaign had never been waged: by the winter of 1742-43 all Finland had been lost.

At this juncture, when an enquiry into the conduct of the war was about to be pressed on all sides, the Hats had a stroke of luck. Owing to the age of King Frederick and to the lack of an heir, the question of the succession had arisen in an acute form, and the Hats saw to it that it was given precedence in debates. Denmark now urged the recognition of her own Crown Prince as heir to Sweden, and prepared to reinforce her diplomacy by a fleet. The revival of the idea of reunion of the Scandinavian crowns found little enthusiasm in Sweden, and it was abhorrent to Russia. Presently came news that the Tsarina Elizabeth would be disposed to moderate her demands in Finland if Sweden's choice should favour her own candidate, her cousin Adolphus Frederick of Holstein-Gottorp.

The opportunity for the Hats to recover by negotiation what they had lost by incompetence was too good to miss. Holstein-Gottorp was an ancient ally whose activities were always of concern to Denmark, and the Tsarina's wishes could be supported by a Russian fleet. Adolphus Frederick was duly elected successor to the Swedish throne, and the country's ships, adequate in ceremony if not in war, were sent to Germany to bring the young man's bride to Stockholm. She was beautiful, talented, imperious and Francophile, and she was sister to a prince who was to become the most remarkable of all Prussian sovereigns. When, in due time, Louisa Ulrica's husband occupied the throne of the Vasas, Frederick the Great might have powerful interest in a northern court.

The Peace of Abo, signed in the summer of 1743, was, under all the circumstances, a favourable compact for Sweden. Although she was forced to cede territory east of the river Kymmene, and so lost the towns of Fredrikshamn, Nyslott and Villmanstrand, she recovered the rest of Finland. It was the third fortunate peace she had contrived within a century, and although she found herself deprived of territory which made the approaches to the new Russian capital more secure, she had at least saved her face.

6. Poland Dismembered

The War of the Austrian Succession and the Seven Years' War, which preoccupied major powers in the middle decade of the eighteenth century, affected the Baltic only marginally. They decided two other principal matters: that supremacy overseas, in America and India particularly, should rest with Britain rather than with France. Supremacy in Germany, in which the contest was between Prussia and the empire represented by Austria, remained undecided, though by reason of his victories in the field and in diplomacy Frederick the Great made it certain that the power of Austria would diminish, while Prussian influence would extend.

The wars were of significance to the Scandinavian countries in that their ships were liable to interference from belligerents. Britain and Prussia at one stage nearly severed relationship over the seizure of Prussian vessels, and when the two countries later combined against Austria and France, Denmark and Sweden sent a fleet into the North Sea to protect their trade. It was an early instance of the principle of armed neutrality, which was to cause serious complications nearer the close of the century. Neutral argument was that neutral ships might trade in safety even along belligerent coasts; that their flag protected their goods, except for agreed contraband of war; and that to be respected, a blockade must be efficient.

In 1757, Louisa Ulrica had the mortification of finding her new country at war with Prussia and allied to Russia, the influence of the Swedish crown having reached its nadir. Little was accomplished except the capture of Memel and an engagement between Swedes and Prussians at Stettin, the first serious action of a Prussian navy, in which the Swedes were victorious. They took six hundred prisoners and occupied the islands of Usedom and Wollin, blockading the Prussian port. Soon afterwards, on the usurpation of the Russian throne by a German princess known to history as Catherine the Great, Russia withdrew from the war, and the Baltic returned to comparative tranquillity.

Catherine, by far the ablest sovereign of her time except Frederick of Prussia, was Peter's true successor, though her reign did not begin until nearly fifty years after Peter's death. Legend has made much of her uninhibited love affairs. It makes less of the fact that these were but one of her many diverse activities, one of her many means of self-expression, and that her passions included politics, philosophy, literature, life in all its colour and variety.

Although a Russian only by adoption, Catherine identified herself so completely with the country that it seemed as if she had been destined from the first to enhance her power. Like Peter, she looked towards the west, and she enriched the Baltic capital by the skills of the best architects and artists she could employ. She found in Samuel Bentham a shipbuilder after Peter's own heart, and it was not the least of her gestures that she re-dressed the four-room wooden house at St. Petersburg, built in the Dutch style, in which Peter lived when he began his city, with durable stone.

"Ambition is in some sort genius," wrote William Hazlitt, and his description of a statesman is as applicable to Catherine as to her predecessor: "To understand character thoroughly, to see latent talent or lurking treachery, to know mankind for what they are and use them as they deserve, to have a purpose steadily in view, and to effect it after removing every obstacle, to master others and to be true to yourself asks power and knowledge, nerves and brain."

Before Catherine's death Russia and Prussia had divided between them most of the southern shore of the Baltic. This came about through the astonishing elimination of Poland. Her independent existence was put to an end by means of a series of

partitions, a strange curtain or, as it proved, an extended inter-
lude in a complicated drama.

The partition of Poland had long been considered in Vienna,
Berlin and St. Petersburg, and would have come about sooner
had not Peter the Great preferred a buffer state on his borders,
across which armies could operate almost at will. After the demise of Augustus II, Catherine was able to secure the election of
a friendly, candidate in Stanislaus Poniatowski, and it was during his reign, in 1772, that the first of three partitions was accomplished. The country which benefited most was Prussia, since
by it she secured West Prussia—though not including Danzig,
which retained an independent status until the second partition. She had, at last, an almost continuous seaboard from the
border of Swedish Pomerania to a point, somewhat north of
Memel, which marked the limit of her original Prussian duchy.
Frederick could now ride from the Elbe to the Memel rivers without trespassing on foreign soil. He had won as much as could
have been achieved by a series of military victories, without losing a soldier.

Russian and Austrian gains were inland; and with the exception of Lemberg, in Galicia, part of the share of Austria, they
were not of comparable importance. Russia's turn came in the
second partition (1793) and above all in the third (1795),
which were resisted, when she secured Courland and the Baltic
littoral as far as East Prussia. By that time Frederick the Great had
been gathered to his fathers, and it was indeed one of the last
achievements of Catherine's own reign. Russia and Prussia had
become the predominant Baltic powers, henceforward challenged
vainly by the Scandinavian kingdoms. This was never better
shown than in the war against Russia waged by Gustavus III, the
son of Adolphus Frederick and Louisa Ulrica. In the course of it
Gustavus won an outstanding sea victory at Svensksund, in
which the Russians lost more than fifty vessels of all kinds and
over 7,000 men, thus avenging serious reverses at Hogland and
Reval, but he did not succeed in regaining any of the territory
lost by his predecessors.

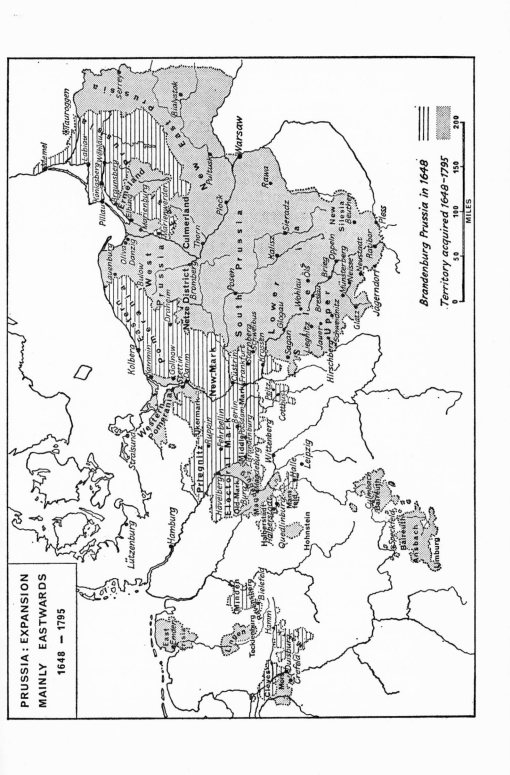

PRUSSIA: EXPANSION
MAINLY EASTWARDS
1648 — 1795

Brandenburg Prussia in 1648

Territory acquired 1648-1795

0   50   100   150   200
MILES

II

Frederick the Great's father, Frederick William I of Prussia, had boasted that he would make his country "a rock of bronze," with a full treasury and a large, disciplined army. He had succeeded in his aims, and as the son he treated so harshly proved himself a military genius of the first order, he was able to fulfil the written injunction of his sire to "keep up what your forefathers have begun and to win the territories claimed by us, which belong to our house by the laws of God and man." Catherine had achieved her ends through her unlimited resources, and by diplomatic skill, backed where necessary by force of arms. Why then had Poland, which even as late as the sixteenth century was the largest kingdom in eastern Europe, whose territory had once stretched from the Baltic to the Euxine, disintegrated in a series of surrenders scarcely paralleled in history? The answers were partly geographical; partly they stemmed from the nature of her people and her constitution.

Poland was a nation of individuals who would never unite under strong direction, as was the case in the countries to which she succumbed. She was a republic with a king, a paradox in keeping with her condition. The elective character of her monarchy prevented continuity of policy and made the Polish crown a prize for intrigue, ambition and corruption alike to foreign rulers and to her own aristocracy, while her land served as the battleground for states striving for mastery in eastern Europe. Even her Diet could on occasion be "exploded," in an apt term, by the protest of a single deputy.

Added to these handicaps, she was not racially compact. Her people consisted of various elements, Poles, Lithuanians and the Little Russians or Ruthenes of eastern Galicia, Lodomeria, Kiev and the Dnieper, together with the White Russians of the area north of the Pripet Marshes, racially and linguistically akin to the Great Russians of Moscow and Novgorod. Probably not more than a third of the population were Poles, while in the two Prussias and in Livonia the influence of the German race predominated.

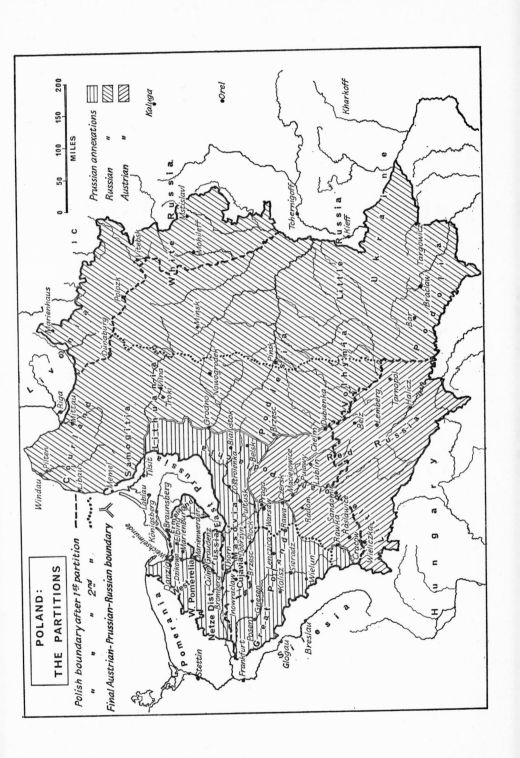

POLAND:
THE PARTITIONS

Polish boundary after 1st partition — — —
    "   "   "   2nd   "   ....
Final Austrian-Prussian-Russian boundary

Prussian annexations
Russian   "
Austrian   "

0   50   100   150   200
        MILES

Denied natural boundaries and readily defensible frontiers, it was clear that unless the Polish monarchy could in itself become more efficient than rivals and neighbours, more capable of organized effort and of the vision that plans and dreams for the future while contriving a current framework upon which that future may take shape, Poland was doomed. Vast, shapeless, unwieldy, lacking racial homogeneity, she was bound to become a Naboth's vineyard if Ahabs flourished on every side.

It was Poland's tragedy, and one of Europe's, that from the time of John Sobieski (who had harder struggles with his own selfish, turbulent and anarchic nobility, than with Turk, Slav or German) her progress was towards helpless disintegration. John Sobieski was her last great king, and although Poland revived, exists and has added store to her history, the disadvantages which led to her first dismemberment remain.

A prime advantage working for health and continuity in any realm is geographical unity, and in that respect island status is a paramount blessing. Another is at least some unity of race. A third and most difficult requirement is fulfilment or at the least tranquility among neighbours. Powers have arisen and flourished without one or even two of these ingredients, but never without a core or "rock of bronze" from which strength will accrue. Lacking all such blessing, Poland went down, and though she was re-created, her condition could scarcely be other than unstable. What she never lost, since these assets are lasting yet intangible, were hope, courage and even gaiety among her diverse people. They know, better than their nobles, that out of suffering and loss may come a renewed sense of national entity.

7 . The Baltic in the wars of France

While Polish affairs were decided between emulous powers, another dismemberment was about to take place on the far side of the Atlantic which was to be of infinite consequence. The Colonies in North America were to engage in measures to free themselves from Britain, their mother country. The resultant war, in which first France and later Spain joined to aid the Colonists, threw a greater strain upon the Royal Navy than at any earlier time in its history.

Britain had long aimed at developing North American supplies of naval stores to replace those which she drew from the Baltic. Her success had been limited, and at the very time when she most needed Baltic materials, she was least able to monopolize them. Norwegian spruce, Danzig plank, Stettin oak, fir and hemp from Riga, St. Petersburg and Memel—the latter a Prussian port with a Russian timber supply—flax from Narva were as valuable as ever, Russian hemp being unmatchable elsewhere. Unfortunately for Britain, the Baltic countries were as glad to supply her enemies with their products as Britain herself. It was therefore inevitable that difficulties should arise and increase, and that the idea of an armed neutrality should re-emerge. The luxuries which Britain carried to her northern customers, West Indian sugar, coffee, tea and tobacco, could, at a pinch, be dispensed with, though by a singular irony the British had won from the Dutch a considerable share in the general Baltic carrying trade, and Cheshire salt was a staple commodity in northern Europe.

From first to last, the War of American Independence spanned nearly a decade, but it was not until 1779, nearly halfway through the conflict, that the northern powers, Denmark, Sweden and Russia, sent a trade-protecting fleet into the North Sea. In the following year a formal agreement was reached to cover mercantile interests, in which the originating powers were joined by Prussia, Holland, Portugal, Austria and Naples. Britain at once declared war on Holland, her ancient rival in trade, and fought so stubborn an action off the Dogger Bank that it recalled the slogging sea fights of the previous century, but she took no steps against the other countries. Activities extended to the Atlantic and the Mediterranean, the Russians at the time having ships both at Lisbon and Leghorn.

The climax came later, when, after 1793, Britain engaged in a twenty-year war against Revolutionary and Napoleonic France, being at times, and then at critical stages, nearly or entirely alone. Almost from the outset Holland and Britain were ranged on opposite sides, which gave Britain an additional enemy to watch by sea, but which allowed her to capture still more of the Dutch Baltic trade, a matter of vital importance to her economy. Denmark and Sweden continued their armed neutrality, the Danes on occasion protecting their merchantmen as far as the Cape of Good Hope, but in 1795, Russia became active against France and for the next few years her Baltic fleet co-operated with the British against Holland, making use of English bases for repairs, replenishments and anchorage.

The Empress Catherine died in November 1796, but her successor, Paul I, at first continued his fleet at sea, joining the English blockading the Texel. Simultaneously a detachment was sent into the Mediterranean, Russia having by this time secured a hold on the Black Sea sufficient to support squadrons which, allowing for Turkish good will and consequent free passage of the Dardanelles, could operate off the coasts of southern Europe. Paul had been alarmed by Bonaparte's expedition against Egypt. After the French fleet had been destroyed by Nelson at the Battle of the Nile, six Russian ships of the line left Sevastopol for Constantinople, where they were joined by a Turkish force with the purpose of recapturing the Ionian Islands, by then in French hands. Corfu, the last French position, fell in March 1799, after which the Turks and Russians contented themselves with a somewhat desultory blockade of the Italian coast, where this was within enemy control.

II

The first year of the nineteenth century saw a sea crisis between Britain and Denmark. The Danish frigate *Freja,* escorting six merchantmen, was met off Ostend by a detachment of English frigates. Krabbe, the Danish captain, refused to allow his convoy to be searched, and fired on a boarding party. Action at once became general, and after half an hour's gallant resistance the *Freja* struck to superior numbers, with the loss of six men. She was taken with her convoy into the Downs, but was left under her own flag.

The incident raised the whole question of the rights of neutrals, and the government in London sent an envoy to Copenhagen, backing his representations with an operational force. The British ships reached the Sound on 20 August, 1800. Nine days later an agreement was reached. The *Freja* was to be repaired at an English port and was to be released, together with her convoy. The entire question of right of search by belligerents was to be discussed later in London; meanwhile Danish merchantmen were to have convoy only in the Mediterranean, where the activity of corsairs from the African shore made this necessary.

Unfortunately, this was not the end of the affair, which was taken up by Russia with a vehemence characteristic of her ruler. The warped, half-insane Paul I, with his catlike face and uncoordinated limbs, had begun to conceive an admiration for Napoleon which was largely the result of an astute stroke of policy. After Malta had fallen to the French in 1798, its garrison was blockaded by British forces, and surrender became a matter of time. Napoleon, knowing Paul's romantic interest in the Knights of St. John, of which he was Grand Master, suggested that Malta should become his, and when, in due course, the garrison gave in, Paul expected occupation. Britain, well knowing the value of Malta to her fleet, thought otherwise. Paul's rejoinder was to form an alliance with the Scandinavian kingdoms and Prussia, to seize all British ships in Russian ports, imprisoning their crews, and to insist on the total abolition of the "right of search." In face of such a combination, and of what was in effect though not in form a declaration of war, Britain assembled an expedition which she placed under the command of Sir Hyde Parker, with Nelson as his second. She must defeat the northern menace speedily, at any cost, and she must begin with Denmark, the state which held one entrance to the Baltic.

Parker, over sixty, rich, disliking his orders, was of the school of British admirals who had appeared in Baltic waters earlier in the century: cautious, dilatory, and perhaps conceiving that his mere presence would bring the northern kingdoms to reason. He was, in fact, a sad choice for so important a mission. Nelson was of another stamp. He believed in what he called a "home stroke" and that nothing furthered an agreement better than a squadron of men-of-war with guns shotted and run out. As soon, therefore, as the Foreign Office emissary returned from Copenhagen to the fleet with news that the Danes were firm in their resolution and were preparing to defend their city, Nelson was for pressing forward instantly. By dint of perseverance he had his way, and was given charge of the force designed to shatter the Danish defences.

As the fleet passed Kronborg on its way south, the Danes opened fire, but they wasted their shot, for none came from the Swedish side of the Sound, and the British kept to the far shore. Although Gustavus IV, then reigning at Stockholm, was as eccentric in his own way as the Tsar, he harboured no anti-British sentiments, and did not intend war unless forced to it. He prepared to reserve his energy for use against the French, whom he detested.

On 2 April, 1801, Nelson, with twelve ships of the line and supporting vessels, sustained for five hours the fire of the Danish fleet and the great Trekroner battery. Three of his larger vessels went aground on shoals, but his tactical genius ensured the defeat of the Danes, and he secured his own terms for an armistice. At one stage in the battle the fire was so tremendous that Parker, away in the distance with supporting deep-draught ships, signalled the fleet to discontinue action, thinking Nelson must be overwhelmed. It was the famous occasion when Nelson turned a blind eye, refusing to slacken pressure until victory was assured.

By singular irony, this battle, which Nelson considered the saddest and hardest of his life, was proved to have been unnecessary. Paul I had been murdered on 24 March in a palace conspiracy, and his northern league thereupon dissolved. Unhappily, the news did not reach Denmark until after the action had been fought. Even so, Nelson did not leave the Baltic before he had made certain that the merchant ships seized by Russia would be released.

The speed and effect of the whole operation had shown that Britain, so uncertain in military affairs, could act like a thunderbolt when her maritime interests were threatened. Napoleon, impressed as well as furious, gave out in an official bulletin that British agents had been responsible for the murder of the Tsar! There was not a particle of evidence behind the assertion, which was fantastic in the extreme, but official propaganda and truth never had much resemblance.

III

The Peace of Amiens, which lasted throughout the year 1802 and the spring of the year following, proved a mere breathing space before those wider operations which marked Napoleon's reign as Emperor. Hitherto the Baltic had played a comparatively minor part in the conflict of Europe. From now until the day when Waterloo at last ensured peace, its importance increased, and it was on its shores that much of the future shape of affairs was decided.

The character of Paul I's successor, the only sovereign with the potential strength to put bounds to Napoleon's conquests, was in sharp contrast to that of most rulers whom Russia had known hitherto. There is no doubt that he had been cognizant of the plot to overthrow the father, by whom he had been humiliated, but he was naturally of a thoughtful, courteous, religious and, in his early life at least, liberal disposition, partly the result of the enlightened education which he had been given and the care of his grandmother, Catherine the Great.

A giant in stature and strength, Alexander I, who attained the throne in his early twenties, seemed to many to be the hope of Europe. It was an attitude which widened and increased in strength as more and more countries bowed before the genius who reigned from Paris, and who controlled a larger extent of territory than any potentate since the heyday of the Holy Roman Empire. "The French are civilized," Talleyrand once said to the Tsar, "their sovereign is not. The sovereign of Russia is civilized, her people are not." The observations were just, and when Talleyrand added that Alexander should stand firm against his rival, he was pleading for a political balance in Europe which Napoleon upset. Some conceived the statesman's warning to be treachery, but Talleyrand's point was that "the sovereign of Russia must be the ally of the French people," since he foresaw the dangers and enmities into which the French were being driven by the will of their leader. Many shattering events were to occur in Europe before Alexander at last, and finally, followed his advice.

At first, indeed, it seemed as if Russia would continue her earlier policy of alliance with Britain, for in 1805 she formed part of one of the more promising coalitions, the countries including Austria and Sweden. Had the powers been able to combine, which they never were, they might, from the extent of their resources, have ensured Napoleon's defeat, since Nelson's victory at Trafalgar signified the fact that France would henceforward recognize Britain's sea supremacy, and would confine French naval operations mainly to a war against commerce, thus allowing British armies to move freely across the world, and to land where they wished.

Yet all went badly. Napoleon's victories against the Austrians and Russians at Ulm and Austerlitz had results which drew Prussia over to the side of France, which led to the formation of a confederation of the Rhine under Napoleon's aegis and which forced Alexander to stand upon the defensive. Although Prussia soon changed sides, she was defeated within a year at Jena and Auerstädt, whereupon Napoleon dictated what he called his Berlin Decree, which established a Continental System or counter-blockade against his most stubborn enemy, Britain. His aim was to destroy her trade. "The sea," he said, "must be subdued by the land." Commerce must be manoeuvred like a regiment.

From the mere size of her forces, Sweden's effort had throughout been marginal. Gustavus IV sent a contingent to Stralsund to co-operate in an attack on the French troops occupying Hanover, an activity pleasing to Britain, since her kings remained Electors of Hanover for well over a century after the accession of George I. Russia sent eleven ships of war and 18,000 men to Rügen to act with the Swedes, but the expedition did little, and Stralsund itself was soon endangered.

In 1806, Russia became at war with Turkey, and it was the disappointing results of Britain's naval effort, after Admiral Duckworth had forced the passage of the Dardanelles and had actually appeared off Constantinople, added to a succession of defeats by land culminating at Friedland, that caused Alexander to treat with his enemy. Soon after the fall of Danzig, in May 1807, the emperors met on a raft specially built on the Niemen at Tilsit, and settled the affairs of Europe between them. Alexander, seduced by Napoleon's charm, bowing to invincibility, agreed to follow the Berlin Decree, and to exclude British ships from Russian ports. "That," said Napoleon, "will soon bring perfidious Albion to her knees"; it also meant that Alexander would become at war with his ally.

Meanwhile Sweden made one further effort at Stralsund. The London government sent a small force to the Baltic, which gave Gustavus IV an excuse to renew the war, but the British were withdrawn almost at once, and the Swedes thereupon left their fortress. In September 1807 they were forced even from Rügen, relinquishing their last opportunity for action within Germany. Britain's move was not an act of treachery. It was because her 10,000 men were needed even more urgently for service against Denmark in a second conflict within little more than six years.

It was considered in London that Denmark would be forced to join the formidable coalition now forming against Britain and Sweden. Napoleon had already dangled the bait of territorial accessions at Sweden's expense, and France, Prussia and Russia could between them undoubtedly coerce the Danes into taking sides. In that case Napoleon would have at his disposal the Danish as well as the Russian fleet. It was known that under the leadership of the Crown Prince, who was about to succeed to the throne as Frederick VI, the Danes had been rebuilding their navy after their earlier humiliation. Such a fleet could play a part out of all proportion to its size in the struggle which was unfolding by reason of the geographical position of Denmark, with its islands and harbours.

As always when her sea domination was threatened, Britain acted decisively. Napoleon made much of her threats to a small country, but the possible closure of the Baltic was never a light matter, and never had it been more necessary for British interests that they be protected in the northern sea. Napoleon might believe he could regulate commerce, but despite all his efforts, British ports were still crowded with foreign shipping. Smuggling became a patriotic as well as a lucrative employment, luxuries originating from British possessions appeared at the Imperial table, and staple Baltic products were needed as never before by every country at war. Britain conceived that she could contain the Russian Navy as well as the French, certainly with Sweden's aid. With Denmark against her, the issue might well result in her defeat upon the element whereon her whole future depended. Her struggle with Napoleon was for national survival, no less. If Britain had learned nothing else from the War of American Independence, it had caused her to realize that there were limits to the burden which her navy could support.

IV

Canning, the British Foreign Secretary, had already proposed a secret defensive alliance with Denmark, the chief terms of which were the handing over of the Danish fleet, to be kept as a "sacred pledge" till peace was established, a subsidy of 100,000 pounds in token of that fleet and the offer of armed assistance if Denmark were attacked by France. Not unnaturally, the offer was refused, and Denmark once again prepared for resistance.

Admiral Gambier was thereupon ordered to the Baltic with seventeen ships of the line and appropriate smaller vessels. He sailed on 26 July, 1807, at the same time that orders were sent to Lord Cathcart, commanding the British at Rügen, to proceed to Denmark. Cathcart would join forces with the troops embarked with Gambier's fleet, giving him a total of some 27,000 soldiers.

In his country's terms, though not in those of the Continent, this was a considerable army.

A landing was made on 15 August at Vedbaek, between Helsingor and Copenhagen, the British having the advantage of Swedish bases near at hand. The actual disembarkation was unopposed, but from the outset, and throughout the operations, great gallantry was shown by lighter units of the Danish Navy, and movements at sea were seldom free from attack. On 21 August a further landing was made at Kjoge Bay, south of the capital, and a pincer movement against Copenhagen began. The future Duke of Wellington distinguished himself in a brisk action following the second disembarkation, where he led what corresponded to a flying division.

Before the final advance towards the capital began, the offer of alliance was renewed, and was once again refused. By 1 September batteries were in position, and Gambier and Cathcart sent Copenhagen a summons to surrender. This was rejected, and on the morning of the 2nd the bombardment began. British gun brigs moved in from seaward, but they were driven off, and it was the army which this time assaulted the Danish capital. Pressure continued until the afternoon of 5 September, when General Peymann, the veteran Hanoverian commanding in the city, reported that fires, particularly in the timber yards, were becoming unmanageable. He thereupon asked for a truce as a preliminary to capitulation.

The British commanders insisted on the surrender of the Danish fleet as an essential to any accommodation, but they stopped the bombardment and sent representatives to draw up an agreement. This was signed on 7 September. The conditions were that the British occupy the citadel and dockyard for six weeks, but that they withdraw as soon as they had secured their objects. The terms were scrupulously carried out, and on 20 October, Gambier, with his prizes, sailed for England.

The operation itself showed how real the threat might have been. Fifteen ships of the line were taken away, six others being destroyed as useless, or in process of building. Fifteen frigates were also removed, including the 40-gun *Freja*, which had already made acquaintance with the British Navy, and over thirty smaller vessels. On the day that Copenhagen's fate was decided, the frigate *Quebec*, supported by the *Majestic*, took the North Sea island of Heligoland from Denmark. It remained in British hands for eighty years, and was then ceded not to Denmark but to Germany. The object of this capture was as insurance against the closure of the Baltic to British merchantmen. If necessary, Heligoland could be turned into a depot and centre for distribution of goods into northern Germany.

Canning keenly regretted the failure of his scheme for a Scandinavian alliance, since he foresaw that without it Sweden must suffer at the hands of Russia, and possibly from a French army operating from Zealand. The sailors and soldiers had a somewhat easy success, and by a curious coincidence, both the greatest fighting leaders produced by Britain in her war with Napoleon served with distinction against Denmark, both helping to draw up the terms of an armistice. Nelson and Wellington each expressed regard for the qualities of the Danes, and Wellington's charger "Copenhagen" became in due time one of the most celebrated animals in Europe.

v

As Canning had predicted, the next moves in the Baltic were against Sweden, for the Tsar's concordat with Napoleon enabled him to embark on a war for the possession of Finland, so long the object of Russian ambition. Alexander's predecessors had limited their conquests; he himself would settle possession once and for all.

The war for Finland began in February 1808, and in the same month Denmark also declared war on Sweden, French troops entering Jutland for the purpose of a combined attack on Scania. Denmark, like Russia, was reviving an old dream at Sweden's expense. In her peril, Sweden looked towards Britain, and with some confidence, although the complexities of a Baltic war on a scale hitherto unknown at one stage led to tragicomedy.

Early in the year 1808, Britain sent a fleet to Göteborg which in composition equalled the forces which had been at the disposal of Parker and Gambier when acting against Denmark. Of the thirteen ships of the line, led by Nelson's *Victory*, four had been present at Trafalgar and others at the Nile. Their chief, Sir James Saumarez, who was a man of fifty-one, had a record of fighting service unsurpassed even in his heroic generation, and many of his captains were of corresponding stature. Saumarez had an extremely difficult task, but his abilities were worthy of it, and for five years his was the master hand in naval affairs of the western and central area. He had to keep the Belt and the Sound open for merchantmen, to protect eastbound and westbound convoys, to fend off incessant attacks by oared gunboats which the Danes and Norwegians were building in great numbers, and which they fought with wonderful determination and sometimes with striking effect, to sever communications between Denmark and Norway, to station a powerful force in the Belt and prevent the passage of enemy troops ready to attack Sweden, to support the Swedes in their war with Russia and to blockade French-held ports such as Lübeck and Danzig. It was a succession of duties such as had never before been laid upon a British commander in chief operating in the northern theatre. In course of service he came to be as much a diplomat as a sea officer, and as much a source of news as a diplomat. It was by way of printing presses organized by the British that the Baltic countries learned truths about the progress of the war which were carefully suppressed in all French-controlled journals.

In May a British army was sent to Göteborg, 10,000 men under the command of Sir John Moore. The intention of the British Government was that they should be used either in Sweden, to help to protect that country, or in Zealand, to oppose an invasion army before it started. Moore, who was as skilled and experienced in the military sphere as Saumarez was in the naval, at once made his way to Stockholm, there to interview Gustavus IV and to place his army at Sweden's service.

The meeting of Swedish King and English general was unhappy. Moore found Gustavus autocratic and eccentric, a disciple of Charles XII without any of that monarch's capability. Moore's army would be no use in Sweden, so the King pointed out, for the country could defend herself. It would not be much better in Denmark, since, with Saumarez in the Sound, an invasion might never be attempted; but in Finland, that was another matter. A royal hand swept across a map of the eastern Baltic, and Moore grasped that Gustavus intended the 10,000 for a land campaign far from Swedish bases, in face of a powerful Russian fleet, and—final horror to a professional soldier—with the King in personal command. When Moore refused even to consider the suggestion, Gustavus placed him under arrest, and the general was able to return to Saumarez only by subterfuge, disguised in peasant costume, utterly certain that Swedish plans would end in disaster.

The troops withdrew, and Moore with them. They were to be used with infinitely more effect in Spain and Portugal, where another war was about to open. This became the "ulcer" which Napoleon in his later years was to declare had "killed" him. Even then there was a Spanish contingent in Denmark under the Marquis de Romana, ready at French orders for the hoped-for descent on Scania, a project which was thwarted not only by Saumarez but by a national rising in Spain. Over 7,000 troops were taken off in British ships, after they had seized Nyborg, to do service in their own country. Truly the Baltic scene was ramified. Spaniards, preparing to invade Sweden in French interest and allied with Danes, found themselves aboard British ships sailing to defend their land against Napoleon. It would be hard to find a happier instance of the advantage of sea power, or a more striking instance of the tergiversations of Continental policy.

If the Spaniards found a happy deliverance, in Finland nothing went right. The Swedish Army had no faith in Gustavus, and the iron generation of generals was no more than a memory. On land defeat followed defeat, while at sea the nature of the Finnish coast line, its rocks and islands providing a series of sheltered channels suited to light craft but less favourable to the manoeuvring of a sailing fleet, gave the Russians an advantage. Ever since the days of Peter the Great they had been well armed with galleys and gunboats, and they used them with much of the resolution of their Danish allies. Even the genius of Frederick Chapman of Karlskrona, the shipwright of Yorkshire descent who built a series of notable vessels for Sweden, could not supply his country with the enthusiasm necessary for successful war; and as the Russians advanced by land, supported where possible by their navy, so the Swedes were ejected from one coastal position after another.

The severest blow was the fall of the fortress of Sveaborg, which surrendered tamely, or as many held, treacherously, giving the Russians possession of nearly a hundred vessels of various kinds which had been protected by the batteries, while the loss of Abo presented the invaders with the chance, which was soon taken, to attack the Aland Islands, thus closely threatening Stockholm. In this instance the danger passed. The enemy were driven out, while no better fortune attended a Franco-Russian expedition mounted from Libau with the purpose of taking Gotland. Visby, the ancient walled town of the Hanseatic traders, fell without a struggle, but when a Swedish squadron based on Karlskrona was sent north, the Russian commander agreed to leave the island without fighting.

On 4 July, 1808, Gustavus IV, wishing to emulate his father's services in the naval war with Russia of five and twenty years before, appeared in person with a squadron off the Finnish coast and engaged in an action with light forces of the enemy. The result had no effect on the course of the war, and it was the one occasion upon which the King intervened in an operation by his fighting services.

In August, Saumarez sent two British ships of the line, the *Centaur*, wearing the flag of Sir Samuel Hood, a veteran of the Nile, and the *Implacable*, to co-operate with the Swedish fleet in Oro Roads. On 22 August a Russian squadron under Admiral Chanykov left Hangö and took up a position south of the allies. Three days later the fleets came in sight of one another, the Russians with nine ships of the line and five large frigates, the Swedes with ten ships of the line and four frigates, reinforced by the two British ships.

The action became a chase, for Chanykov, seeing the nature of the opposition, wisely retreated. All day on 25 August the Swedes and British were in pursuit, but by evening the superior sailing of the British ships was such that they were five miles ahead of the nearest Swede. They were coppered, to prevent marine growth on the hulls below the water line from impeding their pace; the Swedes, in spite of producing the best copper in Europe, had not adopted the practice, and suffered accordingly.

Towards evening the Russian *Sevolod*, which was to leeward of her squadron, was engaged by and struck to the *Implacable*, Captain Byam Martin. Admiral Chanykov gallantly bore up to her rescue, and Hood, in the *Centaur*, was forced to recall his consort, since no other ships were able to come to their support.

Chanykov managed to tow the *Sevolod* to Port Baltic, on the Estonian shore of the gulf, but the ship was forced to anchor outside, and she was once more attacked by the *Centaur*. This time there was no mistake: Hood was now close by, and the *Sevolod* surrendered. As she was too damaged to be got away, she was set on fire, and she blew up a few hours later.

VI

Moore had been right in his view of the Swedish King, and indeed the royal line was bred out. Gustavus III, a man of spectacular gifts, had fallen victim to a conspiracy of his nobles; his son, following the failures in Finland, was deposed in March 1809. He had begun his reign under the tutelage of his uncle, the Duke of Södermanland, and the Riksdag now insisted that the Duke should once more assume the burden of the crown, this time with the formal title of Charles XIII. The Duke was old and of uncertain health; moreover, he had no heir, but he answered the call of his country, agreed with his people that a Danish prince, Christian of Augustenburg, should be declared his successor, and tried to make terms with Napoleon. He did not succeed in his last aim, and was forced to ask for a continuance of British support against Russia.

Help was, in fact, never more urgently needed, for an ambitious plan of invasion had already partly succeeded. Three Russian armies had advanced simultaneously, one across the ice by way of the Aland Islands, another farther north, using the Kvarkens as steppingstones, and a third around the head of the Gulf of Bothnia. The first army was foiled by the breaking up of the ice, and was left stranded in the Alands; the second, under

Barclay de Tolly, crossed the gulf and took Umea; while the third, marching by way of Tornea, defeated and took prisoner at Kalix the remnant of the Swedish forces which had been used to defend Finland.

While in their home country the Swedes were preparing with renewed vigour to eject the Russians from their lodgements, Saumarez, with the daring which belonged to his nature, carried the war to the enemy by a sortie in force into the Gulf of Finland. He himself sailed in the *Victory* to direct and co-ordinate operations, and at one stage a detachment of his seamen landed and destroyed a Russian battery. Alexander did not dare to risk his Kronstadt battle fleet against so doughty an opponent, but his more expendable smaller vessels were continually in action until, in September 1809, the Treaty of Fredrikshamm put an end to the Russo-Finnish conflict. By its terms, Sweden lost the whole of Finland, forever, as it proved, together with western Lapland and the Aland Islands. Alexander transformed Finland into a grand duchy, and promised her a full measure of self-government.

No treaty in Swedish history caused more despondency, for it ended centuries of close alliance. Had Gustavus IV not been deposed, he would never have been forgiven by his countrymen for his failure to hold those Finnish territories in which Sweden took such pride, and which had given birth to so many of her leading spirits.

VII

Even in an era of reversal of alliances, the year 1810 proved notable, fulfilling Napoleon's saying: "Policy is nothing else than the calculation of combinations and chances." Peace was made between Sweden and France, one of the conditions being the exclusion of British ships from Swedish ports, Sweden being given back her lands in Pomerania. Considering the steady alliance of Britain and Sweden by sea, it was likely that the first condition would remain a dead letter. This was indeed so, and it was six months before George III's representative was asked to leave Stockholm. A formal state of war then began, but it was taken seriously by neither country.

Sweden's difficulties were increased by the sudden death of the young heir to the throne and the necessity of seeking another. After much hesitation the choice fell upon Bernadotte, one of Napoleon's ablest marshals, who had already been created Prince of Ponte Corvo. A wiser step was never taken by the Swedes, and it proved more permanent than most arrangements of its time, for Bernadotte's descendants still reign in Sweden, and have provided as many rulers of distinction as any family in Europe.

Bernadotte, married to the daughter of a mercer, a lady who had once been affianced to Napoleon as well as to his brother Joseph, was a Gascon who, apart from his military prowess, had shown himself an able and popular administrator of Hanover and the Hanse towns. He was widely respected and a man of unshakeable confidence. His appearance was as striking as his character. "I have never seen so remarkable a countenance," wrote Sir Hudson Lowe. "An aquiline nose of most extraordinary dimensions, eyes full of fire, a penetrating look, with a complexion darker than a Spaniard, and hair so black that the portrait painters can find no tint dark enough to give it its right hue." This southerner, with a temper as explosive as that of Gustavus Adolphus, had Moorish blood, and was such a consummate actor that it was not surprising that of all his marshals, Napoleon felt the most unease in his presence.

The new Crown Prince felt happier in Swedish society than his better-born wife, even though he had risen from the ranks, and for some years she did not make her permanent home with him. "This clever fellow," wrote one of Saumarez's officers, "has completely renovated the military character of the country, and makes one recognize in the nation that mad spirit of war which we read of in the time of Charles XII." "You are the true hero of the age," wrote Madame de Staël, and she found many to agree with her. Bernadotte quickly showed his independence of his former master by refusing to give Napoleon his word that he would never bear arms against France. He was at once deprived of his Italian principality.

Many signs exemplified the latest change in Scandinavian politics. The sea warfare between the Danes and British increased rather than diminished, and the British more than ever found the Kattegat island of Anholt valuable. They had seized it in the summer of 1809, garrisoned it with four hundred marines, and defended it throughout the war with success. It was the source of an excellent water supply and invaluable as a depot. Saumarez continued to use his anchorage off Göteborg, with which town his relationship remained as cordial as ever. In October 1810 he was called upon to protect a convoy of no less than a thousand merchantmen, bound mainly for British ports, proof in itself of the futility of the Continental System, and in the same month, by mutual consent, Bernadotte was allowed to sail right through the British fleet on his way to the land of his adoption. He told one of his staff that this fleet was the most remarkable sight he ever beheld, "being one of which [he] had never formed an idea." Loopholes and evasions had, in fact, made the whole counter-blockade a farce, and the traveller who wrote: "Heaven help the man who arrives in a Baltic town without a commercial commission!" was speaking nothing less than the truth. British exports to the Baltic had increased tenfold since the war began, though it was not all new trade. Many of the goods had been diverted from ports closed by the enemy.

Such an odd state of affairs could not endure long, but one of the principal events of 1811 was a purely marine disaster. Early in November a convoy left the island of Hano under the protection of a squadron of ships of war. On the night of 15-16th, while at anchor off Laaland, the *St. George*, flagship of Admiral Reynolds, dragged her anchors and went ashore. Her masts were cut away and she lost her rudder, but next morning she was refloated and put under jury rig. On 2 December the ship reached Vinga Sound, the Göteborg anchorage—known to the British sailor as "Wingo," and two weeks later she left for home. But on Christmas Eve, in fearful weather, both the *St. George* and the *Defence*, another ship of the line, were wrecked near Skagen, with the loss of all but a handful of their companies.

This was by far the greatest tragedy in the Baltic naval war. The *St. George*, besides being a flagship, had been with Parker off Copenhagen in the expedition of 1801, while the *Defence*, though nearly half a century old, had not only been present under Parker, but had served at the Glorious First of June, the first fleet engagement of the long war with France, at the Nile and at Trafalgar. In addition to these great vessels, no less than thirty merchantmen foundered in hurricane weather, proof, if any were needed, that the Baltic was no place for large sailing ships to keep the sea in winter.

The year 1812 was memorable for Napoleon's disastrous advance into Russia, and for the destruction of his army during its retreat from Moscow. Although, in reaching the old Russian capital, the Corsican had succeeded where Charles XII had failed, his fate was more humiliating, his loss many times greater. Time had made clear that despite their meetings at Tilsit and elsewhere, Europe was not large enough to contain an Emperor of the West and of the East, and it was Alexander's refusal to abide by the terms of Napoleon's Continental System which, as much as any other single factor, led to their final severance. The Russian campaign led to curious results. England and Sweden once more became friends; Saumarez enjoyed even greater facilities at his anchorages, while Alexander ordered ships from Kronstadt and elsewhere to join the British, a number of them sailing for The Nore.

The wheel had come full circle. A Russian force was now fighting with the men beside whom sailors of Catherine the Great and Paul I had served when the French wars opened.

VIII

With power a hundred times greater, and with equally ruthless determination, Napoleon recovered from his Russian campaign in a way impossible to Charles XII, a century before him. Yet Napoleon, having had a taste of Spanish hatred, was now to find that not all Germans were as malleable as Frederick William III, the monarch he had so humiliated, and who had lost that leadership of the German-speaking peoples which had once been aspired to by Frederick the Great.

The spirit of Prussia, cheered by the Spanish revolt and the reverse at Moscow, revived with such vigour that with help from Austria and Russia it was able to triumph over inevitable checks and setbacks such as occurred even in Iberia. Against Napoleon nothing was easy, but every gain was golden. "In war," he said, "men are nothing: it is a man who is everything." Hitherto he

Gustavus II Adolphus, statue at Stockholm by P. H. Larcheveque (1796)

Gustavus Adolphus at Lützen, portrait at Kronberg Castle by Jan Asselyn

Christian IV, bronze bust at Rosenborg Castle by François Dieussart

Charles X Gustavus, by S. Bourdon

Peter the Great, portrait at Gripsholm Castle by Jacopo Amigoni

Charles XII, a portrait of 1706 by J. D. Swartz

"Image and Superscription": Coins and Medals (reading from left to right):
(Christian IV—Charles XII—George I—Napoleon I—Bernadotte—The Great Elector)

Alexander I, a miniature at Gripsholm by an unknown artist

Catherine the Great, from a portrait at Windsor Castle by Michael Schibanoff

Admiral Sir James Saumarez, later Baron de Saumarez, from a miniature of 1801 by P. Jean

Bernadotte, portrait of 1810 by François Gérard in the Royal Palace, Stockholm

Bismarck in 1894, portrait by Franz von Lenbach

Marshal Pilsudski

Marshal Mannerheim

Hitler as German Chancellor, 1934

The Yalta Conference, February 1945: seated, left to right, Churchill, Roosevelt, Stalin; standing, left to right: Lord Leathers, Anthony Eden, Edward Stettinius, Sir Alexander Cadogan, Mr. Molotov, Averell Harriman

had illustrated his saying at prodigious cost in life; but even the greatest man must decline, and from the days when Romana's Spaniards sailed homewards, when Wellington landed in Portugal and beat Junot at Vimeiro, and when winds from the steppes flayed the backs of his soldiers on their road home from Russia, the Emperor was doomed. No one dared tell him that many of his troops marched on English leather, that his measures against England were becoming so ineffective that the insurance rates for Baltic shipping, which had risen steeply between 1808 and 1811, would never again cost the merchant more than a moderate percentage, and that the common soldier was becoming weary of winning glory for the insatiable.

Napoleon still retained the trappings of empire; he had some of his most remarkable battles before him, including one on the historic field of Lützen, where he beat the Prussians, but older men knew through reasoning, and younger ones felt in their bones, that the limit to French influence had been reached, and that the trend of politics would be reversed. No two men were surer of it than Bernadotte in Stockholm, who knew Napoleon as well as anyone living, and Sir James Saumarez, exercising command in the *Victory*.

It was Saumarez's control of the southern Baltic which had prevented seaward supplies reaching the Grand Army both during its advance into Russia and in its retreat, and Platen, the Swedish Minister, was guilty of no hyperbole when he wrote: "You have been the guardian angel of my country. By your wise, temperate and loyal conduct, you have been the first cause of the plans which have been formed against the demon of the Continent. You were the first cause that Russia dared to make war against France. Had you fired one shot when we declared war against England, all had been ended and Europe would have been enslaved."

The warmth that subsisted between Sweden and Britain was indeed very real, and it has confirmation from an unexpected source—in a letter from Jane Austen. Saumarez's captains at one stage included Frank Austen, the elder of the novelist's two sailor brothers. He commanded the *Elephant*, which had been Nelson's flagship at Copenhagen, and he had himself served under Nelson, though not in battle. Hearing that his ship was off Rügen, then a Swedish possession, Jane Austen wrote to Frank on 3 July, 1813: "It must be a real enjoyment to you . . . to be where you are, seeing something of a new country and one which has been so distinguished as Sweden. You must have great pleasure in it. . . . I have a great respect for Sweden, so zealous as it was for Protestantism. I have always fancied it more like England than other countries." There spoke the amateur historian, the lover of the navy, and a most affectionate sister.

Captain Austen replied that Sweden was very poor, which was true enough, and meant among other things that Saumarez, with all his skill and patience, had had a simpler role to play than Bernadotte, for in order to justify his choice as heir to the Swedish throne, the Gascon must somehow obtain compensation for the loss of Finland, as well as prove good faith to his allies by showing a front against Napoleon. The first matter proved more straightforward than the second, for the Prince conceived that it was in the west, in Norway, that he could find a solace to Swedish pride for their loss to Russia.

The Tsar proved to be Bernadotte's friend, in this respect as in others, and at a personal meeting at Abo he promised his support. Britain proved slower to persuade, while within Norway itself, although there had from time to time been agitation for independence from Denmark, there was no enthusiasm for a union with Sweden. If Bernadotte succeeded in his major aim, it would be a personal conquest.

Meanwhile, and as a first step, there was the new coalition, Russia, Prussia, Austria, Britain and Sweden, each with divergent objects, though each determined on Napoleon's downfall. Bernadotte, so it was hoped, would provide that element of military skill which had been lacking in earlier combinations. The role flattered him, though as he said on more than one occasion: "If I were defeated, I might search Europe in vain to find anyone to lend me six francs!" His position was such that one false step could ruin him; on the other hand, if he played his cards well, a prospect of splendour opened.

When Britain came to terms over Norway, it was agreed that her support for the Swedish claim should be given in consideration of Bernadotte's promise to land 30,000 men in northern Germany to co-operate with the Allies. Britain would pay him a million pounds a year in monthly instalments as a war subsidy, and would try to secure him possession of the West Indian island of Guadeloupe, which had been taken from the French, to balance Danish possession of the Virgin Islands and to give Sweden status overseas. In the end, he got a lump sum instead.

What Britain could not harmonize were Allied aims. Her own traditional interest, Hanover apart, lay in the principle that the Netherlands must be in hands which would not threaten her sea communications: independence was preferable. Bernadotte, in addition to his ambitions in Scandinavia, pressed for France's eastern frontier to be the Rhine, an idea which was inimical to Prussia, who looked for recovery and enlargement in western Germany. Austria dreamed of aggrandizement in Italy, while Russia intended to swallow the whole of Poland, which Napoleon had reconstituted into a grand duchy, though without any seaboard. With such divergence among his friends, when Bernadotte launched his force in Swedish Pomerania in May 1813 it was with a wary eye fixed upon Denmark, and without that unclouded sense of mission which had guided Gustavus Adolphus, Charles X and his grandson in their Continental sorties. Like Agag, he trod delicately—and, in the event, with better fortune.

In the campaigning which led to Napoleon's defeat at Leipzig in October, Bernadotte confined himself to the defence of Prussia, a nation whose military virtues he despised, since he had beaten their generals more than once when in French service, and to "strategic support," which enemies in both camps were quick to describe as trimming. The moment the danger of a Napoleonic resurgence was removed, he turned against Denmark, and by December he had established his headquarters at Kiel.

Helpless before such an army as the Swedes had mustered, Frederick VI made peace, ceding Norway, but being given as compensation Swedish Pomerania, the last of Gustavus Adolphus's German territory, together with the island of Rügen. Denmark, in losing the kingdom which had always been associated with her, paid heavily, not merely for her seven-year loyalty to France and her endurance at sea, but for being a small and somewhat isolated country.

Norway did not submit to her fate without a struggle, and it was not until November 1814 that the Storting gave assent to a

Union of the crowns. It was never more than that, for the country retained a separate Parliament and administration, and although the tie held for nearly a century, it was not as firm as Swedes would have hoped. Bernadotte had a way of sweeping his hand across the map, in the manner of Gustavus IV, and pointing to the geographical entity of Norway and Sweden. What he did not emphasize was the difficulty of their lateral communications —the countries have a backbone of mountains—the strength of independent tradition and the fact that while Sweden was a Baltic country, Norway was not.

Successful in his aim of justifying himself to the Swedes, Bernadotte was at one stage tempted to think in even grander terms. If Napoleon fell, there was the throne of France to be filled, and if Bernadotte was chosen, his son succeeding in Sweden, events would have made him a second Emperor. In order to tempt him to help in the invasion of France, the Tsar at one stage encouraged his ambition, but it would have been wholly unacceptable both to the other allies and within France itself.

When Napoleon was banished to Elba in 1814 and the house of Bourbon restored, it was after Bernadotte's candidature had been disposed of by Talleyrand in a telling sentence. "Why choose a soldier," he asked the assembled statesmen, "when you have just discarded the greatest of them all?"

8. The nineteenth century

The chief gainers by the downfall of Napoleon, and by the Congress of Vienna, which followed upon his overthrow, were Russia and Prussia. Britain retained her maritime supremacy; Russia, whose armies had for the first time operated on a large scale in western Europe, digested Poland and Finland, ensuring for herself the great arc of the Baltic from the Gulf of Bothnia almost to Memel. Prussia, redeeming humiliation by her vigorous revival, was established between Mecklenburg and the Niemen. Sweden, though given responsibility for Norway, disappeared from Germany. Her last possessions in Pomerania, originally ceded to Denmark, were in fact made over to Prussia and Mecklenburg, Prussia granting Denmark the Duchy of Lauenburg by way of compensation, together with a monetary payment. Mecklenburg already held a mortgage on Wismar.

If Sweden may be said to have benefited by treaty once again, finding in negotiation more profit than she deserved from her operations in war, she also had the good fortune, not shared by any other Baltic country, of laying down her arms for what proved to be the last time. Bernadotte brought her enduring peace, an astonishing event when her earlier history is remembered. Denmark was Napoleon's victim. Made bankrupt by the ruin of her trade, she emerged from Vienna a member of the new German Confederation, which was the successor to the old empire, by virtue of possession of Holstein and Lauenburg, but she was an inconsiderable member, liable to become the victim of a powerful neighbour. Denmark also remained what she had long been, a country with overseas possessions. She held Greenland— a fact which was resented in Norway, whose pioneers had done much to colonize the island—and she ruled Iceland, the Faeroes, settlements in Guinea, Tranquebar, on the Coromandel Coast, which she disposed of to Britain in mid-century, together with the West Indian isles of St. Thomas, St. Croix and St. John, which were sold to America in the First World War. She also still ex- acted her Sound dues, an ancient and unjustified privilege which was not abolished for nearly half a century, and then with com- pensation in which the maritime nations, the United States in- cluded, subscribed their share.

Of all Baltic lands, Denmark, diminished and straitened, might have looked forward to the longest spell of peace. In fact, it was in Danish waters that the next Baltic battle was fought, and the cause, as many had anticipated, was the Schleswig-Holstein ques- tion. This was to vex European statesmen for more than a dec- ade, and to bring satisfaction only to Prussia.

From the time of Charlemagne, the Duchy of Schleswig, bor- dering on South Jutland, had been closely associated with Den- mark, while Holstein, to the south, had acknowledged Danish kings as overlords since 1460. Each province enjoyed a consider- able degree of independence, and racially, while northern Schles- wig was purely Danish, southern Schleswig was mainly, and Holstein entirely, German. On the formal dissolution of the Holy Roman Empire in 1806, both provinces had been awarded uncon- ditionally to Denmark, but the founding of the German Confed- eration reopened discussion of their status. Frederick VI, the mainspring of Danish efforts in the cause of Napoleon, joined the Confereration as Duke of Holstein, but refused to allow the en- try of Schleswig, as being an integral part of his Danish realm. The extreme Danish view aimed at making the river Eider the southern boundary of the kingdom proper. The extreme German view held that the two duchies must be regarded as one, and as such should be subject to the new dispensation. The Confedera- tion, it was argued, was German, not Scandinavian, and the di- vergence of opinion led to two separate wars.

Throughout the eighteenth century Danish politics were much in the hands of German statesmen, and little effort was made to safeguard Danish traditions even in neighbouring Schleswig. Officials in both duchies were largely recruited from the Holstein university at Kiel: a customs barrier was strictly maintained; commercial life was orientated towards Hamburg, and the German element in public life was such that a deputy was actually expelled from the Schleswig estates when he insisted on his right to address the assembly in Danish.

Liberals in the duchies became increasingly vocal in demanding a special Constitution, and under Christian VIII "consultative assemblies" were in fact established at Roskilde, Viborg, Schleswig and Itzehoe (covering Holstein). Frederick VII, when he succeeded to the Danish throne in 1848, proposed a "free" Constitution for his entire kingdom, but the idea pleased no extremist, and led directly to a revolt in Holstein, which at first received active support from Prussia.

This was, indeed, a time of political explosions and changing alignments among major powers. There had been serious troubles in France, Austria, Hungary, Germany, Italy, Spain and Poland, and in the matter of Schleswig-Holstein, which involved international and broad strategic factors, Russia, France and Great Britain at first inclined to view with equanimity any development which might tend to weaken the strength of the German Confederation, which was perceived as a revival of the idea of a German-speaking empire within Europe.

If Prussia was the power behind the insurgent Holsteiners, Pan Scandinavians in the kingdom of Sweden-Norway felt sufficiently for the sister realm on the other side of the Sound to regard with satisfaction the fact that a Swedish-Norwegian contingent actually landed on the Danish island of Fünen. The troops were not called upon for more active service than garrison duty, since the Danes believed that they could themselves manage an affair which concerned them and their sovereign. Although in the end they proved that this was so, the revolt was on such a serious and sustained scale that for three years Denmark became the scene of war. This was chiefly on land, though in April 1849 there occurred the first Baltic battle in which steamships were engaged. The fact is additionally curious since only the year before, Holsteiners had built twelve gunboats at Kiel for service in the rebellion and these, though armed with 60-pounders, were designed to use oars as well as sail, in the manner of Chapman's vessels built in the eighteenth century for Sweden.

The encounter took place at Eckernförde Fjord, off Kiel Bay, when the Danes attempted to use their navy to cover a landing. The *Christian VIII* of eighty-four guns and the smaller *Gefion* were sent into the fjord together with two steamers. They were engaged by two shore batteries of twelve guns each, and after a fight lasting all day, both sailing ships surrendered. The *Christian VIII* was so badly damaged that she had to be destroyed, but the *Gefion*, forty-six guns, was taken into the German Navy and re-christened *Eckernförde*, in honour of their first naval victory. The Danes lost over a hundred killed and sixty wounded in proving what their ancestors could have told them from experience, that sailing ships have little chance when pitted against shore artillery in good positions. Even more sinister—and prophetic—was the appearance, shortly after this episode, of a German submersible vessel, the *Brandtaucher*, designed by Wilhelm Bauer. Her details have not been much studied, but her advent was in itself enough to cause a blockade of Kiel to be lifted.

On land, and with difficulty, for the Holsteiners in particular were stubborn and well supported, the Danes gradually gained control, though they always showed more bravery than military skill. Russia and Britain brought pressure to bear on the Germans, and in 1852 an agreement was reached between Denmark, Prussia and Austria—the latter representing the predominant power in the German Confederation. It was confirmed that the duchies would continue to be administered separately from the Danish Kingdom, and that Schleswig should not be incorporated within it. The Germans gained their point, though the territories remained under the Danish King.

Every thoughtful statesman realized that the solution could only be temporary; that a union of countries merely through the person of a reigning monarch implied far more spirit of co-operation than existed between Danes and Germans, and that when the increasing force of German nationalism was faced with a new development in Danish affairs, trouble would recur.

The Baltic peace in fact held for a mere two years, though when next it was disturbed it was in the Russian sphere. A strange successor to Sir James Saumarez was called upon to lead a British fleet to tasks which more realistic planners would have known to be a waste of time.

II

If to some degree they had been drawn together by the matter of the duchies, since the instincts of both countries were against helping Germany to become once more what a league of German towns had been in the distant past, a great Baltic power, Russia and Great Britain were at odds in their eastern policy, which was a principal cause of the Crimean War. Russia believed Turkey's days in Europe to be numbered. Britain supported Ottoman power as a bulwark against Russian expansion.

For Britain, the danger signal came when the Russians destroyed the Turkish fleet, and when she realized that nothing formidable stood between Russian dominion of the eastern Mediterranean, and hence of the approaches to her remoter possessions and interests. Allied with France, which since 1848 had been ruled by Louis Napoleon, the great soldier's nephew—at first as President and later under the title of Emperor Napoleon III—Britain declared war on Russia for reasons which were thought insufficient by many responsible statesmen at the time, and which have not since been justified by more protracted scrutiny. Napoleon III, whose personal position both as a usurper of power in France and as the self-appointed heir of the most outstanding warrior the country had produced, needed to acquire every particle of prestige abroad which policy or meddling could achieve. The Emperor had already embroiled himself with Russia over the question of the protection of Catholics within the Tsar's sphere of influence, and by joining himself with Britain, a power with at least some valid reason for wishing to curb Russian aspirations, he hoped to win at least some military glory at modest cost.

Britain sent forces to the only areas where the enemy was vulnerable to sea power: to the Crimea, where an army landed unopposed, and to the Baltic, where Russia had a principal naval base and the seat of her government. The war itself exposed the weaknesses of more than one power, and it checked Russian expansion, while, by maintaining neutrality in matters where her

interests could have been seriously affected, Austria began to lose
that influence in western Europe which she assumed after Napoleon's defeat.

The man chosen to lead the British Baltic expedition was Sir
Charles Napier. He was an officer approaching seventy who had
joined the Navy at the close of the eighteenth century. Since that
time he had been remarkable for vigour and independence, but
also for the violence of his disagreements. His language was in-
temperate, while his lack of discretion would have ruled him out
as a possibility for chief command had the choice not appeared
to be so narrow. Only veterans had had previous experience of
war, and the navy itself was undermanned, equipped with untried wooden ships powered with engines of uncertain quality.
Of staff work and strategic planning the service was innocent.

Lord Clarence Paget of the *Princess Royal,* who at one stage
was Napier's flag captain, gave a revealing glimpse of his admiral
as he appeared when he first took over command. "He began by
lighting his cigar," the captain noted, "and saying he had a
deuce of a job in hand, to go into an enemy's waters and attack a
force numerically superior and of greater efficiency than his
own . . . but by the time he had finished half a dozen, he had
informed me of such bloodthirsty resolves that, what with them
and the thick tobacco smoke, I slept little that night."

Napier was in Baltic waters before war had been declared,
and before the ice of the Gulf of Finland had broken. His fleet
made its passage through the Belt, not the Sound, using charts
which were based on experience built up in days when Saumarez
controlled the sea lanes. The Admiralty had suggested that he
enter reinforcements abroad *sub rosa,* but neither in Norwegian
ports nor at the old anchorage at "Wingo" had he found volunteers. Scandinavia was curious, but noncommittal. Everyone
feared Russia. Veterans remembered the older British fleets and
admired the appearance of the expedition; on the other hand, it
was soon clear that Baltic towns were doing a thriving business
in supplying war matériel, just as they had done in the heyday
of the great Napoleon's embargo.

Napier's duty was threefold. He had to blockade Russian-con-
trolled ports, in so far as his limited resources permitted; he had
to prevent the Tsar's fleet from getting to westward of his own;

and he was expected to achieve something worthy of the country then recognized as mistress of the seas.

His blockade was only mildly successful. Steam tugs had altered conditions so radically that ships were no longer imprisoned in harbour by onshore winds; evasion of cruisers had to that extent become simpler. The Tsar, sensibly enough, kept his Baltic squadrons safe under the guns of Kronstadt and Sveaborg, protecting their approaches by mining. His mines—a type new in warfare—were described as "submarine shells reported to contain 450 lbs. of powder, fired by galvanic batteries."

When a French squadron, led by Admiral Parseval-Deschênes, joined that of Napier, the Allied force was provided with a military contingent under the command of General Barraguay d'Hilliers, who as a youngster had lost a hand from frostbite during the retreat from Moscow. Napier described his fellow admiral as "a very gentlemanly man," and Parseval-Deschênes, who had been present at Trafalgar, certainly hoped to win glory for his Emperor serving side by side with the British. "The French admiral," wrote the First Lord of the Admiralty to Napier, "has some high-sounding instructions. Your duty does not extend to the impossible." Napier was also warned to "hold hard in the expenditure of shells for practice"; they were not too plentiful.

A distant survey of Kronstadt was made, but the difficulties, particularly the "infernal machines" for which Napier had a wholesome respect, seemed insuperable. Yet the Baltic summer was short—something must be attempted, and there were the Aland Islands. Their chief fortress, Bomarsund, was said to be garrisoned with 2,500 Russian troops, and it appeared a worthy object. In August 1854 a landing was made amid friendly people, their simple log houses gay with roses. Guns were manhandled along atrocious surfaces, and then, following a heavy bombardment, French and British took the fortress by storm, and over 2,000 prisoners, many of them Finns. One of Napier's flag officers, Henry Chads, actually had his wife with him on the expedition, while yachts owned by men of fortune also visited the scene of operations. One of them enjoyed a tow behind the *Princess Royal*.

In making choice of the Alands as a scene of operations, the British admiral, perhaps more by chance then by design, hit upon the one area above all others about which the Swedes were sensitive. The islands, as Napoleon I had once pointed out, were in a sense both a key to and a threat to Stockholm, and their geographical position enabled a garrison to seal the approaches to the Gulf of Bothnia.

When in 1809, at the Treaty of Fredrikshamm, Russia secured Finland from Sweden, the Swedes, though bereft of the country they had ruled so long, were at least guaranteed that the Alands would never be fortified. Russia had in fact disregarded this obligation, and thus provided an excuse for a declaration of war on the part of Sweden. Long, hard and bitter experience made her wary. Bernadotte's son, King Oscar I, might have been willing to act, but he could not have carried his country with him, even though fighting beside two major powers. Napier got courtesy, but nothing more substantial in the way of practical help, within Swedish waters. "It is true that Russia is rather a formidable neighbour," said the King to the British admiral, "but I do not know how an alliance with any other powers would mend the position."

In the upshot, Sweden had the benefit of war without the cost of participation, for some two years after the reduction of Bomarsund, as the result of a convention related to the peace settlement, Britain, France and Russia signed a guarantee that the Alands would not be refortified, and that naval and military garrisons would not be maintained within the group. It was half a century before any further cause for alarm was given to Sweden because of islands about which she was so naturally sensitive.

Elated with a success won at modest cost, the Allies thought once more of Sveaborg, but summer was going, and General Barraguay d'Hilliers had been ordered home. "No man in his senses," wrote Napier to the Admiralty, "would undertake to attack Sveaborg at this season of the year," the month being then October. He had not done much, but Bomarsund was better than nothing. The fleet returned, and in December 1854, Napier struck his flag. For the seven years that remained to him, he carried on a private war against the Admiralty, who, so he maintained, had expected the impossible.

Napier's successor, Sir Richard Dundas, though a younger man, did little better. His single summer campaign had for its high light a bombardment of Sveaborg. This was noisy, diverting to the sailors and quite useless. His orders to find out more about the Russian "submarine shells" proved the ingenuity of an enemy wise enough not to risk his ships at sea. Tradition also credits him with being the cause of forest fires on a scale which he certainly would not have intended, the result of too zealous use of his ordnance, and with the destruction of a full year's supply of pitch. This had been awaiting an opportune time for shipment to England, whose government had already bespoken it!

Ambitious plans were made for a third Baltic sortie, but peace prevented it, and the British Navy resigned itself to living on its past, while the soldiers redeemed by valour in the Crimea gross ineptitude in leadership and administration. The sailors indeed had the lesson which the Russians once taught Gustavus III of Sweden—that in the eastern Baltic the country which is dominant by land can render a sea effort nugatory. Other powers observed that while Britain's navy might still, in the long run, be the decisive factor in a European or in a world war, the uses of a fleet were circumscribed. In that respect the failure had bearing on renewed troubles in Schleswig-Holstein.

III

In 1857, when Denmark relinquished her Sound dues for the sum of four million pounds, she attracted an expression of opinion from the far side of the Atlantic which Europeans were to have occasion to remember. During the negotiations Mr. William L. Marcy, acting on behalf of the United States, permitted himself a generalization which found an echo among his countrymen, and caused wry smiles in Copenhagen. "Of the utility or wisdom of the political theory of the Balance of Power, in its application to the European family of nations," wrote the representative, "it is not proposed to express an opinion; but enough of its operations have been seen to impress upon this Government a fixed determination to avoid being brought within its vortex." Mr. Marcy might write as he would from Washington; for Denmark herself, the vortex was inescapable. She gained handsomely from abandoning her Sound dues; less welcome was the future loss of a third of her population.

It so happened that two events, closely connected, occurred in successive years. Frederick VII of Denmark died in November 1863, childless. Fourteen months earlier Bismarck had become Prime Minister of Prussia. Bismarck was then a man of forty-seven, at the full height of his powers. Superficially his character held contradictions. A high-pitched voice, a nervous tendency and a gift of expression which resulted in some of the most masterly summaries which have ever been written might have be-tokened the literary artist. Bismarck's gifts were otherwise employed. His energies centred upon his undisguised appetite for power. He had huge zest for the turmoil of life, for the food and drink which did so much more than merely sustain him, and he relentlessly savaged all who crossed his path. His grasp both of immediate realities and long-term possibilities was uncanny, and his statement that the most important fact in nineteenth-century history was that Britain and America spoke the same language showed a world grasp rare among his countrymen. Finally, his exact perception of how to handle his fellow men, how to bend them to his purposes, made him feared in every capital, particularly his own.

Bismarck worked, by devious routes, towards one single end: this was the aggrandizement of Prussia, and ultimately of the German Empire, which he created. Entirely free of scruple, scorning unpopularity, brutal in speech to enemy and ally alike, he succeeded in his purpose by means of three wars. The first, in the north against Denmark, proved Prussia's army, and made it certain that she could also become a naval power. The second, in the south, against Austria, gave his country predominance in central Europe. The third, against France in the West, broke Napoleon III and ensured the Hohenzollerns an Imperial crown. It was a lifework for which men and women suffered for a century. "It is unworthy of a great state to fight for anything that does not form part of its own interests," wrote Bismarck. He did not add that a clever man could extend these "interests" to include anything on which he set his mind.

In the Denmark of the 1860's a situation developed of which Bismarck made more use than any contemporary would have believed possible, since neither the kingdom itself nor the duchies which were the cause of the war actually marched with Prussia. Bismarck saw the difficulties so clearly that he wrote: "I have not the smallest doubt that the Danish business can be settled, in a way desirable for us, only by war. The occasion for such a war can be found at any moment we consider favourable for waging it."

Different succession laws applied to Denmark and to the duchies, where the same Salic rule applied disregarding the status of women as had been the cause of the separation of Hanover from Britain at the accession of Queen Victoria. In Denmark, Prince Christian of Glücksburg succeeded his uncle Frederick, and he was also proclaimed Duke of Holstein and Schleswig, though no German admitted his right to the duchies. According to the Salic law, the heir to the duchies was the Duke of Augustenburg, who had already taken part in the war of 1848.

In fact, the Duke had given up his right of succession in consideration of 400,000 pounds, but his eldest son, Frederick, announced that he had assumed his father's inheritance, and the Germans in the duchies supported him. Conflict, armed or diplomatic, was inevitable, and the man who knew best how to profit by it was ready. Bismarck's aims had to be kept secret even from the Prussian King, who was friendly to the Augustenburgs, and only Sir Andrew Buchanan, British Ambassador at Berlin, guessed something of the truth. "I shall be surprised," he wrote, "if Bismarck does not endeavour to obtain more solid advantage for Prussia than the honour of having placed a Prince of Augustenburg on the throne of a Schleswig-Holstein state."

As the German Confederation did not admit the new King of Denmark to be a member of their body, German troops marched into Holstein, from which the Danes withdrew without firing a shot. Bismarck's plan was now to move into Schleswig, which Denmark had annexed, and to bring about a war with Christian IX. To do this, the support of Austria, as head of the German Confederation, was essential. It was achieved because Rechberg, the Austrian Minister, believed, like Bismarck, that a weak independent state such as Schleswig-Holstein would become, if in Augustenburg hands, no proper bulwark against revolution. In the Austrian Parliament someone asked Rechberg a pertinent question. "We let our troops play their nice regimental music and conduct the Prussians into the duchies with drum and trumpet; but to what tune will we be conducting them out again?"

On 1 February, 1864, Prussian and Austrian troops crossed the Schleswig frontier, and the Danes decided to fight, as Bismarck hoped they would. He needed resistant enemies to win his ends, and his agents had encouraged the Danes to believe that they would have support from Britain. Bismarck knew well enough that active help was unlikely, and that even if it came it would be ineffectual. Britain would make Denmark powerful by sea, but she had no considerable army, and the German statesman judged rightly, that when it came to the point the London government would not go to war. Nor did he fear the pan-Scandinavians in Sweden and Norway. They were vociferous, but the few hundred volunteers who crossed the Sound to help a sister kingdom were the measure of their activity. Their feebleness resulted in the embitterment of Ibsen and led indirectly to *Brand* and *Peer Gynt*.

The Allies carried all before them, and by 18 April, Prussian troops had stormed the Danish stronghold at Düppel. It was the second time it had fallen, the first occasion being almost exactly fifteen years before, when Saxons and Bavarians had fought on behalf of the Holstein rebels. Alsen, together with most of the Danish Army, was the next capture, and it was followed by a threat to the larger islands. At this stage Britain convened a conference at which Austria and Prussia were compelled to state their aims. Bismarck himself did not attend, but Rechberg (who now wished for nothing but to end the war) declared that German demands were the complete separation of the duchies from Denmark and their union as a single state under the Prince of Augustenburg. As Denmark would not accept this proposition, the conference broke down and war continued.

Three days after Rechberg's declaration Bismarck had a conversation with Frederick of Augustenburg. The Prussian Minister left the Prince no doubt that his conditions would be such that Frederick was likely to remain without territory for the rest of his life or lose all self-respect. "At the London Conference," Bismarck told a friend a few months later, "I hitched the Prince to the plough as an ox, to get it moving. Once the plough was in motion I unhitched the ox." It was as simple as that. Within weeks Denmark was compelled to sue for peace, and Britain gave vent to righteous fury. In August 1864, at Vienna, Christian IX ceded his rights in the duchies not to Frederick of Augustenburg but to the Emperor of Austria and the King of Prussia, the sovereigns whose troops had conquered them.

What of Rechberg's declaration and the Prince of Augustenburg? Bismarck soon settled that little matter. First he invented a new Pretender, in the person of the Archduke of Oldenburg; he then proposed that the duchies be administered under an Austro-Prussian "condominium." That meant, in practice, that Prussia would advance to her goal step by step, while Austria was reluctantly compelled to follow her. Ten years earlier Prussia had induced Oldenburg to cede some territory at the mouth of the Jade on which she could build a naval station, later known as Wilhelmshaven; now Bismarck proceeded to build up the port of Kiel. He was several moves ahead, but certain of success. By a series of insults and provocations he made the "condominium" intolerable to Austria; he whipped up popular enthusiasm in Prussia to support annexation, and by the winter of 1866 the duchies were Prussian by right of conquest and diplomacy. Lauenburg went to the King in consideration of a cash payment to the Emperor of Austria.

Lord Clarendon called the whole procedure the most infamous business since the partition of Poland, grimly adding that King Bismarck I was the only man among forty million Germans who not only had a purpose but the will to implement it. The Prussian Ambassador in Paris wrote sadly to Count Bernstorff in London that the affair has "put us permanently on the path of trickery, force and violation of law."

Prussia had clamped an iron collar around the neck of Jutland. She had also, and for the first time, shown herself to be a power with naval as well as with territorial ambitions. For the rest of his active career, which extended until 1890, Bismarck contented himself with consolidating his gains not only in the duchies, but in Hanover, Hesse-Cassel and other territories which were the harvest of his later war against Austria. Finally, when he had robbed France of Alsace and Lorraine by his defeat of Napoleon III, he proclaimed his sovereign German Emperor in the Hall of Mirrors at the palace of Versailles. All this is well remembered;

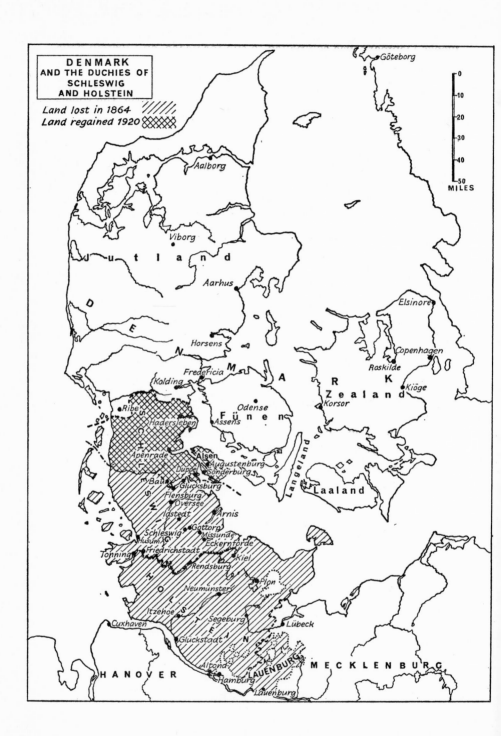

DENMARK
AND THE DUCHIES OF
SCHLESWIG
AND HOLSTEIN

Land lost in 1864
Land regained 1920

0
10
20
30
40
50
MILES

Göteborg

Aalborg

Viborg

J u t l a n d

D

E

N

Aarhus

Elsinore

Horsens

M

Copenhagen
Roskilde

Fredericia
Kolding

A

R

K
Kiöge

Ribe
Haderslev

Odense
Assens

Fünen

Zealand

Korsor

Apenrade

Alsen
Augustenburg
Düppel Sönderburg

Langeland

Laaland

Bau
Glücksburg
Flensburg
Oversee
Idstedt

Arnis

Schleswig
Husum
Tonning
Friedrichstadt

Gottorp
Missunde
Eckernförde

Kiel

Rendsburg

H

O

L

S

Neumünster

Plön

Itzehoe

E

Cuxhaven

I

Segeburg

N

Lübeck

Glückstadt

HANOVER

Altona

Hamburg

LAUENBURG

MECKLENBURG

Lauenburg

what is overlooked, because Bismarck was not himself permitted to carry it out, is that it was his foresight, his ruthless pursuit of his single end, which enabled Germany to build the Kiel Canal.

The war of the duchies was, in fact, the final blow to Scandinavian predominance in the Baltic, since, through the annexation, followed by that of Hanover, Prussia commanded the mouths of the Weser, the Elbe, the Oder and the Vistula, a formidable succession of North Sea and Baltic egresses. As reactionary Mecklenburg could always be relied upon, the construction of a deepwater canal between Kiel and the mouth of the Elbe, a project which had been partly realized in the eighteenth century, transferred the key to the Baltic (which nature had bestowed upon Denmark) to Germany. With a strong navy, she could keep it.

The completion of the canal in 1898 followed the transfer of Heligoland to Germany, and the waterway was then secure at both ends. Henceforward Germany was able to steam her ships of war from the North Sea to Königsberg and beyond without political or maritime let or hindrance. It was a prime example of how the sea can be made to unite as well as to divide. Supreme in north Europe, Germany was now to aspire to world power. She had nothing to fear from Denmark or Sweden, and she had the will and means to build a high-seas fleet. Her people, arrogant with success, began to call the North Sea, the ancient scene of struggle between British and Dutch and Scandinavians, the German Ocean. So far can national horizons be extended in the course of a few decades.

9 . Disasters and new hope

Few statesmen could have predicted, before the war opened, the effect upon affairs in the Baltic of a Russian reverse in the Far East, though with time its bearing became ever clearer. The conflict with Japan which broke out soon after the turn of the present century had among its causes Russian determination to garrison Port Arthur and use it as a naval base—which was a direct threat to the island kingdom. Japan acted against Russia without declaring war, and early setbacks so reduced his eastern fleet that the Tsar, from sheer necessity, was forced to order his Baltic squadrons to Vladivostok, in the hope of reversing the balance. Nicholas II reviewed the force he had entrusted to Admiral Rojdestvensky in October 1904, bidding it Godspeed on its immense journey around the world.

Rojdestvensky sailed, in no sort of order, and without much notion of how to set about his task. His armada of battleships old and new, cruisers, torpedo boats and a fleet train which ranged from transports to colliers, was motley and ill organized. He expected to replenish at French ports, hospitality which was duly extended, but anxieties were acute. He believed he might be attacked by enemy "scouts" even before he quitted Baltic waters, and at one stage his gunners made a target of a Swedish merchantman, mistaking her for an armed Japanese.

In the North Sea things were worse. Fishing vessels were fired upon off the Dogger Bank, lives being lost as the result of wild shooting. At the time there was in fact an Anglo-Japanese alliance in existence, its object being the maintenance of the *status quo* in Asia: even so, Rojdestvensky's apprehensions were unrealistic, and most landsmen would have recognized trawlers for what they were. Such was the state of affairs in ships which, seven months later, met destruction at the hands of Admiral Togo.

Defeat was expected. What was not so readily perceived was its effect on Germany. Admiral Rojdestvensky's departure had left Kronstadt almost empty, and in some of the remaining units, notably the battleship *Potemkin*, serious trouble occurred, as it did in the capital itself. Russia, politically unstable as seldom before, had eliminated herself as a formidable naval power in the Baltic, and since fleets cannot be built, equipped and trained for modern war with the speed of armies, Germany would have little to fear from her at sea in a struggle to which her planners already looked forward with confidence. Her maritime resources could be reserved for a major antagonist, and that was likely to be Britain.

The Russo-Japanese episode affords an example of Russia's earlier dilemmas as a naval power. While her armies could operate freely on immense "interior lines," her men-of-war had four possible spheres of activity. Each of them, the White Sea, the Baltic, the Black Sea and the Sea of Japan, had handicaps hard to overcome. The White Sea is intersected by the Arctic Circle. Both the Baltic and the Black Sea are virtually landlocked, the Baltic at times and in part being ice-conditioned. In the Far East what could be achieved by Russian sea power was restricted; such were geographical and political factors.

Over the course of time Russia has achieved temporary or local dominance in one area or another: for instance, in the eastern Baltic under Peter the Great, and in the Black Sea under various successors; but the separation of aims and problems has never yet enabled her admirals to obtain all-around experience and mastery in every sea upon which they may be required to exercise command. Since Rojdestvensky's defeat Russia has established no claim as a considerable maritime power in war, though squadrons and even single ships have been used in support of land fighting, sometimes with effect. About future possibilities it is rash to speculate, for the completion of a waterway system linking Leningrad with ports in the far North, and with the development of polar routes to the East, Russia's situation has radically altered and improved.

II

Six months after Rojdestvensky's ships went down in Asian waters, Sweden became a kingdom solely Baltic. Bernadotte's union worked but never prospered, and in November 1905, Haakon VII, a Danish-born prince, was recognized as the independent sovereign of Norway. Haakon VI, the last Norwegian King, had died in the fourteenth century, and now at last, after more than five hundred years, the country could develop those world-wide interests which attracted her seamen and traders, without the need to look across the Sound, or over a mountainous shoulder. Sweden was alone. Once she had possessed an empire. For long she had been considerable. Now she became one of three more or less equal Scandinavian kingdoms, moderate in resources, progressive in outlook.

Separation was not effected without a struggle. All through the nineteenth century Norwegian restlessness had grown. Bernadotte himself could not address his original subjects in Swedish; how could he hope to identify himself more than superficially with a sister kingdom not disposed to be friendly, and with no reason whatever to be grateful? His successors were enlightened men, but the cleavage did not disappear. As was the case with Denmark and Schleswig-Holstein, a union of crowns was not enough.

Under the Fundamental Law of 1814, Norway had been declared "free, indivisible and independent." These were big words, but as the years passed, it seemed to Norwegians that only "indivisible" made sense. They recalled with nostalgia one day when, after they had repudiated Bernadotte's arrangements with Denmark, they had acclaimed, and for a few months enjoyed, a king of their own choosing. The celebrations, in course of time, became forbidden, but it was impossible to stifle the aspiration of a vigorous people.

A clash might have come much earlier, but restraint postponed it until, after a succession of difficulties of forming an administration, the Storting announced: "As King Oscar II has declared his inability to form a government, he has automatically ceased to reign." For some perilous weeks an inter-Scandinavian war seemed possible, but when a vote was taken and Norwegians proved to be overwhelmingly in favour of breaking away, the Swedish King bowed to majority opinion. No one in Norway has found cause to regret the decision, for the reigning house has shown wisdom and fortitude under trials which Sweden has avoided.

III

Three years after the Swedish-Norwegian separation two agreements were come to, worthy in purpose, though in practice "scraps of paper." They concerned the "regions which border upon the Baltic Sea" and those which "border upon the North Sea." The signatories to the first were Germany, Denmark, Russia and Sweden, and to the second Germany, Denmark, Britain, France, the Netherlands and Sweden. All countries involved proclaimed their wish to maintain the existing state of affairs and the sovereign rights of those represented. In the event of a menace to either, they would, so it was agreed, concert measures by mutual consent. Separate negotiations covered Norway, a treaty guaranteeing her territorial integrity being ratified in 1907 by Great Britain, France, Russia, and Germany.

Seven years later large-scale events made it certain that the agreements would be forgotten under the pressure of far greater problems, and the Scandinavian kings, Gustav V of Sweden, Christian X of Denmark and Haakon VII of Norway met urgently at Malmö to consider their attitude towards the struggle which was raging elsewhere. Their hope was to remain neutral, and at a later meeting, held in 1917, they had reason to express satisfaction that they had realized their wish. Their kingdoms had become a refuge of sanity in a disordered and cruelly damaged Europe, although Norway, with the fourth-largest merchant fleet in the world, had by that time suffered immense losses, nearly half her prewar tonnage, through the unrestricted submarine campaign conducted by Germany.

The spark which set alight the train of powder which blew an older European dispensation into fragments was the assassination, on 28 June, 1914, of the Archduke Francis Ferdinand of Austria by Serbian nationalists. "Some damned foolish thing in the Balkans," as Bismarck once predicted, did just what he said it would do. Such was the pressure of fear, suspense, design and political combination that no more than six weeks later Germany, Austria-Hungary, Russia, France and Britain were at open war. Belgian neutrality had been ruthlessly violated, and Germany was executing her plan to crush France within six weeks. Her armies marched by way of the traditional "cockpit of Europe," where Napoleon had fought his last battle.

Broadly speaking, only one power stood to gain by war, and only one welcomed it. "History," said Bismarck, "teaches one how far one may safely go." His nation, having sabre-rattled for half a century, getting its way in the process, believed it might safely go anywhere. As always, the Germans had the wish to be loved, but they never for an instant felt the need to deserve it. The country had a superbly trained army, a newly created and most powerful navy and people as eager for expansion as their ancestors had been under Frederick the Great.

German statesmen argued that war must come, and that by delaying longer their relative strength would suffer, since the Russians had taken everyone by surprise by their speed of recovery, in a military sense, from the humiliations of the clash with Japan. Nominally, Germany armed on behalf of Austria, who feared Russian aspirations in the Balkans. Her true reasons were otherwise. As Prince Lichnowsky, the German Ambassador in London, said to his Austrian colleague when they received their passports: "We wanted the war, not the Austrians, and I have told the English so."

All classes were involved. The army considered itself invincible, as indeed it almost proved to be; Tirpitz, at the German Admiralty, sought a trial of strength, and the Imperial Navy did much to fulfil his hopes. Diplomats and businessmen regarded Britain and France as semi-moribund, and they wished to inherit Britain's share in world affairs and finance. The general public, nurtured on memories of Bismarck's victories, believed in a quick breakthrough, and triumphant entry into Paris. What no German welcomed, and few visualized, was a serious war on two fronts before everything was secure in the west. By taking the initiative and the offensive, Germany would fight her battles on foreign soil. There she would stay until enemies made peace at her bidding.

Her plans were scientific, and her strength and efficiency were such that they nearly came off. What marred sucess was a combination of circumstances which included failure on the part of certain generals, notably von Kluck; unexpectedly quick help given to France by a small though well-trained British army, and a threat to East Prussia by Russian armies under Generals Rennenkampf and Samsonov. It was this threat which helped to ensure a long war, and which afforded the Western Allies priceless relief at a time when the capture of Paris seemed an instant probability.

A purely Russian treatment of her earlier military problems would have led to a holding campaign until full mobilization was completed. Instead, with an ardour which did honour to the Tsar and his government, France's call for help was answered. Two converging forces, Rennenkampf's marching from Vilna, near the Baltic shore, and Samsonov's from Warsaw, advanced towards the German border. The immediate result was the withdrawal from France of two army corps and a cavalry division, and consternation at the Kaiser's headquarters. This was a development not according to the book.

The defence of East Prussia had been confided to General von Prittwitz, a Falstaffian figure renowned at the table. He faced a double threat from armies each of which was numerically equal to his own. He advanced to meet Rennenkampf near the eastern border of the Fatherland, and on 20 August, 1914, began to fight the Battle of Gumbinnen. The day was indecisive, although the superior training of the Germans soon became apparent. In the evening von Prittwitz, alarmed at reports of the movement of the army from Warsaw, which appeared to be threatening his line of retreat, broke off the battle and telephoned to general headquarters with the news that in the face of overwhelming numbers he must retire behind the Vistula, and that in view of the low state of the river he did not feel able to guarantee to hold even that position.

The German High Command decided there and then to su-
persede the rattled general. Telegrams were sent to Major General Ludendorff, who had distinguished himself before Liége,
and to von Hindenburg, an officer of approved qualities, and
they were ordered north to restore the situation. At the same time
the Austrians were urged to hasten an offensive, a plea which resulted in disaster.

Hindenburg and Ludendorff proved a successful and long-last-
ing combination, and as they worked with plans already prepared by General Hoffmann, a staff officer of von Prittwitz's, they
were able to defeat the Russians at Tannenberg, and near the
Masurian Lakes (scene of a medieval victory by Poles and Lithuanians over the Teutonic Knights), where the Russians lost at least
100,000 men and five hundred field pieces.

Not until the very end of the war was Germany again to suffer invasion, and when it came an armistice was in force. Hindenburg, who at the time the East Prussian campaign opened had
been retired for some years and was nearing seventy, henceforward became the symbol of Prussian and hence of German sol-
dierly virtue. It was a reputation he maintained for the rest of a
long life, although, as everyone knew, the brains of the Hinden-
burg-Ludendorff combination were with the younger man.

Later in the war Hoffmann, who remained on the eastern front,
would sometimes conduct awe-struck visitors over the field of
victory. "Here," he would say, "is where the field marshal slept
before the battle. Here is where he slept after the battle. And
here," he would conclude with solemn expression, "is where he
slept during the battle."

IV

For some months after Tannenberg the Baltic became a back-
water in the struggle. Germany's naval strength and her geographical advantages were such that, so far as Britain was concerned, there could be no Saumarez exercising control over any
area, while the Russian Navy presented so little threat that the
sea was German-dominated, an unprecedented state of affairs

in time of war. Even so, Russia had her value for the Western Allies, as was shown in a striking way. As early as September 1914 the German cruiser *Magdeburg*, operating at the entrance to the Gulf of Finland—significantly far to the east—was wrecked off the isle of Odensholm. The dead body of an underofficer was picked up by the Russians, and upon it were found signal books, ciphers and minutely squared maps of the North Sea and the Heligoland bight. The Russians set to work at breaking down the codes, and by November they were able to give information of importance to their naval allies. It was further proof of the value of Russian co-operation, even in a sphere where they were far less able to afford help than by land.

Not long after Tannenberg the Germans established a line which ran from near Riga southward into territory which had once been Polish, the great battles between the Russians and Austrians being fought out in Galicia and elsewhere. On the western front a thread of trench and fortification, stretching across Flanders and France from the English Channel to the Swiss frontier, became the scene of some of the most dreadful warfare in human history, in the course of which millions died and millions more were gassed or wounded. After a few months of move and countermove, it became a locked struggle, attrition in which gains were reckoned by yards, and in which a generation of manhood drained away.

In the north, warfare was apt to be less static, if only because ground was less precious, and how decidedly both Germans and Russians regarded the Baltic sphere as one in which the land predominated is shown by such activity as the Tsar's fleet was prepared to display. From the outset the Russians generated much enthusiasm for that mining warfare which had once intimidated Admiral Napier. It was essentially defensive. Although on paper the Tsar could oppose four battleships, four cruisers, over sixty torpedo boats and six submarines against the scratch force which was all that could be spared by the Germans, yet the shadow of Rojdestvensky's defeat lay heavily upon the Russians, and they allowed the ships at the disposal of Prince Henry of Prussia, commanding in the Baltic, to keep the initiative. This was made easier for him from the practice of the high-seas fleet of

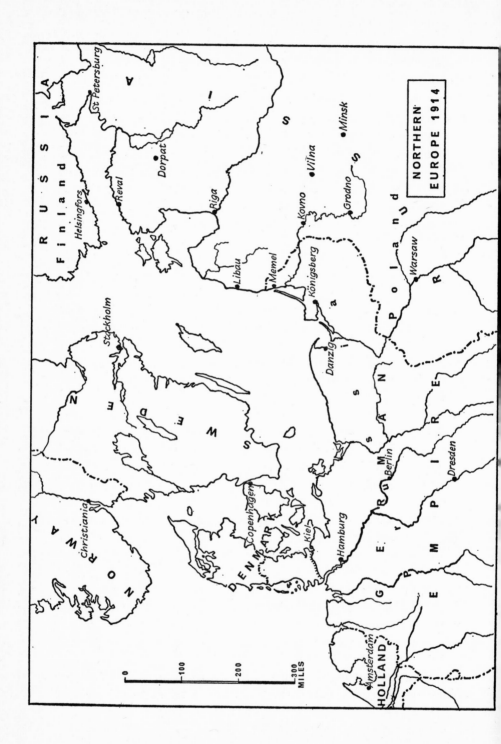

NORTHERN
EUROPE 1914

RUSSIA

Finland

Helsingfors

St Petersburg

Reval

Dorpat

Riga

Libau

Memel

Kovno

Vilna

Minsk

Grodno

Königsberg

Poland

Warsaw

Danzig

Stockholm

N

S   W   E   D   E   N

A

N

s

i

a

Christiania

NORWAY

DENMARK

Copenhagen

Kiel

Hamburg

Berlin

Dresden

Prussia

GERMAN   EMPIRE

Amsterdam

HOLLAND

0   100   200   300
                              MILES

making occasional training exercises in his area, which had been made accessible to larger units since the deepening of the Kiel Canal.

The Russians had some success with their mines, by means of which they had once done appreciable damage to the Japanese, but they rarely showed tactical skill even on the few occasions when, by good fortune, they caught German ships at a disadvantage, and their attempts at interference with the essential ore traffic from Sweden were ineffectual. Professionals noted that the conning tower of Russian submarines would as often as not break surface after a torpedo attack, a sure sign that the chief engineer had inadequate control of the trim of the vessel.

In the summer of 1915, at the request of the Russian Government, a few British submarines were sent to the Baltic, outstanding results being by Lieutenant Commander Max Horton, in E.9, prophetic of his success in the Second World War as Commander in Chief of the Western Approaches at the height of a far greater campaign. In July, Horton torpedoed the armoured cruiser *Prinz Adalbert*, and throughout that summer activities increased to an extent which delayed, though never seriously menaced, German advances.

In the later stages of the war Russian naval effort grew steadily less effective, while the Germans got the better of their mines. The mutinies of 1905 recurred on a far more serious scale, inactive steel hulls breeding such steely thoughts that the time arrived when the sailors of Kronstadt became the *sans-culottes* of a new disorder. Far off in Kiel and Wilhelmshaven, German sailors became similarly affected, undermining the unity of their service while more active fellows, roaming the sea lanes in their lethal submarines, were doing their utmost to sever the western supply line.

This disintegration, occurring at both ends of the Baltic, was symptomatic of a profound change in the aspect of Europe. If at sea the mine and the submarine were destroying the freedoms and traditions of the older surface navies, on land, and in the north, armies began to advance and retreat as of old, and events assumed such significance for the future as to demand a different scale of examination.

In the Baltic the clash of nations radically altered. There were new alignments, even swifter changes, and a startling emergence of nationhood in smaller countries. Finland freed herself, setting an example which was to be followed by neighbour states. Elsewhere a form of society began to take shape as alarming to entrenched interests as the French Revolution had proved nearly a century and a half earlier. Out of the midst of devastation and misery ideas which were charged with hope began to take on reality. For the first time Russian regiments began to ask what they were fighting for, and for the first time someone was at hand with an answer.

That answer affected the entire world. For this reason, and because events since the end of the First World War continue to have repercussions—many of the men who helped to shape them being still alive—a more detailed scrutiny seems necessary to the understanding of the conditions under which the peoples of the north, like their fellows elsewhere, now live.

Part Two ♆ THE BALTIC REORDERED [1917-1945]

"No one, except Winston, who matters just now has read history.
Statesmen and warriors pick their way through the dusk."

LORD ESHER, in 1914.

I O . Russian fragmentation

Mankind's capacity for sustained suffering brought about by rulers and governments seems limitless. If the Thirty Years' War left Germany a desert, Russian history is one protracted agony, while the Scandinavian countries, with slender reserves of man-power, were upon the rack almost continuously throughout the seventeenth and eighteenth centuries. Charles XII of Sweden provides the extreme illustration of a ruler to whom sacrifice to purpose meant everything, but he was not unique. Even today every adult Russian and German is in a sense a mere survivor from a struggle lost and won. A principal difference between them, as their literature shows, is that while the Russian has qualities which include an ingrained suspicion of authority, even when he has had some hand in choosing it, the average German exercises no such private relief, being conditioned from childhood to like being led.

It was a virtue in Lenin, who brought new hope to his country, where he is honoured as a god, that he rejected the necessity for man merely to endure. "I never met anyone in Russia," said his friend Gorky, "where the inevitability of suffering is preached as the general road to salvation, who hated and despised all unhappiness, grief and suffering as much as he did." Such was Lenin the individual. Lenin the doctrinaire spoke differently. "It would not matter a jot," he said, "if three quarters of the human race perished. The important thing is that the remaining quarter should be Communists." The purging of "unhappiness, grief and suffering" must come by Marx's method.

The contrast between the wish for human happiness and obliviousness of the cost at which it is achieved is in fact no more startling than that provided by a climate in which seasonal temperatures may range between 115 degrees Fahrenheit and 47 below zero in a single place. Russia is a country of extremes, though few will dispute the opinion of Carl Mannerheim, who served the old Russia and fought the new, that human life and personal freedom were held in far higher esteem under the Tsars than under their successors. Lenin's purpose was "to apply to politics, both national and international, one doctrine of war."

"Insurrection is an art," so he declared. It was the creed of a man who dedicated his life to it. "If you are not prepared to adapt yourself," he said, "if you are not inclined to crawl on your belly in the mud, you are not a revolutionary but a windbag."

The state of Russia, when Lenin was born in 1870 at Simbirsk, on the middle Volga (a town now called Ulyanovsk, after his family name), was like nothing else in the universe. A crust of aristocracy, headed by the Tsar, owned vast estates upon which peasants lived in medieval conditions. Such little industry as had been developed owed everything to foreign capital, and was to increase its dependency. Priests suggested a beatific hereafter to believers who had little to look for in the present, and even they were required to reveal the secrets of the confessional in the interests of a state whose agents were the police, the taxgatherer and the bureaucrat. Lenin's elder brother was executed at the age of nineteen for being implicated in a plot to assassinate Alexander III. He is said to have believed in government by consent, a notion then ridiculed not merely in Russia, but in far more advanced societies. Russia had no middle class in the sense that other nations knew it, and it was one of Lenin's views that certain elements which such a class represented should be encouraged, not least in revolutionaries. They, so he argued, should be "no less professionally trained than the police." As for the proletariat, the means of change from below, he pointed out that it was "trained for organization by its whole life." Factory workers and peasants knew discipline: their lives were ordered by the production line and the needs of beast and crop. Once they chose and obeyed their own leaders, their battle was half won.

The European war provided Lenin not with an excuse but with an opportunity. Ever since he had learned to think, which was at an early age, he had worked for change in Russian life with a single-mindedness which no setback discouraged. He discovered in the writings of Karl Marx a body of political doctrine suited to his needs, and Marx had written: "All philosophies have sought to explain the world; the point, however, is to change it." Lenin was pre-eminently practical, and needs came first. Marx provided the theories upon which revolution was built, but his First International Working Men's Council, founded in 1864, collapsed when Lenin was in the cradle, and it became necessary to rebuild.

Marx had solutions which Lenin believed to be enduring. As he expounded in *Das Kapital*, Marx argued that a diminishing number of capitalists appropriate the benefit of improved industrial methods, while the artisan is left in increasing dependency and misery, which was indeed true in his own age. He held the view that the price of a commodity should be the remuneration of the work required to produce it, and that it fails to be so because capital exacts an inequitable share, while competition among workers obliges them to accept less than their proper due.

Marx pointed to a remedy in the total abolition of private property, to be brought about through a "class war" between the haves and have-nots. "Workers of the world, unite!" That was his slogan and crusade. His idea was that when the community had acquired possession of all property and means of production, it would distribute work to each individual and provide for his welfare. "From everyone according to his faculties, to everyone according to his needs."

This gross oversimplification, which begs many questions and omits many steps in logic, was the doctrine as presented to people many of whom could neither read nor write, but all of whom could feel and vote. What more realistic approach to an earthly paradise could be offered them? The old worker who, driving back to Petrograd from Tsarskoye Selo a few days after the Revolution, swept the far gleaming capital with an exultant gesture, crying, "Mine . . . All mine now . . . *My* Petrograd!" had caught the spirit of hope.

Strictly speaking, there is no such thing as a Communist state, which represents an ideal, perhaps unrealizable. The official title of the present Soviet constituents, whose people inherit Lenin's work, is that of Socialist Republics, state socialism being a stage towards a stateless goal which comparatively few Marxists consider practicable.

A possible alternative to Marxism, based on a guaranteed minimum standard of life, with freedom of belief, freedom of combination and freedom of incentive, was inapplicable in the circumstances of the time and in the country where revolutionary crisis broke out. That this should have happened in Russia was in a sense ironical. Karl Marx, who was born in Rhenish Prussia of Jewish descent, and who wrote much of his best work in London, owed nothing to the country whose future leaders were to adopt him as political savant and scientist in chief, and he was dead before Lenin reached manhood. Marx never believed that effective revolution would come out of Russia. He spoke of the "idiocy of rural life," and in a country which was so largely peasant he saw little promise. His was an urban creed. Time proved him wrong because special conditions prevailed in the Russia of Lenin's day, and Marx's dialectical materialism, which, robbed of its jargon, means reaching reasoned conclusions on matters which concern the actual world, was one of the ways by which Lenin most successfully proceeded.

Lenin, fanatic for Marxism as he became, based his actions on realism, and on the seizing of opportunity. As a student he read law, and for a time he practiced in peasant communities. By 1897 he had become well known as a subversive, and he was actually condemned to a term in Siberia, to which he travelled at his own expense, and where he found conditions far from pleasant. In the abortive revolution of 1905 he was active but escaped re-arrest, and he then spent some years abroad. At the outbreak of war he was in Switzerland, living with his wife on slender resources, but, as always, doing a prodigious amount of work, and already recognized as an outstanding personality.

Early in 1917, when the Tsarist armies were showing every sign of collapse, after prodigious losses in the cause of the

Western alliance, the Germans perceived in Lenin a possible tool to serve their purposes. Even though working with clear aims of his own, he might help to undermine the remaining military value of a country which still presented a standing danger, so remarkable were her proved powers of recovery. The Germans made their arrangements, and Lenin, with a party of about thirty others, returned home from Switzerland by way of Berlin, Denmark, Sweden and Finland. His journey could, so they thought, do the Germans no harm. Lenin was determined that it should do his country, through himself, much good. For one thing, he intended to stop the war, and that in itself suited the Germans. Their Austrian allies were demoralized, and by a prodigious effort a clear-cut victory might still just be possible.

In March the Tsar abdicated, and the army, tried too sorely, refused obedience. The Duma, the remaining seat of authority, which was a token of such success as the risings of 1905 had achieved in making heard the voice of the nation, never enjoyed power, and it was not respected. Government was, in fact, breaking down altogether, and in the capital the people looked increasingly to the Workers and Soldiers Soviets, or Councils. There were, in fact, nominal and actual seats of authority, and it became only a matter of time, of finding leaders, before they coalesced. Over the next few months Lenin and Trotsky asserted that leadership.

Succeeding events included some of the most remarkable in Baltic history. Kerensky, the son of Lenin's old schoolmaster at Simbirsk, formed what was styled a Provisional Government and arrested the chief revolutionaries. Lenin went into hiding. The United States, which had by then been forced into the war largely by the pressure of the submarine campaign, which was unsparing of neutrals great or small, offered Russia a 75,000,000-dollar loan in consideration of an offensive. Kerensky ordered the Russian armies to fight, but his efforts merely resulted in fraternization. His policy defied and his position made impossible, Kerensky fled from the Winter Palace in a car flying the Stars and Stripes. It was Lenin's chance. The October Revolution placed him in power. His announced aims were peace, the land for the peasants and a new Communist International. The Bolsheviks, the extreme radical wing of the Social Democratic Party, had triumphed. Once it had gained a position of authority, there it intended to stay. Russia, the country of extremes, was also the country of absolute rule.

The peace claimed first attention, though the Treaty of Brest-Litovsk, named after a town on a river owning to the name of Bug, represented what the Germans so complained about when it was applied to themselves—a *Diktat*, or forced measure. Lenin, who signed the treaty, refused to study it, once again showing his sense, for the terms deprived his country of a quarter of her territory, a third of her population, the granary of the Ukraine, the Baltic states, and three quarters of her coal and iron. They were impossible. As Lenin remarked, it was now the turn of the Soviets to "take up the burden of Peter the Great." Russia must be re-created.

By the time matters between Germans and Russians were negotiated, the last full winter of the European war was over, and President Wilson, who appeared as the hope of the universe, had announced his own Fourteen Points, which summarized what he thought could be the basis for a lasting general settlement.

These points are more often alluded to than remembered, and they may be worth recalling as the considered view of one of the most powerful men then living, and one of the best intentioned. The President spoke from a detachment impossible in statesmen whose countries had endured nearly four years of confusion and suffering on a scale unparalleled. Some of the points concerned the Baltic powers directly, others had a bearing upon them, and most of the ideas found expression in later treaties and those international agreements which redrew the map. Perhaps the most impressive aspect of the President's statement was that the sharp end of more than one point was directed at his own allies.

Point the first required open diplomacy. The second sought freedom of navigation, even in war, outside territorial waters, except when seas were closed by international action. This was thoroughly impractical. Its allusion was both to the murderous undersea campaign then going forward and to the system of blockade which, in the earlier stages of war, had led to friction with Britain. The third aimed at removal of economic barriers

—it was a plea for free, or at any rate free-er, trade. The fourth required guarantees for the reduction of armaments.

Points five to thirteen all concerned adjustments of territory, and were related to the right of self-determination for all nations. Point five, which expressed American suspicion of British and to a lesser degree of French imperialism, suggested impartial settlement of colonial claims, the interests of peoples having equal weight with claims of governments. The sixth demanded the evacuation of Russian territory by the Germans; the seventh the restoration of Belgium; the eighth that the wrongs of France should be righted in the matter of Alsace-Lorraine; the ninth, tenth, eleventh and twelfth concerned Italy, Austria-Hungary, the Balkans and Turkey, a proposal being made that the Dardanelles should be free to all shipping.

The last two points, thirteen and fourteen, were to be of great consequence. Poland should be restored to independence, which was an idea implanted in Wilson's mind by Ignace Jan Paderewski, surely the most influential musician ever to have entered politics. The country's autonomy had been declared as early as 1916 by Germany and Austria in a bid to attract enthusiasm, but the gesture, coming from such a source, had been so obviously a propaganda move against Russia as to excite derision. American beneficence was a very different matter.

Finally, a general association of nations should be formed under covenants which would afford mutual guarantees of political independence and territorial integrity to great and small states alike. This was the germ of the League of Nations, whose tragedy it was that the United States herself refused participation, while Russia ended a brief membership by acts of aggression which led even the well disposed to the view that there was no place for her within a pacifically minded assembly until she had learned forbearance.

So far as the Baltic was concerned, it was points six and thirteen which were of most weight. The evacuation of Russian territory and the re-creation of Poland entailed vast operations, but even by the time Lenin had seized power, the first results of Russian fragmentation were beginning to appear. Finland was in turmoil, and the wind of change had been felt in the forests of the eastern shore of the Baltic. In February 1918, the month after the publication of the President's manifesto, Lithuania and Estonia declared their independence, and Latvia would have done the same but for the presence of a German army.

II

Finland proved as restless under union with Russia as had Norway when joined to Sweden. Her people, neither Slav nor Teuton, with their own language, traditions and qualities, had long been equipped to guide their own destinies. Now, like the Russians themselves, they saw their chance.

When Alexander I first occupied the country during the Napoleonic wars, his policy had been ameliorative. The Finns were politically far more advanced than his Russian subjects; they had a long history of contact with the West, and during their six centuries under Sweden they had enjoyed comparatively enlightened rule. Alexander needed Finland for strategic protection if for no other reason, but wisdom led him to try to govern by co-operation, and one of his first acts was to restore Viborg to the country from which it had been severed by Peter the Great. The Finns were granted a "free Constitution" with a Senate and a Governor General, and in the time of Alexander II the Diet, with its four Estates of nobles, clergy, burghers and peasants, was reconvoked, after being in recess for almost a lifetime.

By the end of the reign of Alexander III two Finnish parties had come into being, neither of them inclined towards Russia. One sought reunion with Sweden, the other was nationalist pure and simple. These, and other parties, had grown so strong by the time Nicholas II succeeded as Tsar that his government grew seriously alarmed, and a manifesto dated February 1899 virtually abrogated the Diet's legislative power. A process of Russification then began, which was so unpopular that by 1905, the year of abortive revolution, the Finns showed in clear terms where their aspirations lay. Nicholas, alarmed at the fierceness of national sentiment, restored power to the Diet, at the same time granting universal suffrage to men and women alike, freedom of the press and freedom of association. These concessions

were regretted once the alarm had subsided. It was embarrassing for Russia to have a subject country exercising liberty so near
her capital. Reaction was almost inevitable.

Finns were not liable to compulsory service in the Russian
Army even in time of emergency: there was a system of exemp-
tion by purchase, and in fact, when the European war opened,
volunteers were almost equally divided between those who opted
for Germany and those who served the Tsar. The country's more
serious problems began later, when fighting reached their doorstep and it became a case not of volunteering but of choosing the
right side.

This might have been Sweden's great opportunity to revive historic ties, to use her resources to aid the Finns in their struggle.
It was missed. Sweden feared Germany, and she could not dis-
cern, any more easily than her neighbours, the shape of a new
Russia. She took no official part in the Finnish War of Liberation,
though her sympathies were made clear. There are those who
wonder at what they perceive to be underlying sadness in a country which has enjoyed an almost unparalleled span of peace and
prosperity. It may arise, in part at least, because many of her people believed that had they dared greatly, even at the cost of suffering, they would have known an exhilaration now denied them.
Neutrality is often wise, and it sometimes requires sustained
courage, but it carries its own penalties.

Finland's freedom was gained through the circumstance of a
world at odds, through the determination of her people, and
through the skill of Carl Mannerheim, a Swedish Finn of aristo-
cratic family who has claim to be the most outstanding leader
the Baltic countries have ever produced, not excluding Gustavus
Adolphus. Mannerheim not only ensured independence, he twice
occupied the highest office in the state—each time in a moment
of crisis—and he thrice led Finnish armies against the world's
most formidable land power. His aims were wisely limited, and
even success brought with it on two occasions inevitable loss of
territory. Even so, Mannerheim's resolution and military genius
saved Finland from being re-engulfed into the maw of her gigantic neighbour. As his last campaign ended when the marshal was
nearer eighty than seventy, after a lifetime of action, stress and
responsibility, he need yield place to no one, living or dead, as

the hero of a free country, or to any warrior in the span and variety of his achievements.

Born in 1867, near Abo, where his family held property, Mannerheim took service as a youth in the army of Imperial Russia. He fought in the Russo-Japanese War, made a valuable journey of exploration into the recesses of Asia and later commanded the Tsar's Cavalry Guard. By the time of the great war he had become a general officer, and he served with distinction in the opening campaigns against the Austrians. In 1917, at the age of fifty, he returned to his homeland by way of Petrograd, which was then in the throes of revolutionary change. He reached Helsinki in December, to find the country on the verge of a civil war in which the Whites of the central and northern districts were opposed by Reds of the south, aided by forces from Russia who fought under the Bolshevik banner. There was never any question where Mannerheim's sympathy lay. He was a Finn and a White. He saw his first duty in disarming the Russian garrisons stationed throughout the land, in organizing armies where none had existed before and in ridding the south of what he considered to be disruptive elements. He believed his country could free herself through her own efforts, without the need of intervention. Volunteers he welcomed, and during his four-month campaign he had useful service from Swedes, Norwegians and Danes, the Swedish contingent including eighty regular officers.

The Germans had formed those Finns who had enlisted in their armies into a unit of their own—the 27th Jäger Battalion, which had already proved itself in battle on the eastern front. Mannerheim requested its recall to serve in the war which he was now conducting, and the Jägers fought from February 1918 onwards, when they were at last able to return to Finnish soil. More difficult problems arose from the advent, two months later, of a German general, von der Goltz, at the head of a regular Teuton formation.

Before taking over his command, Mannerheim had made it a condition that official help should not be sought since, like the late Earl Balfour, he believed that next to being enslaved by Germany, there is no worse fate than being liberated by her. "I insisted," he wrote, "that a people's freedom to be lasting must be

paid for with its own sufferings and the blood of its own sons."
Unfortunately, Pehr Svinhufvud, a statesman who had already
been Speaker of the Finnish Diet, who had served a term in Siberia for anti-Russian activities, and who saw no hope of salvation without Germany, had already invited aid. Von der Goltz's
forces were useful, though not essential, in the final episodes of
the struggle. Later they were to prove an embarrassment, for by
the time Finland had been restored to peace, Germany had virtually lost the war, Russia was in a state of chaos and it was necessary for the country to seek friends elsewhere.

At this stage Mannerheim was requested to go on a mission to
Sweden, thence to London and Paris to sound opinion and to
seek economic help for a country in which supplies were gravely
short. He learned while in Sweden that the pro-German party
had offered the throne to Friedrich Karl of Hesse, a prince who
spent the summer of 1918 in a frantic attempt to learn the difficult Finnish language. It was wasted effort. His summons never
came, for it was soon clear that, away in their northern world,
politicians had become sadly out of touch.

By the time Mannerheim had landed in Britain on his European journey, the Flanders fighting was over, and a cable from
Helsinki offered him the status of Regent. This he accepted, since
it enabled him to negotiate with plenary powers. When he returned to Finland, having achieved recognition of his country's
autonomy, it was to be saluted by a guard of honour drawn
from the Civil Defence Corps, headed by Sergeant Major Pehr
Svinhufvud. Seldom can a more manly gesture of political con-
trition have been made. Henceforward Finland belonged in sympathy with the Western nations. She enjoyed the particular favour of the United States, who sent her practical help in the form
of much needed foodstuffs and negotiated a considerable loan,
which, as every American learns in history books, was duly re-
paid in full.

Mannerheim says not a word in his modest *Memoirs* to indicate
what was among his more striking attributes: the skill in languages, and the gift of friendship which enabled him to confer on
the highest level with Swedes, Russians, Germans, French, Americans and English. There is a tradition that his Finnish was in-

different, but he never had difficulty in making himself understood in his native tongue, and his countrymen proved gratefully
aware of his unique services.

The last immediate problem which might have disturbed Finnish harmony was that of the Aland Islands, that important
group which lie strung across the approaches to the Gulf of
Bothnia, to which it forms a natural defence. The Alands had
long been administered as an integral part of Finland, but the
people were Swedish-speaking, and Stockholm regarded foreign
possession as a strategic threat. The islands proved a matter of
contention for some years, and one of the earlier acts of the
League of Nations was to decide, after considerable hesitation,
that although the islands should continue to belong to Finland,
they should not be fortified. This solution proved acceptable to
all parties. With Bornholm to the south of her in Danish possession and the Alands to the east under Finland, Swedish apprehensions were natural, particularly as the islands had been mili-
tarized by Russia in the earlier stages of the war.

III

One of the first actions of the British Admiralty, after the signing of the Armistice with Germany on 11 November, 1918, was
to obtain charts of the inhibiting Baltic mine fields, and to send
men-of-war to the area. It was intended to re-establish British influence in a part of the world which had always been important
to her trade and sea power, but from which she had for long
been excluded.

The presence of forces friendly in intention yet without territorial stake in the Baltic resettlement soon proved to be of value,
for as early as 18 November, Latvia—mainly the old Livonia—
joined Lithuania and Estonia in declaring her independence,
and by February 1919 a squadron under Admiral Sir Walter
Cowan had orders to proceed to Libau. Cowan's task was mani-
fold, though largely unofficial. He was to encourage the aspiring
nations; he was to ensure the flow of maritime traffic of all kinds;
and he was to watch any movement by Bolshevik ships to cross
his purposes, or to intervene in the affairs of the nascent states.

Cowan's tasks were not unlike some of those which had been entrusted to Sir James Saumarez at an earlier time of upheaval, when the armies of Napoleon were marching and countermarching across Poland and Russia. They were rendered additionally complex by the presence of the undefeated Count Rüdiger von der Goltz (who liked to describe himself as "the last of the German generals") in the Baltic provinces, and by the fact that no one knew the exact whereabouts, or the future intentions, of those partly reorganized Russian armies, now under the Red banner, which were regarded with suspicion not unmixed with horror by Europe at large. Wherever they moved, rapine was probable, and although Lenin had announced his policy of encouraging Baltic autonomy, it remained to be seen how sincere was his aim, or how closely his definition of "autonomy" matched that of other statesmen.

It was soon perceived that while Lenin was ready enough in theory to grant "freedom" to constituent Russian states, yet having done so, he expected them to rejoin his own Soviet system voluntarily, and this was in fact what happened, sooner or later, in various parts of the country. It was not so in the north, where countries were influenced from abroad and where, in the last resort, independent political bodies might look for help from Western sources. It was also remembered that although Lenin had at an early stage recognized the aspirations of Finland, this had not prevented a savage war in which Russian forces had taken part. It was in fact the closeness of Kronstadt to Finland which had enabled Red sailors to give aid to comrades ashore in the Finnish War of Liberation, and lent special bitterness to the fighting. Thousands of Reds were rounded up when the struggle ended, and many died of starvation in concentration camps, but this was due more to the food shortage which affected every section of the community than to cold-blooded brutality. The fate of landowners or student prisoners of war at the hand of the Reds was generally swifter and more drastic. They were shot out of hand. In due time little more mercy was shown to the Red sailors themselves, when they became less docile towards central authority than was judged appropriate.

Allied intervention within Russia itself, so unfortunate and so rightly resented, was already beginning, but the leaders who were given support were too often of poor quality. This was certainly true of Yudenich, who commanded the White Russians assembling in the Baltic states for an attempt to advance on Petrograd, while insistence by Whites on the "indivisibility of Russia" lost them what would have been invaluable help from Finland, and support from Estonia and elsewhere.

It seemed at that time impossible, as for many years it proved, that plenipotentiaries sitting around a conference table reordering the world should include representatives of a power not yet internationally recognized, but formidable, intractable and growing increasingly united by misguided opposition from beyond its frontiers. In the meanwhile Baltic affairs must, so it seemed, proceed step by step. Finland had shown the way, but Finland was a special case, as the world was quick to see. Never before, at least in modern times, had Estonia, Latvia or Lithuania enjoyed anything approaching freedom. They could be test cases for President Wilson's principle of self-determination: they could also form part of that *cordon sanitaire* against Bolshevism" which was spoken of in Paris and elsewhere.

In each country the pattern of affairs was roughly the same. An indigenous population, having survived many vicissitudes of oppression, had managed to preserve language and traditions, though standards were not comparable with those in Finland. The Letts of Latvia and the Lithuanians belonged to the Indo-European group of nations, distinct from both the Slavonic and the German races; the Estonians to the Finnish-Ugric group, with a somewhat different origin. All three countries were religious: the Estonians and Letts mainly Lutheran. The Lithuanians were Catholic, the peasants notable for handicrafts, their village greens famous for geese.

In Latvia and Estonia, great landowners, the "Baltic barons" who were successors of the medieval Teutonic Knights, an Order which had been formally abolished by Napoleon as lately as 1809, managed vast estates often with supreme skill, and in Latvia they owned sixty per cent of the soil. In Lithuania landowners were mainly Poles or the descendants of commanders and soldiers who in the past had been rewarded with estates by the Tsar. One family, the Radziwils, had property here and elsewhere which was equal in extent to most of Belgium.

The local political parties which were busily forming were made up of a core of professional men (in the case of Lithuania, of priests), generally with some knowledge of other countries, backed by representatives of land-hungry peasants. There was no "proletariat" since there were no industries to speak of, and in none of the three countries would Marxian ideas, as presented by the current Soviets, have found wide acceptance. Only at Riga, the city seaport which had flourished since the days of the Hanseatic League, was there a considerable urban population, and stresses of war had reduced its numbers by half.

The politicians had three kinds of opposition to deal with, and no ready source of help unless the Western Allies, through the agency of the British Navy, should be able to provide it. There were the landlords, the old ruling class who, whether they served a medieval Order, the Russian emperors or merely themselves, had never done anything considerable for the peasants, and monopolized most positions of authority. In Estonia, Latvia and to a lesser extent in Lithuania, there were Germans, mobile or in garrison, who were experienced in war and had adequate weapons. All three countries were subject to forays by the armies of Bolshevism. These were strong in Estonia, the territory nearest to Petrograd, while in Latvia they had at one stage occupied Riga, the commissar, Stutzka, driving the people almost hysterical with his unreasonable orders, his capricious executions and his apparent aim of reckless disintegration.

An early result of the freeing of Finland had been the release of Soviet forces to attack Estonia, which they did in the summer of 1918. Many Estonians had thereupon fled to Helsinki either from the mainland or from the islands of Dago and Osel, at the entrance to the Gulf of Riga, and had been hospitably received. The Finns did more for their neighbours. Two infantry regiments and some batteries of artillery were organized with speed, and on 30 December, 1918, they landed at Reval, where they engaged in a counteroffensive, organized under the Estonian general Laidoner. The first campaign was even shorter than Mannerheim's in Finland. Before the end of February 1919, Laidoner announced that the country was free of Bolshevik troops. His news was premature. Petrograd did not give up so easily, while the Estonians still had to deal with von der Goltz, who saw possibilities in the country for the resettlement of his troops. The Baltic barons, anxious to re-establish permanent German influence, promised them land both in Latvia and farther north, and the prospect to soldiers whose principal armies had been defeated was refreshing. Von der Goltz also saw himself as an important factor in the *cordon sanitaire.* The Western Allies, so he considered, would have need of his services against the Bolsheviks, and like Pehr Svinhufvud in Finland, he even favoured a project for a German royal house in the Baltic, an idea which had been put forward, even after the Western Armistice, by the Livonian land marshal, von Strych, who actually offered the crown of Livonia and Cour-land to Duke Adolf Friedrich of Mecklenburg. At one time, in-deed, von der Goltz, resolute and optimistic, seems to have hoped for a complete reversal of the general fortunes of war.

Even as things were, the German commander was able to make considerable trouble in Latvia, where he tried hard to es-tablish the protectorate envisaged in the Treaty of Brest-Litovsk. Karlis Ulmanis, the head of the Provisional Lettish Government, had originally established himself in Riga, but with the advent of the Bolsheviks he had moved to Libau, where he had the sup-port of the British Navy. The Bolsheviks were in control of much of the interior, which they made little attempt to organize. Von der Goltz's army was also in the country, his own headquarters near Ulmanis's at Libau. When Admiral Cowan's ships arrived, with a representative of the British foreign service on board the cruiser *Caledon,* one of those tangled situations arose which were to be discovered in many parts of Europe until the terms of a peace settlement had been realized.

Ulmanis, without any army, represented the Letts. Von der Goltz and the Russians, both with armies, stood for occupying powers. Cowan, with no land forces at his disposal, represented law and order and the victorious Western Allies. Finally, the party of the Baltic barons, who had scraped together a contingent to fight Bolsheviks or Letts, but not Germans or Britons, were waiting hopefully upon events, so that they could repossess their estates and the key positions which they felt were theirs by right of inheritance.

As had been the case with the Germans and the Finnish Jägers, the Tsar's army, during the earlier part of the European war, had encouraged the formation of Lettish rifle brigades with their own officers, and with commands given in their own language. Released from service, the survivors of these units returned home, some to join the Bolsheviks, but others ready to be the nucleus of a national army, and to carry out the orders of Ulmanis's Provisional Government. Early attempts to establish Lettish regiments were frustrated by von der Goltz. He would have had no objection to their helping him fight the Bolsheviks, but had no intention of allowing a force to be raised which might be used against his own troops, or against the party of the pro-German barons.

In the spring of 1919 the general, assisted by Herr Winnig, the German diplomatic representative at Libau, carried out a *coup d'état* which overthrew the Ulmanis government, members of which sought refuge with the British Mission. The new authority was composed of Balts, and it was headed by a German pastor, Niedra, but von der Goltz's action, together with an unpopular choice of ministers, was calculated to increase support for Ulmanis throughout the country, while his personal safety was ensured by the presence of British ships. Ulmanis continued to exercise authority from the merchantman *Saratov*, and continued to be regarded as the representative of his country by the Western Allies.

Leaving a garrison behind him at Libau, von der Goltz next advanced his main body from Mitau towards Riga, intending to occupy that great city. He met with little opposition, and on 18 May, 1919, entered it in triumph. As his next move was to deplete his Libau forces, Cowan took the opportunity to offer to transship the small army of the Balts to Estonia, where they would be of use to the Whites under Yudenich. This plan was accepted, and it opened the way for Ulmanis to return to Libau, where he reestablished authority based on popular opinion.

Von der Goltz's occupation of Riga was a means to an end. His mind was on Estonia, which to many of his 25,000 Germans represented the promised land. Advancing due north, following the line of the Baltic coast, he was able to rout such Bolsheviks as had not already been disposed of by Laidoner, but when it became clear that he intended to overthrow the Estonian Government in precisely the same way that he had acted at Libau, local hostilities against Bolshevist forces ceased and the Estonians faced about, ready to meet the new enemy. Assembling their full strength, they surprised and routed the Germans on 23 June, 1919, near Cesis, forcing them to retire to Riga. There an Allied Mission was able to arrange an armistice, by the terms of which the Germans were required to withdraw to a line fourteen miles beyond the capital, von der Goltz establishing his personal headquarters at Mitau. This was the opportunity for the Letts to regain their capital, and they wasted no time. Ulmanis sailed early in July on the S.S. *Saratov*, and henceforward Riga remained the seat of government.

Ulmanis's first and most essential task was to organize an army with which he could rid his country first of the Germans and then of such Russians as remained. Within a few weeks over 30,-000 men were recruited, but they were largely untrained, and such small arms as could be supplied by the British ships and by French units which had now joined under Commandant Brisson were scarcely a match for the equipment of German veterans. Von der Goltz, moreover, had a final trick up his sleeve. His *coup d'état* frustrated, his plans for colonization unrealized, he decided to turn his force into a Russian army—not quite White, and certainly not Red. He found for his purpose a Cossack adventurer, Bermondt, who consented to take over nominal command. The Germans were also reinforced by some 6,000 Russian ex-prisoners of war, a few of whom had fought at Tannenberg.

In October 1919, Bermondt and von der Goltz attacked the Letts and drove them back to the outskirts of Riga. The German-Russian force then took up a line along the southern bank of the river Dvina, keeping the city itself under shell fire. The Letts soon planned a counterattack. They crossed the river farther down, at Bolderaa, where the British ships *Dragon* and *Vance* and the French cruiser *L'Aisne*, stationed in midstream, covered their boats and bombarded German outposts in the sand dunes. Surprised by the effectiveness of naval gunnery, the invaders withdrew in disorder. The Letts pressed forward with great gallantry, attacking the enemy flank at Regensburg and Thorenburg. Although both places were defended by the German Iron Division, they were taken by storm, together with most of von der Goltz's artillery.

On 11 November, 1919, the anniversary of Armistice Day, the

Germans withdrew altogether from the neighbourhood of Riga, and their officers, for the first time, failed to rally their men. The Letts advanced to Mitau, where they captured a mass of stores, and where General von Eberhardt, who had taken over the conduct of affairs from the Bermondt-von der Goltz partnership, proposed an armistice. The Letts took no notice of his request, and during the course of a month's further fighting, Courland and Lithuania were rid of intruders. But for Allied intervention, it is possible that the jubilant Letts would have advanced upon East Prussia. That, at least, was a humiliation von der Goltz was spared.

II. Versailles and after

If Finland and the Baltic states solved, through self-help, most of the problems which concerned their immediate future, this was not so elsewhere, and one of the thorniest subjects which faced the triumvirate upon whom the burden fell of reordering Europe was that of Poland. President Wilson, *primus inter pares*, had already pledged Poland's restoration to the comity of nations: Georges Clemenceau, the old "Tiger of France," saw in Poland renewed a bulwark both against Bolshevism and a resurgent Prussia, while David Lloyd George, representing Britain, was content in this matter to hold a watching brief. If at any time Lloyd George may have thought that the future of Poland could be of no urgent consideration to his own country, time brought a shock which affected even his resilient spirit, for Poland proved to be the source of as much concern as most smaller countries put together. Her old nature reasserted itself, and statesmen with a sense of history recalled at least some of the perplexities of their predecessors.

The reconstitution of Poland had been one of the crucial tasks of the Congress of Vienna needing to be faced after the exile of Napoleon and the collapse of his system. In general, the powers had then agreed with the archconservative Metternich that it was better to aim at restoration of the old than to experiment with the new. Alexander I had wished to create, under Russian suzerainty, an autonomous Polish state which would include the whole of the Napoleonic Grand Duchy of Warsaw. He had suggested that Prussia annex Saxony by way of compensation, an arrangement that would have been acceptable to both countries, even though it would have brought the Polish and hence the Russian frontier within ninety miles of Berlin. It is not the least of the ironies of history that it was British and French opposition, combining with Austria's fear of Russia, which caused the plan to be so substantially modified as to result in an altogether different settlement.

A kingdom of Poland was indeed set up under Russian protection, but it was a diminished realm. Prussia retained Thorn, Danzig and the modern province of Posen, thereby pushing her eastern frontier back double the distance from Berlin than would have been the case had the earlier idea not been rejected. Austria recovered eastern Galicia, while the ancient city of Cracow, with a strip of territory, was constituted as an independent republic. The general results, therefore, of the eighteenth-century partitions—the dismemberment of the Polish race under Prussia, Russia and Austria—were confirmed.

The autonomy of the Congress kingdom lasted only sixteen years. In 1831 the Poles staged one of the characteristic revolutions, and when it failed, autonomy ended, the constitution being withdrawn by the Tsar. Fifteen years later Austria annexed Cracow, and Polish leaders, who for all their divisions never ceased to work for independence, went underground. From time to time they rattled their chains, for Poles loved Russians even less than did the Finns, and in 1861, Bismarck, who was then representing his country at St. Petersburg, wrote in characteristic terms of how he thought they should be treated. "Strike the Poles in such a way as they will despair of their lives!" he said when considering a fresh outburst of nationalism. "I have every sympathy with their situation, but if we want to exist we cannot do anything else than *exterminate* them. The wolf, too, is not responsible for being what God has made it, but we kill it, nevertheless, if we can." Bismarck was at one with the Russians in recognizing a Polish danger as well as a Polish problem. His countrymen in due time actually attempted to apply his solution to another perplexing race, the Jews, with results which have added a searing memory to modern consciousness.

As reconstituted by the Treaty of Versailles, and by a succession of agreements or *de facto* recognitions which followed it, Poland was re-formed as a republic larger in area than any of its neighbours except Russia and Germany. Not only so, but her boundaries, except for the line of the Carpathians in the south, being largely artificial, raised as many difficulties as they solved. Although the Vistula flowed for most of its length through the country, Poland did not command its mouth, for Danzig, traditionally a German city, was given independent status under the mandate of the League of Nations. The Poles were therefore obliged to build their own Baltic seaport at the valuable, though less useful, site of Gdynia, to the west of the course of the river. Although, by acts of aggression at Lithuania's expense, the Poles pushed their northern frontier as far as the Dvina, yet Riga, at the mouth of the river, was secure in Latvian possession. Nor had the Poles a Baltic outlet by way of the Niemen, for that river, which flowed through Lithuania, debouched into the sea near Memel, which was at first administered independently, and later ceded to an otherwise portless country.

The most doubtful measure of all, one over which no powers of prophecy were needed to perceive a source of future trouble was the Polish "Corridor." Germany, who in Churchillian phrase is as a rule either at her neighbours' feet or at their throats, had, in respect of the Corridor, her most legitimate grievance, for at Versailles a crowning work of Frederick the Great was undone. The Königsberg enclave was separated from the rest of the Fatherland not merely by an independently administered Danzig, which might just have been tolerable, but by a wedge of Polish territory which included a stretch of the Danzig gulf, taking in that well-known Baltic landmark, the "heel" of sand dune extending along many miles to shelter the waters in northerly and western winds. Germany was to make much of her wrongs, real and fancied, and the results of plebiscites held in areas both of East and West Prussia soon showed that the affiliations of the majority were indeed with Germany, not with untried Poland.

The revived country soon showed herself, despite her extensive area, as land-hungry as any peasant, and her greed brought about near disaster. Having occupied Vilna, the ancient capital of the Lithuanians, the Poles turned upon their hereditary foe, Russia, and with a blend of recklessness and stupidity which was

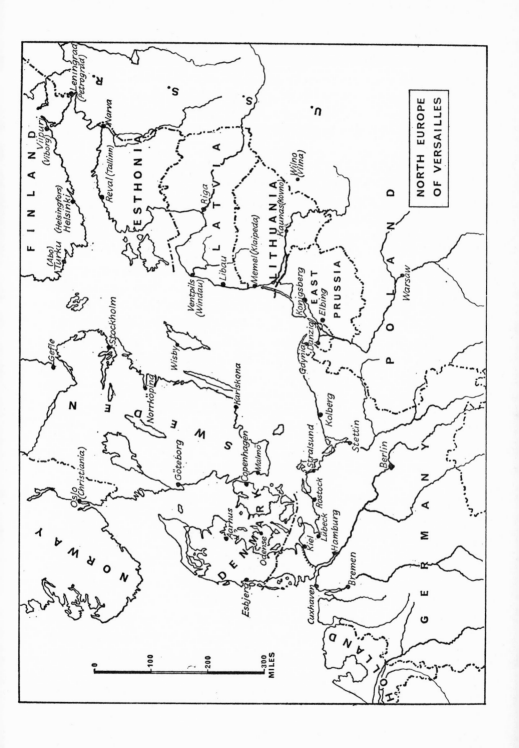

NORTH EUROPE
OF VERSAILLES

0   100   200   300
MILES

FINLAND

Leningrad
(Petrograd)

Viipuri
(Viborg)

(Åbo)
Turku

(Helsingfors)
Helsinki

Narva

Reval (Tallinn)

ESTHONIA

U.S.S.R.

LATVIA

Riga

Libau

Ventpils
(Windau)

Memel (Klaipeda)

LITHUANIA

Kaunas (Kovno)

Wilna
(Vilna)

Königsberg

EAST
PRUSSIA

Elbing

Gdynia

Danzig

Warsaw

POLAND

NORWAY

Oslo
(Christiania)

SWEDEN

Gefle

Stockholm

Norrköping

Wisby

Karlskrona

Göteborg

DENMARK

Aarhus

Copenhagen

Malmö

Odense

Esbjerg

Kolberg

Stralsund

Rostock

Kiel

Lübeck

Hamburg

Cuxhaven

Bremen

Stettin

Berlin

GERMANY

HOLLAND

calculated to inspire even the most war-weary Soviet unit with a thirst for battle, armies marched into the Ukraine, from which they were very soon ejected. As she had not been invited by the Versailles powers to consider the implications of Polish independence, or to decide the frontiers, the action of Soviet Russia in advancing on Warsaw was in every way justified. The Poles had a bitter lesson, and it was partly the skill of the French general Weygand which saved the capital from a fate which it had suffered so often before, that of occupation by a hostile power. The Russians withdrew, and for a time Poland exercised her freedom in other directions. The Peace of Riga, which was the outcome of the Lithuanian-Polish-Russian troubles, left seven million non-Poles in the new Poland, which was two thirds the size of France. Her future problems would demand all the skill of which her leaders were capable, since she had added discontented minorities to geographical handicaps.

If Paderewski had influenced American opinion in favour of his native land, to which he was to return in the capacity of Prime Minister, it was to Józef Pilsudski that Poland owed much of what prestige she acquired in the earlier years of her resurgence. Pilsudski was the same age as Mannerheim, and when he took office in 1919 as President he had already experienced many of the perils and most of the frustrations which belong to a life dedicated to a political cause with more enemies than friends. He lived long enough to see ambitions realized, and he died, honoured at home and abroad, before the next holocaust. Official Poland has ceased to revere his memory, since history, if written to the pattern of a doctrine, can be made to serve ends other than that of objective enquiry, but between the world wars his country owed much to Pilsudski, and was glad to say so.

Pilsudski was born near Vilna, and claimed descent from an illustrious Lithuanian family, a fact which gave impetus to the early and successful acts of aggression in the north, but the whole cast of his mind was anti-Russian, and against that country his activities were remarkable. He was sentenced to Siberia nearly a decade before Lenin, and spent five years in exile before returning to Vilna to found and inspire a paper devoted to the Polish Socialist Party, his proclivities, thoroughly well known by now to the authorities, leading to further terms of incarceration at Warsaw and St. Petersburg, under far worse conditions than Lenin was to know.

After the European war broke out, Pilsudski showed himself as able at soldiering as in propaganda work. He took service under the Austrians, but insisted that his Polish riflemen, who became troops of high quality, form an independent command. When at last they were disbanded, as a result of the collapse of the eastern front, Pilsudski himself fell foul of the Germans, who imprisoned him at Magdeburg, a confinement from which he escaped by feigning madness.

Pilsudski was always popular with the Polish Army. His standard of discipline was good: his men knew what they were fighting for and respected the man who led them, and until the end of his life the marshal—for so he became—found more satisfaction in the unity of a fighting service than in the parliamentary democracy which was tried after he had established his government at Warsaw. Pilsudski refused a second term as President, and shortly after the ending of the Russian war retired into private life. He hoped that his fellow Poles would learn with experience to rule themselves wisely, but democracy on the Western pattern requires a long and patient apprenticeship. Tired of the wrangling which seemed to him to turn the Warsaw Parliament into an undignified resurrection of the ancient Diet, Pilsudski staged a *coup d'état* in 1926 which was the prelude for a stage of single-party control. Never again was it possible for him to relinquish the burden of political responsibility, and to the end of his life he remained the statesman to whom his countrymen turned in their times of perplexity. When he died, in 1935, he was buried in the storied Cathedral of Cracow, the religious centre of a Catholic land.

II

Although Polish reappearance as a Baltic country had severe limitations, owing to her very restricted coastal area, the treaty powers were at least able to do an act of delayed justice to "sea-girt Denmark." They restored territory in North Schleswig, together with the islands of Romo and the larger Alsen, which had been lost to her after Bismarck's war.

At the peace which had followed the Schleswig-Holstein conflict, a clause had been inserted in the treaty, at the instance of Napoleon III, which provided that North Schleswig should have the right to be reunited with Denmark if a free vote of the population should show this to be the general wish. In the outcome, negotiations on this particular matter were delayed by Germany, and conditions were then put forward which were impossible for Denmark to accept. Finally, in 1878, the clause itself was repudiated, an action which made Germany lasting enemies in the northern kingdom.

Bismarck went further. He subjected North Schleswig to a systematic process of Germanization, one which was scarcely calculated to endear the masters of the country to their new subjects; yet in spite of this, and of continued Danish emigration, over thirty years later almost the entire population were still Danish-speaking. The Treaty of Versailles restored the clause of the earlier settlement, and in the first and larger zone, that of South Jylland, 75,000 voted for re-incorporation, and only 12,000 against. In the more southerly Flensburg area, which contained the city itself, an even larger number preferred to remain under the German flag, this being a case where language and sentiment coincided, irrespective of the recent fortunes of war.

The territory which was restored to Denmark included the site of the Düppel stronghold, where the Danes had made their last stands against the invader. The tall mill, several times rebuilt, which is a landmark in the district, became an appropriate symbol of national resistance.

III

Matters might be ordered in Denmark by referendum and ballot, by means of which, though the majority had their way, the minority need not suffer. In Russia things were different. Marx's "class war" was waged with a vengeance, first against the Whites and the "haves," and then, when they had been extirpated, against other "national enemies," deviationists, freethinkers, old-fashioned worshippers of God and in due course anyone and everyone who was even fancied to stand in the way of the ruling circle or of the recognized dictator. It was thus that Trotsky came in time to be expelled, the man who inspired the Red armies in their first ordeals, one whose services were spoken of with those of Lenin.

As with the greater, so with the less. No more dynamic revolutionary force was ever congregated than the sailors of the Baltic fleet, who were advanced even in their excesses. The suppression of their activities, an episode which is not given weight in chronicles of the time, showed how far Lenin was prepared to go, even against one of the citadels of his new order.

It had been said of the naval mutinies of 1905 that the tension existing between the officers and men of the lower deck had been aggravated by conditions and discipline severer than those which obtained in the army. A more likely reason, since both then and later subversion was greater at Kronstadt than in the Black Sea, was that recruits were drawn mainly from literate and class-conscious industrial workers, including metallurgists from Petrograd and the Baltic areas. Lenin, at a lecture delivered at Zurich immediately before his final journey home, said that while the sailors started mutineering with great ferocity, yet "with the same ease they committed the naïve stupidity of liberating the officers whom they arrested: they allowed themselves to be taken in by promises and arguments from their superiors. This is how commanding officers gained valuable time, obtained reinforcements, and followed this up with the cruellest suppressions and the executions of the ringleaders." If his own turn came, he would do better.

When the first, and comparatively bloodless, revolution broke out in March 1917, resulting in the formation of Kerensky's Provisional Government, the Baltic sailors showed themselves far in advance of their competitors. Not only did they murder Admiral Nepenin, the commander in chief, together with over a hundred others favourable to Kerensky, they took over all political authority in the navy and set up their own committee, known as the Tsentrobalt. At a later stage, in Helsinki, they publicly tortured a number of officers to death, and during the funeral service broke into the church and tossed the corpses out of their coffins, an incident worthy of Peter the Great in the days of the Strieltzy. By such acts they were committed as extremists even among the Bolsheviks, and the shelling of the Winter Palace by the cruiser *Aurora*, which was the immediate cause of Kerensky's flight, was symbolic as well as effective, though only three projectiles hit the massive building. Six months later the Tsentrobalt Committee was dissolved, its functions being transferred to a Council of Commissars, a body of Party officials appointed from above.

In the years of civil war the Kronstadt sailor became a familiar and dreaded figure whenever he appeared as commissar, as head of the secret police, as agitator and organizer of action by local Soviets against suspected Whites and other intransigents. The bluejackets, whom Trotsky once called the "glory and pride of the Revolution," became guardians of Bolshevik conscience in its purest forms. However poorly they might have shown themselves when defending their country's shores against the Germans, Baltic sailors were champion upholders of the extreme left wing.

Guardianship was one thing—independence another. Shortly after he took over power, Lenin transferred the capital back to Moscow, and the sailors began to feel that they were being unduly interfered with by central authority, now increasingly remote. Towards the end of February 1921, just as a Congress of the Party was about to meet, disturbances occurred at Petrograd. A delegation of sailors was sent to find out what was going on. They returned to report to a mass meeting held in defiance of the order of the commissars in the battleship *Petropavlovsk*. A resolution was passed demanding the re-election of all Soviets by secret ballot, freedom of speech and press for all left-wing socialists, the abolition of Communist methods of control over peasants cultivating their own land and the end of the Communist monopoly of propaganda and agitation. The sailors asked for their resolution to be made known to the country, and had this been allowed, it would have been the first public protest against the methods of Party dictatorship. Lenin saw the red light. When the sailors sent thirty delegates to the Petrograd Soviet to explain the standpoint of Kronstadt, he had them arrested as hostages. Preparation for military action was already in full swing.

The sailors' resistance extended over eighteen days in March

1921. After an attempt at reducing the fortress had failed, owing to the strength of the defences and defection of some of the troops to the rebels, Kronstadt was finally captured by Marshal Tukhachevski (who was liquidated sixteen years later by Stalin), defiant to the last. The attackers were mainly Red Army trainee officers, whose morale was boosted by the presence of three hundred delegates from the Moscow Congress. Some of the survivors were lucky enough to escape over the ice to Finland; among the remainder retribution was severe. Executions and heavy prison sentences were kept secret, except for the shooting of thirteen selected people, whose social background was useful in creating the myth of the White character of the insurrection.

Commenting on the tragedy to the Party Congress, Lenin explained that its nature could not be fully divulged to the press, and admitted that it represented a movement more dangerous than that of all the White generals put together. The wavering semi-proletarian masses, he said, might if allowed political initiative swing away from support of the Soviet Government and make a restoration of Tsarism inevitable. Having used the Baltic sailors as instruments in the civil war, Lenin ended by suppressing them as soon as they showed signs of putting forward constructive political demands, shadowing their memory by alleging that they were counterrevolutionaries. Even the Paris of Robespierre and the Terror scarcely yielded a more macabre incident.

IV

The delegates who met in the *Petropavlovsk* assembled in a ship which, less than two years before, had been attacked in one of the most daring operations carried out in the Baltic during the present century. Under the general direction of Admiral Cowan, who was working from Estonian bases and was helped by the beneficent neutrality of Finland, British forces mounted a direct assault on the main Russian position at Kronstadt, the object being to prevent interference by the Bolsheviks with independents in the Baltic states. The units employed were fast motorboats, armed with torpedoes, in one of which Lieutenant Augustus Agar had already earned the Victoria Cross by sinking the cruiser

Oleg while that vessel was bombarding Whites holding the fortress of Krasnaya Gorka. Agar, helped by westerly winds which
raised the level of the water in the area, on more than one occasion penetrated the stone breakwater system built by Peter the
Great and his successors to guard the sea entrances to St. Petersburg. This was part of a series of incidents in which he and others
were concerned which were so explosive politically, as well as in
fact, that not only were details kept secret at the time, but they
have not yet been fully incorporated into an official history. The
Kronstadt raid itself, which did much damage at small cost, was
on a scale and of a sort made familiar during the Second World
War. A number of aircraft, one of them piloted by a Swede, were
effectively used to distract the Russian gunners from surface targets.

With Reval as their principal harbour, Cowan's cruisers and destroyers penetrated so far up the Gulf of Finland as to secure the
Estonian littoral, a fact which was made good use of by forces
ashore. Being nearest to the source of Russian power, Estonia was
by far the most vulnerable of the new countries, and had she not
possessed a staunch ally in Finland, she would almost inevitably
have suffered the fate of those inland regions whose attempts at
independence met with no lasting success. Between the Bolsheviks, the Germans and the party of the Baltic barons, her patriots
had a hard struggle to win freedom, and it did not prove easy to
preserve it, even during those twenty years between the world
wars in which it could be cherished.

Her first escape was one which she shared with Finland and
Lithuania. This was the possibility of a German ruler, for the
leader of the barons' party, Dellingshauser, had made a suggestion, before the war ended, that the country might be united with
Prussia, an idea which the Kaiser favoured. Wiser counsels prevailed, here as elsewhere, and Päts, a local leader, became the
first Prime Minister, and later President.

After recognition by the Western powers, which was given *de
facto* in 1918 and *de jure* three years later, the Estonians were
faced with a protracted struggle with their own Communist
Party, the country being the last of the three Baltic states to declare Communism illegal. Within little more than a year, in the
winter of 1924, a *Putsch* was attempted by conspirators at Reval,

aided by Red Guards, immigrant workers from Leningrad and a supply of Russian weapons. The insurgents, about two hundred in all, attacked government offices and military installations, took the railway station and telegraph office by surprise, and murdered the Minister of Communications, but after some street fighting the rising was put down without serious difficulty, and Civil Guards were then enrolled, on the Finnish model, to safeguard future security.

Another crisis occurred two years later, after which martial law was declared and all political parties were abolished, without distinction. Although Estonia was no riper than Poland for parliamentary democracy as practiced in the West, for a few years peace ensued. The country steadily developed her trade in cattle, rye, flax, oil shale, and in the products of her forests, the fir, pine, birch, aspen and alder, which grew over so much of the land. Her prosperity was short but real. Large expropriations gave the peasants that stake in the country to which they had looked forward so long, and they made the most of their blessings.

v

Away in Germany, economic depression, political division and the consequences of defeat made it inevitable that, sooner or later, a messiah would appear to point a way to salvation. Bismarck's successor was, in fact, a painter, agitator, author, demagogue, politician and strategist who was born in Austria in 1889, and that Hitler came from this country was ironical, since the overthrow of Austrian hegemony had been one of Bismarck's main achievements. Hitler's father changed his name from Schicklgruber into something more manageable, and could never in his wildest moments have guessed the hidden potentialities in the being to whom he helped to give life.

After an unhappy youth, in which he knew the frustrations of poverty, Hitler found himself among the crowd cheering at the news of the European war, but he did not fancy service in the Austrian Army, and joined up with a Bavarian field unit. "The six years which I spent as a German soldier," he said, "were the foundation for my hardness, my resolution and my perseverance. Everything which I have won of virtue and of worth was given me in the unique, the incomparable old German Army."

When the struggle ended, Hitler was in hospital in Pomerania, temporarily blinded and suffering from the gas poisoning which the Germans themselves had introduced into warfare. This gave him time to think. One of the results was the composition of his testament, *Mein Kampf*, which he wrote later, while imprisoned after his part in the Beer Hall Putsch, in 1923. The two volumes are an extraordinary blend of secondhand ideas, many of which were unsound, shrewd observation and readable narrative. The importance of *Mein Kampf* lay not in its thought or originality, but in its programme. Hitler spoke of his struggle not only in the past tense. He outlined his future, and that of his adopted nation, when he came to power. His opponents were provided with blueprints of all he purposed. That he was allowed to achieve so much, and in so short a time, was due to his own ability, to the backing of a virile people and to a mixture of stupidity and weakness on the part of opponents, who may have had good excuses for what they did or did not do, but not for ignorance of Hitler's character and aims. In this respect, all that was necessary was to read. His success was comparable with that of Bismarck, who was equally frank, but Hitler had the advantage of being able to rid himself of interference from above, which his forerunner, being the servant of a crowned head, could never do.

He was also aided by a flexible voice. He could rant and rave with all the actor's appearance of spontaneity, enthusing or frightening hearers at home and—over the radio—abroad by the machine-gun-like rapidity and force of his sentences. Master of the mass audience, Hitler, through this gift, affected first his own compatriots, and very quickly the world beyond the German borders. Before he ever moved a soldier, Hitler had begun to demoralize his opponents, and of those he marked down as his victims, it was only Britain that he feared—for her tenacity, her mastery by sea, and her way of drawing others to causes which in a historical view have seldom been hers alone.

Some of the world's most attentively studied works, the Bible, the Koran and—to descend earthwards—*Das Kapital* and *Mein Kampf*, have brought destruction and immeasurable suffering from and upon crusaders acting on their precepts. Only in the Bible, perhaps the most varied symposium ever assembled (and its messages, therefore, apt to be ill digested), is it easy to discover the basis for a constructive life, with values acceptable by fully developed men and women. The Koran promises little but struggle, leading the faithful to an Oriental conception of paradise. Marx, the advocate of straight class war, imagines power seized and kept by the more astute proletarians, leading to a workers' millennium on the lines of an all-embracing trades union. Hitler's tenet was the racial paramountcy of the German. His dream was of living space in which still more could breed, and this could be won at the expense of the patient Slav. The abortive Treaty of Brest-Litovsk had in fact been a near approximation to what he wanted, though it did not go far enough. Given a chance, he would do better. "Guns or butter?" asked his henchman Goering in a much quoted phrase. Despite the bitter experiences of 1918, which were attributed to a "stab in the back," and despite the fact that they were not under threat, the Germans once more acclaimed themselves Europe's cannon makers, accepting the corollary that there must be cannon fodder on a worthwhile scale.

After years of agitation and alternations of hope and discouragement, taking in at least one spell under arrest and many scenes of violence, Hitler attained power through a party which, in its early stages, was constitutional. The situation in Germany was at best unstable, conditions were ripe for change. After the Kaiser's abdication in 1918 and his departure for Holland with a train of treasure, the government had been taken over by a Council of People's Commissioners in Berlin. Under the terms of a new Constitution, the federal legislature consisted of a Reichstag, representing the whole nation and elected by popular suffrage, while a Reichsrat represented the separate states.

For the first decade of its existence the Reich was ruled mainly by Cabinets supported by the middle and moderate left parliamentary parties, of which the Social Democrats and the Catholic centre were the largest, the extreme conservatives and the Communists being in opposition. Successive elections practically obliterated the moderate conservatives and the Democrats, the Social Democrats remaining relatively stable and the Communists gaining. Hitler's party, the National Socialists, or Nazis, rapidly grew at the expense of the middle parties, winning its first substantial successes at the Reichstag election of September 1930— over a hundred seats. Once with a foothold in the Reichstag, Hitler was as incapable of letting go as Lenin, though he had to create his own crises, since he was not favoured by a state of war. In 1932 the Nazis gained 230 seats, and in the following January a joint Nazi–German-National Cabinet was formed with Hitler as Chancellor, von Papen as Vice-Chancellor, and Hugenberg as Minister of Economy. Within weeks this Cabinet assumed the form of a revolutionary body of exclusively Nazi tone. Papen and Hugenberg were driven out, and Hitler, after a landslide election in March, pursued a policy which abrogated constitutional guarantees, excluded all non-Nazis from office, ordained persecution of Jews, liberals and plain socialists, and within a short time transferred the states' sovereignty to the Reich.

At the first signs of discontent, which were described as an "anti-government plot," over seventy people were murdered, including Roehm, a leading Nazi in whom Hitler saw a rival. The President, von Hindenburg, monumental and honoured, died in August 1934, after which the presidential office was fused with the chancellorship, Hitler taking the title of Führer and assuming absolute powers. The world was now warned, for domestic politics soon fell into the background, to be replaced by international issues arising out of German denunciation of Versailles and its consequences. Concurrently, violent propaganda was pursued against Russia and the whole Communist system. Secretly at first, and then with increasing assurance, preparations were made for rearmament on a breath-taking scale, and the first moves were planned for amending the look of the European map.

In the earlier stages Hitler's plans did not affect the balance of power in the Baltic, though every successful step taken under his direction to restore Germany's strength in Europe made it apparent that when, in due course, he was free to give his attention to the affairs of East Prussia, Poland and Lithuania, it was unlikely that he would be less far-reaching in his aims than his hero, Frederick the Great. Hitler took first things first. Having gained complete power at home, he challenged the Western Allies by reoccupying the demilitarized Rhineland, an act of calculated boldness in which he succeeded early in 1936; then came the annexation of Austria, which took place two years later.

All was writ large, for the first page of *Mein Kampf* contains the sentence: "German Austria must return to the Great German Motherland." This is an astonishing statement if read in the light of history, for the Holy Roman Emperors ruled from Vienna, not Berlin. Hitler was now their successor, and he would soon boast that he was building a Reich which would endure for a thousand years. Such statements, as the Greeks knew, are apt to provoke the gods.

Between the German Army's return to the Rhineland and the absorption of Austria, Ribbentrop, who was then German Ambassador in London, had a two-hour conversation with Winston Churchill, at that time a private, though famous, member of Parliament. Ribbentrop unfolded his Führer's plans to his guest, hoping, as he confessed, that Britain would give him a free hand in eastern Europe. Danzig and the Polish Corridor must be absorbed, he said. Western Russia and the Ukraine were indispensable as German living space; nothing less would suffice. Mr. Churchill said that if what the Ambassador said was true, then war was inevitable. "And if," he added, "you plunge us all into another great war, England will bring the whole world against you, like last time." At this plain statement, Ribbentrop rose in heat. "England may be very clever," he retorted, "but this time she will not bring the world against us!"

The Ambassador had already caught the habit of rash prediction from his master, but as Hitler had gone so far so quickly, this was not to be wondered at. Hitler, so his countrymen believed, would succeed in everything he undertook, and what more natural than that Germany should wish to regain ascendancy in the Baltic? There Russia was her only serious challenge, and about Russia, statesmen in the West were halfhearted and suspicious when they were not actively hostile.

VI

After Austria—Czechoslovakia, which might have proved a tough problem for Hitler, since the country was allied with France and had promise of support from the Soviet Union if France fulfilled her obligations. The Czechs themselves possessed enough military strength to resist the first thrust of any attack, provided backing came speedily, and when Nazi activities led to a serious crisis in the Sudetenland, which had a German population, the government in Prague was forced to order partial mobilization. There is no doubt that the Czechs would have fought to defend their integrity if they had been assured of help, but this was never likely to be forthcoming. France was unstable, Britain was unready and the Soviet Union would not move alone. The Western powers, to whom the prospect of war seemed the ultimate tragedy, declared themselves willing to negotiate with Hitler on the whole question, and Neville Chamberlain, the British Prime Minister, umbrella in hand, flew to Berchtesgaden to meet the dictator. Their conversations led to an agreement made at Munich on 29 September, 1938, between Germany, France, Britain and Italy (Germany's ally), under the terms of which the Sudetenland was ceded to Hitler and was promptly occupied.

Czechoslovakia, a country deriving its independence and status from the Treaty of Versailles, had been openly and grossly betrayed by the successors of the architects of that treaty. It was a fact which registered deeply in the conscience of the British, who had no direct obligation in the matter, and oddly less so in the case of the French, who had become supine in foreign policy, being prepared to be led in a sphere where they had at one time directed. Russia, isolated anew, drew her own conclusions from an arrangement over which she had not been consulted, and began to revise her policy, a matter for which she could scarcely be blamed.

Three days before the Munich Agreement, Hitler announced that he had "assured Mr. Chamberlain that the German people desires nothing else than peace. I have further assured him that when this difficulty is solved there is for Germany no further territorial problem in Europe . . . We want no Czechs!"

Within six months of the "settlement" German troops, advancing from the Sudetenland and elsewhere, occupied the rest of the country. So much for words; but the time of the seizure was the spring of 1939, and in that year, although words never ceased to flow, event followed event with dazzling speed. Czechoslovakia was no sooner swallowed than the Germans took Memel from the Lithuanians, and it was clear to even the most sanguine that fighting must occur before the year was out, and that Baltic countries would be involved. Poland was the next victim marked down for destruction.

I 2 . Baltic prelude to the Second World War

Poland had not behaved well at the time of the dismemberment of Czechoslovakia, for on hearing the terms of the Munich Agreement, she had sent an ultimatum to her neighbour, demanding the cession of the frontier district of Teschen, which was rich in minerals. As soon as it was seen that the Czechs were deserted, the region was occupied by Polish cavalry, the door being shut in the faces of the British and French ambassadors, who called in protest.

Such an action might have justified the Western powers in leaving Poland to her fate, but it was overlooked in view of the menace with which every country whose territory marched with Germany was now faced. In spite of Britain not having reached any understanding whatever with Russia, no sooner had Hitler revealed his political shamelessness by his violation of the Munich terms than Mr. Chamberlain, in the name of his country, gave a guarantee to Poland. His example was followed, with more reason, by France, with whom Poland was allied. On 31 March, 1939, with Memel already in German hands and Czechoslovakia prostrate, Mr. Chamberlain announced in the House of Commons that "in the event of any action which clearly threatens Polish independence, and which the Polish Government accordingly considers it vital to resist with their national forces, His Majesty's Government would feel themselves bound at once to lend the Polish Government all support in their power. They have given an assurance to this effect."

It remained to be seen whether this belated gesture, which risked the bombing of British and French cities by a newly equipped German Air Force, and which held no promise of effective aid to Poland (since geography precluded it), would have the result of deterring Hitler from further aggression. In view of Ribbentrop's earlier conversation with Mr. Churchill, it seemed unlikely, and so indeed it proved, although before Hitler made his next move in expansion, he electrified the world by a *volte-face*. He came to an agreement with Russia, the country which the Nazis had execrated above all others. Many of the clauses were secret, but the declaration itself was open. It spelled doom not merely for Poland, but for the other Baltic states whose brief day of independence had been so welcome and so unexpected—and perhaps for Finland also. Estonia and Latvia were recognized as falling within the Russian sphere, while Lithuania now became a German interest, a fact which had already been made apparent in the affair of Memel. Nearly 60,000 Latvians, faced with the alternative of Germany or Russia, chose what they considered the lesser of two evils, and migrated south.

The German-Russian agreement was signed in Moscow on 23 August, and the principal Russian originator was Joseph Stalin, the self-styled "man of steel." He had recently discarded his Foreign Minister, Litvinov, who was a Jew and therefore an anathema to Germany, in favour of Molotov, who had survived the hazards and ordeals to which all the Bolshevik leaders had been subjected, "thriving," as Mr. Churchill says of him, "in a society where ever varying intrigue was accompanied by the constant menace of personal liquidation. His cannon-ball head, black moustache and comprehending eyes, his slab face, his verbal adroitness and imperturbable demeanour were appropriate manifestations of his qualities and skill . . . I have never seen a human being who more perfectly represented the modern conception of a robot."

Ribbentrop, who signed for Germany, had originally inserted in the preamble a high-sounding phrase concerning the history and growth of friendly relations between the two countries. To this Stalin objected, with typical realism. He remarked that the Soviet Government could not suddenly present their public with "such a declaration of friendship, after the Soviet has been cov-

ered with *pails of manure* by the Nazi Government for six years."
The clause was deleted.

The agreement signalized the complete diplomatic humiliation
of the statesmen who became known as the appeasers, or the
Men of Munich. It was reached when a Franco-British military
mission was actually in Moscow, unable to come to any arrangement with Stalin, who thought in terms of military divisions, for
he was a land animal, concerned with what must largely be a
land struggle. "We formed the impression," he said later, "that
the British and French governments were not resolved to go to
war if Poland were attacked, but that they hoped the diplomatic
line-up of Britain, France and Russia would deter Hitler. We
were sure it would not." Stalin had asked how many divisions
France would send against Germany on mobilization, and was
told about a hundred. And Britain? How many could she send?
"Two, and two more later," had been the reply. "Ah, two and
two more later," Stalin repeated ironically. "Do you know how
many divisions we shall have to put on the Russian front if we go
to war with Germany—more than three hundred."

"Since the month of May," wrote Edouard Daladier, then Premier of France, "the U.S.S.R. had conducted two negotiations,
one with France, the other with Germany. She appeared to pre-
fer to partition rather than to defend Poland. Such was the
immediate cause of the Second World War." This was an oversimplification of Russian policy, and took no account of the longer-
term views of Hitler, which Britain, with her agelong tradition of
resisting the attempt of any single power to dominate Europe,
was beginning to fathom.

When his negotiations with Russia were nearing completion,
Hitler summoned his commander in chief, to hear his directions
for the immediate conduct of the war with Poland, as well as his
future plans. He was under no delusions as to the risks he ran, for
he knew the tenacity of Britain—he had written about it in *Mein
Kampf*—and he believed, though he was not yet absolutely certain, that both she and France would honour their pledge. "We
must be determined from the beginning to fight the Western
powers," he said. "Conflict with Poland was bound to come
sooner or later. I made the decision to fight in the spring, but I
thought I would first turn against the West and only afterwards

against the East. We need not be afraid of a blockade, for the East will now supply us with grain, cattle, coal. I only fear that at the last moment some *Schweinhund* will make a proposal for mediation . . . My political aims go far. A beginning has been made for the destruction of England's hegemony; the way will be wide open, once I have finished my preparations."

In the course of the same address Hitler, in less than fifty words, made a general statement which, in its sinister way, no powermonger in history could have bettered. "I shall give a propaganda reason for beginning the war," he said. "Never mind whether it is plausible or not. The victor will not be asked afterwards whether he told the truth. In starting and waging a war it is not right that matters, but victory."

II

The Hitler-Stalin agreement, the cynicism of which appalled civilized nations, was in fact neither so surprising nor so shocking as it seemed. For many years after the First World War, Germany and Russia had been treated as semi-outcasts, one of them defeated and disgraced, the other barbarous and incomprehensible. Both countries had known humiliation and interference. To be appeased on the one hand and courted on the other nourished thoughts of grandeur. If they stood together, anything was possible, or so Stalin argued. Hitler's ideas, as he had already disclosed, were more precise.

By the terms of Versailles, the German Army had been limited to a token or policing force of 100,000 men, but to a nation who above all things loved the soldier's calling, such restriction was intolerable, and it was soon, if secretly, evaded. There was only one country where German professionals could equip and train on the scale at which they aimed, and that was Russia. They had skill and ideas to offer. The Russians welcomed both, and could provide limitless space in which to exercise and experiment, behind a convenient curtain of words put up by the politicians. The Germans despised the Russians, but were glad enough to use them. It was an arrangement which suited both sides, and the period between the wars was, in fact, one in which technical part-

nership, though intermittent, was not unfruitful, civil war in
Spain giving both countries an opportunity to prove in action,
on conveniently opposite sides, lessons learned on the sand table
and in areas of manoeuvre.

It was this cloaked military collaboration which indirectly led
to the great Russian "purges" of the prewar years, so startling to
the outside observer, so devastating in their effect within Russia
herself. Being essentially reserved in public matters, highly selec-
tive in the preservation of their written records and capable of
deceit on a grand scale, the Russians will probably never reveal
the full truth about the reorganization of their forces under Stalin's rule. Nevertheless, certain facts emerge which afford a thread
of evidence to show the state of affairs at a time when Russia
made ready to seize opportunities presented by the apparent
willingness of Hitler to share in a new European order.

The matter of control of the Red Army by the Communist
Party began on a regular system shortly after Lenin's assumption
of power, when commissars were posted to every important unit,
to see that the commanding officer did what his political superiors
wanted. As early as 1920 a feud developed within the Party itself,
the result of defeat before Warsaw by Pilsudski's shock troops, in
a battle which then saved Poland. It was the beginning of strife
between Stalin and his ally Voroshilov, and Trotsky and his
ally Tukhachevski, which resulted in such acrimony and recrimination that Lenin, in the course of time, forbade the campaign
to be discussed in public. The ban was observed, but Stalin, who
had a long memory, nursed resentment against members of the
High Command long after he had emerged victorious from his
duel with Trotsky, and in due course he was able to take a revenge so far-reaching as to be scarcely credible to a normal
mind.

In 1924, the year of Lenin's death, Party control was eased—
except in the navy and in certain non-Russian units—by the
appointment of assistants to military formations, instead of fully
fledged commissars. These Party officials took upon themselves
the comparatively modest role of education officers, leaving military command where it properly belonged, to the regular officers.
In 1933 the old Tsarist titles of army rank were revived, with
modifications, and Russian garrisons and ports were graced with

uniformed grandees in whom, with the expansion of the forces to meet threats real and fancied, Stalin soon detected the danger of Bonapartism, which was a natural apprehension in any revolutionary versed in history. Alarm increased so much that three years later the commissar system was restored in all its rigour, and Gamarnik, whose original idea it had been to replace the commissars by assistants, shot himself to avoid "liquidation." The army was now fairly warned that purges were likely, but no one in their wilder moments could have guessed their scale.

In the years immediately preceding the European war, the historian of the Soviet High Command, Mr. John Erikson, has calculated that the great majority of the principal Soviet officers were removed on Stalin's orders, including three out of five marshals, among them Tukhachevski, Stalin sparing neither his enemy's aged mother nor most of his family. Moreover, out of a grand total of over 75,000 officers and principal commissars—for even the guardians of the Party were not sacrosanct, the watchers themselves being watched under an insanely suspicious system—at the very lowest estimate 15,000 were shot, and probably very many more, after secret denunciation, from which there was no appeal and no escape. Only Russia could have afforded such slaughter, and only ingrained and measureless distrust could have achieved it. The most fantastic element in the story was that use was made of documents, forged by the Nazis, showing collaboration by the victims with the Reichswehr to destroy the Soviet regime. Of all Hitler's successes, this purge, of which he naturally could not boast, was one of the most outstanding, and it cost Germany nothing. Stalin, it then appeared, would believe anything except the simple fact that an officer or commissar strictly educated under the Communist system, and therefore knowing no other, was unlikely to have the means or the wit, much less the will or the courage, to try to betray it.

A new kind of man was in fact being evolved in Russia. He thought in slogans, talked in bullets and believed—if he survived—in Comrade Stalin. More innocent men died to keep Stalin powerful in the Kremlin than were ever sacrificed to the passions, schemes and ambitions of Peter the Great. It will presently be seen how one rogue may fool another and go on fooling him, and it is scarcely surprising, after the review of

Stalin's protracted tyranny which followed his death, that he himself was purged from the higher level of Communist sanctity. In
a moment of truth Stalin might have savoured a sentence by
George Orwell, who said: "History consists of a series of swindles,
in which the masses are first lured into revolt by the promise of
Utopia and then, when they have done their job, are enslaved
over again by new masters." Stalin witnessed the process full circle, and indeed went one better, for he contrived to eliminate all
masters but himself.

An episode which renders the story of the Russian purges more
credible was related by Mr. Churchill in his account of conversations with Stalin at Teheran a few years later. Stalin told him
that there were many Communists in the German divisions with
which the Russians were then engaged, and that when they were
taken prisoner they were asked why they were fighting for Hitler.
The invariable reply was that they were obeying orders, and the
invariable result was that they were shot. Stalin said later that the
whole German General Staff must be rounded up and similarly
disposed of, since the impetus of Hitler's forces derived from
about 50,000 officers and technicians. When Churchill said that
the British Parliament and public would never tolerate mass executions, Stalin pursued the subject. "Fifty thousand must be
shot," he repeated. Mr. Churchill, with his roots in another way
of life, said that he would rather be taken out into the garden
then and there and be shot himself than sully his own and his
country's honour by such infamy. The conversation, which had
an abrupt ending, showed the depths which separated the hu-
manist from the ruler to whom individuals were nothing. It was
not Stalin but Trotsky who once said of the Revolutionaries: "We
were never concerned with the Kantian-priestly and vegetarian-
Quaker prattle about the sancity of human life," and Stalin was
utterly of the same mind.

III

Hitler chose the first day of September to strike at Poland. The
first shots on any scale were fired by the old German training
battleship *Schleswig-Holstein* at the Westerplatte, where there

was a fortification. Hitler had made every preparation. He had removed Danzig from the care of its nominal guardian, the League
of Nations, by fermenting German xenophobia within a predom-
inantly German area and then causing a Nazi inhabitant to proclaim himself "head of the state." To crown the pantomime, the
day before war opened, Hitler declared that he had received a
formal application from the Free City to "rejoin the Reich," and
announced that he had been graciously pleased to grant the request.

Hitler could spare only the *Schleswig-Holstein* and a few similar units from the North Sea area to operate in Baltic waters,
and could not prevent the most modern Polish vessels from making good their escape from Gdynia. The destroyers *Blyskawica,
Grom* and *Burza,* together with the submarines *Wilk* and *Orzel,*
proved a valuable reinforcement to the British Navy. The *Orzel*
endured hair-raising adventures in a cruise which might have
ended in internment in an Estonian port, where she landed her
sick captain, had not local guards been overcome and the second-
in-command, chartless and low in fuel, found his way through
intricate waters to safety.

On land, and in the air above it, there was no such refuge except for a remnant of brave men who were able to cross the
Rumanian frontier and, in time, to re-form to fight elsewhere, the
fate of so many former Polish exiles. German efficiency and ruthlessness ensured that a campaign, planned to the last detail, was
executed with economy and without serious hitch. Hitler showed
Europe that if in diplomacy he was entirely without scruple, he
had the means to take what he wanted by force, and when he
wanted it. Whatever doubts may have troubled his generals before the *Blitzkrieg* in Poland were removed by its speed and success: moreover, the sinking of the passenger liner *Athenia* in the
Atlantic with the loss of over a hundred lives, including that of
twenty-eight Americans, showed that Hitler was as well prepared
by sea as by land, and that, here as elsewhere, he would stop at
nothing. Napoleon would have approved his bland announcement that Mr. Churchill had personally ordered a bomb to be
placed on board the ship in order to prejudice German-American
relations, oblivious of the fact that the statesman had not been
given his old post of First Lord of the Admiralty at the time she

sailed. The idea was no more outrageous than the suggestion that British agents arranged for the murder of Tsar Paul I. In war, as Hitler had already pointed out, only losers are asked questions.

Poland was exposed to German invasion from East Prussia and Pomerania, and to compass his enemy's destruction, Hitler employed over fifty divisions, including all his armour. From East Prussia eight divisions were to advance on Warsaw. From Pomerania twelve divisions were ordered to destroy Polish troops in the Corridor, and then to move southwestward to Warsaw along both banks of the Vistula. The frontier opposite the Posen bulge was held defensively by German reserve troops, but on their right, to the southward, were seven divisions whose task was to cover the left flank of the main thrust of seventeen divisions directed straight upon the capital. Yet farther south, further divisions were given the task of capturing the important industrial area west of Cracow, and afterwards Lemberg.

The Luftwaffe disposed 1,500 modern aircraft with which to overwhelm the Polish Air Force, if possible on the ground. Thereafter they were to support the army in the battlefield, to attack military installations and to disrupt all communications by road or rail. They were also to spread terror far and wide, a mission which could be achieved by their mere presence, unopposed.

Only some thirty Polish divisions, two thirds of their regular army, were available to meet the shock, and they were ranged along the frontiers, with no central reserve. They were outclassed in artillery, and had but a single armoured brigade to oppose no less than nine German *Panzer* or tank divisions, the *élite* of Hitler's forces. The Poles had twelve brigades of cavalry—smart troops, excellently horsed and trained—but they belonged to an arm which had long been proved obsolete: admirable for ceremony, but inviting massacre by modern weapons. Of some nine hundred Polish aircraft, only scattered flights were able to annoy the Germans, for within two days airfields and ground equipment were rendered unserviceable, and with bases wrecked, an air arm was as useless as a navy without ports.

Within a week the Germans had thrust deeply into Poland, and only on the borders of East Prussia were they for a time held at bay. Even here the Poles were soon outflanked, though they were able to fall back on a fairly strong defensive position on the river Narew, which they defended valiantly for some days. One other instance of strong resistance was that of General Kutrzea, who commanded in the Posen area. For ten days his counter-attacks caused concern, though not undue alarm, to the Pomeranian divisions.

By the end of the second week, after bitter though sporadic fighting, the Polish Army had ceased to exist as an organized force, and German armour advanced to the outskirts of Warsaw, where it was halted by resistance organized by the townspeople. A German thrust from East Prussia now menaced the capital from the east, and a column reached Brest-Litovsk, a hundred miles from the main battle fronts.

By 19 September, German pincers met and closed, and Hitler was able to announce that the Battle of the Vistula, now in its final spasms, had been "one of the greatest battles of extermination of all time." The statement was neither lie nor exaggeration, and the use of the word "extermination" was deliberate. Hitler had inherited Bismarck's attitude towards the Poles. They were a race he was to treat with a brutality exceeded only by his measures against the Jews.

Polish trials were now to be crowned by the appearance of the hereditary foe whom they had last driven from their country nearly twenty years before. On 17 September, when the defeated army was in its death throes, Soviet columns advanced across the eastern frontier, unopposed. Next day they occupied Vilna, and thereafter they met their German collaborators at Brest-Litovsk, scene of the abortive agreement which signalized Russian withdrawal from the First World War. Immediately after the Russo-German forces had ranged themselves on the agreed line of demarcation, Lithuania, apart from Memel, was removed from the German sphere of influence, and by the middle of October, Russia's advance parties were in the country.

All was not quite over, but the remaining resistance was more of a desperate gesture than a serious check. Warsaw, and Modlin, a little to the north, still held out, but after many days of bombardment from the air and by heavy artillery, the capital surrendered, and Hitler himself was able to survey the battered city. Modlin fought on until 28 September, when supplies ran short, so that in one month all was over, and a nation of thirty-five million people bowed before dictators. On the 29th the Germans and Russians signed a treaty of partition, the fourth of its kind since 1772. This document recorded what was already fact— that the ancient kingdom was to be shared between the two strongest European military powers.

Hitler and Stalin were now free to direct their attention elsewhere, and the first moves were made by Stalin, for whereas Hitler held the Baltic shore from Schleswig to Memel, the Russians were still hedged in by little states. The main protagonists had already secretly agreed on the elimination of such anachronisms of Versailles as were represented by Lithuania, Latvia, and Estonia, and this was a matter which could be remedied by actions as straightforward as those by which Hitler had secured Danzig, though the methods were slightly different.

Estonia, threatened with invasion, was forced to sign a pact by which bases were leased to Russia, and a garrison of 25,000 men was thereupon admitted. Then came Latvia's turn. A similar pact gave military bases and airfields to the Russians, a garrison of 30,000 men was provided and it was agreed that the Soviet Union should have the use of Libau as a naval base. Mr. Ulmanis, the Latvian who had presided over the rebirth of his country, lived to see its return to Russia before himself disappearing into captivity.

In any future struggle for a further share of Baltic lands, Stalin was now almost as well placed as any of his predecessors, except in respect of Finland, and his gains had been made without expense. In view of his immense resources, and of the fate which had overtaken Poland in face of a modern army, it was unlikely that Finland would cause Stalin loss of sleep. In due time, as Foreign Minister of a victorious power, Molotov was to describe Finland to a visiting admirer as "a peanut." This was not an expression he would have employed with any assurance at a slightly earlier stage of his career, unless, and unthinkably, he had wished to invite ridicule.

IV

The Western Allies had watched the destruction of the country to which they had given their pledge, entirely unable to come to her aid. The French mobilized, manned their intricate and costly Maginot Line, which was believed to be impregnable against direct assault, while the squadrons of what they described as *l'armées de l'air*, equipped with indifferent machines, indulged in no sorties which could draw upon them reprisals from the Luftwaffe. Only at sea were the Allies extended, and from the first day of war it was apparent that the Royal Navy, with its world-wide commitments, would bear the burden it had so often assumed in the past. It had already safeguarded the passage of the Expeditionary Force to France, and if in mere size this justified Stalin's scornful reference, an allusion by the Kaiser, five and twenty years before, to Britain's "contemptible little army" had in the end come home to roost, for that same army, nourished and increased by sea power, proved to be among the most formidable of his victors.

At the Admiralty in London, Mr. Churchill, ever fertile in ideas, spoke and wrote of the attraction of the Baltic as a sphere within which to damage Hitler. This was reviving a favourite idea of Lord Fisher's in the previous war, which in the end had come to nothing. It was soon perceived that air power, and lack of Scandinavian bases, precluded the possibility of an operation which was given the code name "Catherine," after the Russian Empress. Mr. Churchill's scheme had been to use old battleships, specially armoured and protected against mines, as the core of an assault force. In fact, the only solution of the problem might have been by submarines, their range and endurance extended by submersible supply ships or "milch cows" such as the Germans were later to develop in the ocean warfare which they were to wage from the time of the sinking of the *Athenia* to the day, nearly six years later, when their U-boats surrendered in startling numbers.

The period which Mr. Chamberlain first christened the "Twilight War" gave no opportunity for the provision of such refinements as reinforced battleships for the Baltic, for if Hitler waited, digesting his Polish loot and preparing for his next thrust, Stalin, stimulated by the bloodless subjection of his neighbours, made preliminary moves to secure the other shore of the Gulf of Finland. The rigours of winter would soon be upon him, and it was time to arrange matters to his advantage with the men of Helsinki.

Early in October, Mr. J. K. Paasikivi, who had been one of the signatories to the peace treaty made with the Soviet Union after the Finnish War of Liberation, was summoned to Moscow to hear Russian demands. They were put forward on the grounds of the future security of Leningrad and the base at Kronstadt. The idea in itself was not unreasonable, for Leningrad was indeed vulnerable, and all strategists knew it. The question was whether Finland could retain her independence while making acceptable concessions. Russian procedure was different from that of Germany, for her statesmen knew by long experience the character of the Finns. Although this was so, Russia was fresh from participation in the carving up of a country which had afforded glory to Hitler at a price which no militarist would have judged excessive, and she saw no difficulty in adding to her own inexpensive gains. She did not anticipate that the newly organized Red Army, whose formations had recently fought creditably in ferocious actions against the Japanese in Manchuria, of which the West knew little and cared less, would be reblooded so near home. On the other hand, she was as prepared to go to war with her small neighbour, if this should prove necessary, as Hitler had been to crush Poland. Russia had never shown herself unduly sensitive to world opinion, though she still subscribed to the idea of the League of Nations, which the Germans had discarded, and her representative sat at Geneva.

In their abortive discussions with a Franco-British military mission, before the conclusion of the agreement with Germany, the Soviet authorities had disclosed their requirements in the Baltic. These included Hangö, the peninsula thrusting from the south of Finland and serving as her guardian; Libau, the Latvian port second only to Riga, together with the Estonian islands of Osel and Dago, which commanded the Rigan gulf. They also suggested temporary occupation of the Alands. With such bases, so it was pointed out, the Russians could extend cruiser operations as well as submarine and mine-laying activities along the coasts of East Prussia and Pomerania, and submarines would be able to raid supply ships carrying raw materials from Sweden to Germany. With such concessions an active Red Navy could harass Germany by sea while keeping its own bases intact.

When meetings began in Moscow on 12 October, the Russians made it clear that they wanted a "local treaty of reciprocal aid." Hangö was emphasized, and concessions were required at Petsamo, where the Finns had an Arctic outlet. The border would need to be altered in Russia's favour in the area of Lake Ladoga, and the Finns were asked to cede the islands of Suursaari and Koivisto, in the Finnish gulf. Territorial compensation was offered in eastern Karelia.

Two days later Stalin was still more explicit. "We must be able to bar the entrance to the Gulf of Finland," he said. "Against what enemies?" asked Paasikivi. "England or Germany?" Stalin explained that although Soviet relations with Germany were then good, "everything in this world may change." After the meeting a written proposal requested a thirty-year lease of Hangö, which would become a Soviet naval base and be armed with coastal defence guns capable, in conjunction with batteries on the opposite shore, of closing the Gulf of Finland to enemy shipping. The Russians proposed a Hangö garrison of 5,000—an infantry regiment, two anti-aircraft batteries, two aviation regiments and a tank battalion.

At a meeting on 23 October, Stalin stressed the possibility of a Franco-British threat in the Arctic, and he recalled the activities of British units operating from Finnish bases at the time of the civil war. "I well understand your wish to remain neutral," he said, "but I assure you it is not possible. The great powers simply will not allow it." After ten days the Finns made up their minds. If they leased Hangö, they would themselves have insufficient protection and they would become in effect a Russian satellite. The proposals were rejected, and Molotov, who had already proclaimed the aims of the talks at the Supreme Soviet, could not climb down without losing face. He let fall the ominous words: "We civilians can see no further in the matter; now it is the turn of the military to have their say."

There followed one of those propaganda campaigns which so bedevil international relationships, in the course of which representatives of great powers address opponents in terms of vituperation, not reason, in a style so repetitious that the least-experienced cleric would be ashamed of it if delivered from a pulpit, and in which zoological and other similes are employed which are more appropriate to the schoolroom than for the ears of grown men and women. On 26 November the inevitable happened. Seven artillery rounds were fired by the Finnish frontier guard at Manaila. These were described as "provocative discharge of artillery directed against Soviet forces," although in fact it was a far less serious incident than several which had arisen between German and Soviet units when in process of occupying Poland. Moscow sent a formal note of protest to Helsinki, and on 30 November, after a thirty-minute artillery barrage, the Red Army took the offensive against the Finns.

v

The shock of the Soviet attack on a small country, following the recent agreement with Hitler and the division of Poland, will never be forgotten by those who were of an age to appreciate its significance. Here was a nation ringed around by powerful neighbours, willing to negotiate on fair terms, yet assaulted by a giant. Indignation was almost universal. There was talk, fortunately none of it responsible, about "switching the war," and the Russians were expelled from the League of Nations, a gesture which they treated with the derision which could have been expected. The Western powers made what plans they could to send Finland aid, but with Baltic outlets controlled by Germany, all depended on Scandinavian countries' allowing the transit of troops and stores overland, a contingency which seemed unlikely. In Sweden the Russian action was felt with far more force than at the time of the Finnish War of Liberation, when the country itself was split into factions, and for the Winter War, as the campaign came afterwards to be known, considerable, though always unofficial help in men and supplies was sent across the frontier. Even so, as Sweden and Norway refused to abandon their neutrality, the Finns soon realized that their geographical situation was as hopeless as that of Poland. They were Baltic prisoners.

They had two assets—national unity and a very great soldier. Unity was made even stronger by Russian air raids on Helsinki, in which civilians suffered, and by the enemy's crude device of setting up Kuusinen, a Marxist puppet-politician, as "Head of the Democratic Republic of Finland" in the hamlet of Terijoki. Kuusinen's platform was that he was to "liberate the Finnish proletariat from the Fascist military clique." This was language which had been made sickeningly familiar in the propaganda war, but it could scarcely deceive the most innocent. The soldier, Field Marshal Mannerheim, was seventy-two at the time of the attack, but for some years he had been Chairman of the Finnish Committee of National Defence. Although his protracted efforts to strengthen the defences of a peaceably minded country had had all too little result, yet such forces as were available were of high quality, and when his countrymen once more turned to him for leadership in their hour of need, Mannerheim, despite his age, assumed the burden of command.

Finland was wide open to attack on a front stretching for some eight hundred miles, the possible area of operations extending from the outskirts of Leningrad to the Arctic Ocean. Along it were deployed four Soviet armies. The task of one, under Meretskov, commander of the Leningrad Military District, was to strike up the Karelian Isthmus, break the defences of the "Mannerheim Line"—which was not so much a line as a belt of defences, fire points, anti-tank traps, barriers, small forts and trenches. Having pierced this belt, Meretskov was to drive on to Viborg and lay open the way to Helsinki. North of Lake Ladoga, the next army would drive into the flank and rear of the Finns who were defending the isthmus. Still farther north, another army was organized to drive towards the northern edge of the Gulf of Bothnia, and to sever land communications between Finland and Sweden, slicing Finland in two at its "waist." In the Arctic, the fourth army would seize the Petsamo neighbourhood, including the port itself.

The Finns, with their small standing army and limited resources, could not be strong everywhere, nor could Mannerheim enjoy the luxury of any substantial reserve which he could direct at need from point to point. In recalling his achievement, it is necessary to reflect upon the means which were to his hand. Brains, coolness, judgement, trust in subordinates right down to platoon level—these were the qualities he brought to his task. He had to rely mainly on his front-line men, on the resource of local commanders accustomed to individual action, on knowledge of the country and on the ingenuity with which the Karelian line had been sited in depth, where every use had been made of watery and marshy ground.

Meretskov launched his men on 6 December on a seventeen-kilometre front, and for ten days twelve rifle divisions and a tank corps kept up their pressure. Mass frontal attacks were the order of the day. After an opening barrage infantry, preceded by tanks, would assault the Finnish positions. The Russians met with no success whatever, and when a change was made to night attack, the infantry leading and the tanks ready to prize open gaps, the Finns switched on searchlights, and across the excellent fields of fire provided by frozen lakes and rivers they poured machine-gun bullets into the serried Russian infantry. By the end of December the Soviet High Command called a halt to the slaughter, which had yielded next to nothing. The outside world, amazed, drew comfort from this new version of the story of David and Goliath.

Near Petsamo, at the other end of the front, a Soviet division began to advance down the Arctic highway, and sealed off any likelihood of succour which might have been given by way of the sea routes. A strong garrison was instilled in the coastal area, and Russian mine layers stood by. North of Nauts, the attackers halted before a local defence belt. Their immediate task was accomplished, and they could await with confidence news from the Finnish "waist." It came very soon, but not in the form expected. The Russians met with disaster.

The northern division of the army of the "waist" drove for the important road junction at Suomussalmi, advancing along a highway built in great secrecy for this purpose. Another formation approached Suomussalmi from the south, the divisions uniting on 9 December. From Suomussalmi the force would make towards Oulu and the Bothnian gulf. The Finnish commander, Colonel

Siilasvuo, disposing of a force markedly inferior in numbers, determined to strike at the junction of the two divisions.

Harassed by small battle patrols, the Russians were first compelled to quit the ruins of the village. Having split his enemy and harried him back into the open country, Siilasvuo then prepared for a miniature version of Tannenberg. He held the southern force in check and deployed such strength as he had against the northern. As the temperature dropped steeply and sharper cold arrived than any known for a quarter of a century, Siilasvuo attacked in flank and rear, striking also at a supply dump in the middle of a frozen lake. The Russians withdrew in an orderly manner, the remnants of the infantry at the centre of columns of tanks. Although they made good their retreat, they were finished as an effective formation.

Siilasvuo then turned to the southern force, which by this time was strung out along five miles of road. Blocking this road at the Soviet frontier itself, the Finns, working in four groups, harried and cut up the helpless Russians, cold and hunger adding considerably to casualties inflicted by the machine guns and snipers. At the end of two days' fighting the Finns were mopping up a dreadful battlefield, and war correspondents were able to send home photographs of the death throes of a force which had been massacred by opponents whom every professional soldier admired.

Things were no better on the Lake Ladoga front. Every Russian advance was checked, the Finns aiming to cut the supply routes of enemy formations, and generally succeeding. Two divisions were surrounded. A tank brigade, sent to the relief of one of them, was in its turn sealed off from its communications, surrounded, and after fifty-four days of siege was stormed by the Finns. The Ladoga front drained away Russian men and materials, sacrificing them uselessly, but it had the effect of forcing the Finns to divert troops from the vital isthmus.

By the last week of a bitter December the fiasco, redeemed only by the dogged and traditional fatalism of the Russian infantry, was plain to see. Six major offensives had been mounted, and only one, in the least vital area, had enjoyed success, and even that had been halted. After the catastrophe at Suomussalmi it became a matter of pride to retrieve the Red Army's name, high though the cost had been already. Stalin even turned to his German friends for help, and Admiral Raeder agreed that German ships proceeding to northern Sweden could supply Soviet submarines, detailed for operations in the Gulf of Bothnia, when ice conditions permitted, with oil and supplies. Meanwhile the entire method of attack was revised and a new strategy prepared. At the turn of the year 1940, Timoshenko, shortly to become a marshal and to survive many more vicissitudes in a career of soldiering which stretched back to a time when he was a noncommissioned officer in the Tsar's army, took over the general command. He would supervise the second round.

Mass attacks were to be discontinued. More and better use of ski troops, which the Finns employed so well, was to be made. What could not be improved was the general condition that, owing to the policy of rigid control from above, the Russians must always remain uncertain in any situation which involved individual initiative. Under the new dispensation, if enemy pillboxes were not smashed by preliminary barrage, infantry was not to be committed to slaughter. Above all, lines of communication were to be secured against flank attacks before an advance was made.

No detail of the Finnish war escaped German eyes, and their observers were given every facility. A report to Hitler's General Staff spoke of the Red Army as: "In quantity, a gigantic military instrument . . . Organization, equipment and means of leadership unsatisfactory: principles of leadership good, but leadership itself . . . too young and inexperienced . . . Troops not very uniform (i.e., in quality). Fighting qualities in a heavy fight, dubious. The Russian 'mass,'" it concluded, "is no match for an army with modern equipment and superior leadership." The Führer no doubt read this conclusion with satisfaction.

At the end of January the Soviet Government put out peace feelers, tacitly dropping the fiction that the Communist Kuusinen represented his country, but their insistence on Hangö was made as plain as ever. To the British and French, aid to Finland and the possibility of cutting off supplies for Germany of Scandinavian ore became closely intertwined, while the French at the time favoured a plan for trying a landing at Petsamo. Yet even while statesmen and soldiers were meditating these plans, the Red Army facing the Mannerheim Line was being heavily reinforced with supplies which included new tanks, armoured sledges, electric digging machines and an improved infantry rifle. The General Staff was also working on a new plan for outflanking Viborg and for severing it from the capital.

A general offensive began on 1 February, the air arm, which had very limited opposition to encounter, being better co-ordinated with the ground movements than in the early weeks. Pressure was exercised north of Lake Ladoga, where success would have enabled the Russians to cut a railway link from north to south, to outflank the Mannerheim defences and to take Viborg in the rear. The aim was never achieved, but the mere possibility diverted Finnish troops which would have been invaluable to meet the thrusts in the Karelian Isthmus. If the Mannerheim defences remained inviolate and the Finns were equally stubborn on the Ladoga front, Timoshenko believed that as a last resort the war could be brought to an end by large-scale operations across the ice of Viborg Bay.

The Finns held out in one Karelian position after another, disputing every yard of the way and counterattacking whenever they could, for almost the whole of February. It was a feat of arms by a small and incompletely equipped army of free men pitted against the latest weapons, including massed tanks and bombers applied with all the ruthlessness of a totalitarian state. The defence was the wonder of Europe, but in the end, sheer weight of numbers, merciless persistence and unlimited ammunition told. By 26 February the fortress of Koivisto was encircled, and the shattering of the right flank of the Finnish defence belt was an accomplished fact.

Timoshenko's battle of Viborg Bay proved necessary after all, but it was made costly to the attackers. Launching columns across the ice was a perilous undertaking, and Mannerheim's men made the Russians win every painful inch. With the few bombers available to them, the Finns blasted tanks, armoured sledges and infantry as they advanced, blowing up the ice in front of them and using their machine guns with deadly effect. Even so, numbers told. After three days Soviet troops had gained a hold on the northwestern shore of Viborg Bay, and they were launching attacks on the islands which defended the town itself, their artillery, mounted on ice platforms, shelling positions inland.

By early March, Western help had still not materialized, and Mannerheim described the situation on the ice of Viborg Bay as impossible. "We are short of men on every hand," he stated with bare truth. A request for an armistice was turned down flat by the Russians unless Viborg and its bay were evacuated. A delegation thereupon left secretly for Moscow, where Molotov was ready to deliver terms so harsh as to verge on the barbarous. Four days later Mannerheim reported that in the isthmus battalion strengths had fallen to a quarter of their establishment, and that Soviet aircraft made movements and supply "decidedly difficult." These were not words of panic, but they indicated the exhaustion of a people who had been cheered by words of encouragement from the world beyond the Baltic, but not with the sinews of war, except for the help, on a necessarily limited scale, of Swedish and other volunteers. They were faced with the full strength of a power which had been sharply awakened from its earlier idea of an easy campaign.

When fighting ceased, the Finns found themselves forced to sign away the fortified positions and the isthmus they had so wonderfully defended: tracts of country to the east and north of Lake Ladoga, and crowning humiliation, land near the Finnish "waist," the scene of Russian disaster.

Even with all this Finland was still independent. She had suffered cruelly and alone, but she had given an example of courage and endurance which the free world would be unwise to forget. In the Karelian Isthmus some 13,000 Finns had held at bay more than eleven times their own number, and with an army which possessed no tanks and captured or destroyed 1,600 of these kings of the modern battlefield, some by means of a device known ironically as the "Molotov cocktail," which was a bottle filled with chloride of potassium, coal oil and noulen, ignited by an ampule holding sulphuric acid. It was a weapon needing desperate courage and a close approach.

South of Petsamo one Finnish battalion had checked an entire Russian division, while at Tolvajarvi as well as at Suomussalmi the defenders had won battles of annihilation. An air force consisting of less than three hundred machines had defied opponents numbering over two thousand. As for the High Command, that, said Mannerheim, required "sure intuition, realistic imagination and great strength of will, and entailed a strain on the physical and mental forces which was sometimes overwhelming."

To their honour, over 11,000 volunteers fought on the Finnish side. They included 8,000 Swedes, nearly 1,500 Norwegians and Danes, and a number of Finns from America. Memories of the sorrows and endurances of the Winter War grow fainter with the passage of time, but Baltic history shows no more astounding episode.

VI

Peace terms with Finland were dictated on 12 March, 1940. Within a month Hitler made his second move in the war. He occupied Denmark, thus sealing the entrance to the Baltic, and sent task forces to Norway to land at strategic points in the country. The plans were made with his usual minute care, and they were marvellously executed. In Norway fighting by air, sea and land was protracted for some weeks, during the course of which Hitler lost a substantial part of his surface navy. As his attack led to the securing of the greater portion of the large Norwegian mercantile marine for the service of the Western Allies, their gains, though made at the expense of loss and damage to many of their own ships of war and ancillaries, were substantial.

German command of the air conditioned the land fighting, and although Franco-British lodgements were made at Narvik and elsewhere, by the end of the spring Hitler could boast of the control of territory which would provide innumerable bases for his submarines and aircraft. His pupil, the Norwegian major Quisling, added a new word to the dictionary by traitorous conduct towards his sovereign, and in the end suffered a fate he had prepared for himself at the hands of his countrymen.

Denmark, so Hitler had boasted, could be taken at any time on the telephone, and this was not much of an exaggeration. Armed parties arrived in the harbour of Copenhagen concealed in the holds of coal ships, and from the eminence of the old mast tower, which had been in use when Nelson was in action off Amager, Danes saw steel-helmeted troops land and make their way to Amalienborg Palace, where the decoratively uniformed sentries, guarding their royalties, made a forlorn gesture against machine guns. German aircraft soon roared overhead, and henceforward Denmark, islands and mainland, came under the swastika flag and knew the habits of Himmler's secret police. It was the neatest invasion in Baltic history. An entire people became prisoners of war, for there was no chance, as had been the case in Norway and Poland, that detachments of such armed forces as were ready could escape. Danish resistance took the form of sabotage, cautious at first, but soon gathering strength. Danes had old scores to remember, and it was soon a favourite story that after the exaction of a monstrous sum, following the killing of a private soldier, the entire country began saving madly for their first German officer.

There was now no stopping Hitler, not even for purposes of digestion. Scarcely were Denmark and Norway disposed of than he turned upon France, outflanking the Maginot Line in a sweep through Belgium, disposing of Holland, which had escaped the First World War but which still gave sanctuary to the aged Kaiser, on the way. France, supposedly the land bulwark of the Western alliance, proved to have the fastest field army in Europe, and it seldom paused to fight. In June the British Expeditionary Force found itself isolated and pressed within the perimeter of Dunkirk. It was taken off by means of improvisation, leaving behind most of its heavier equipment. Hitler, who once claimed that his Germans were encircled, now controlled an immense arc of coast line from the northern tip of Norway to the frontiers of Spain. By reason of this fact alone, Britain was in infinitely more peril than she had ever been before throughout the centuries and—apart from kinsmen and countries beyond the seas —she was alone. Europe was ranged against her, for Spain was unfriendly, and Italy, seeing France prostrate, joined actively with Hitler, hoping for a share of the spoils. It seemed only a matter of time, perhaps of weeks, before Britain would be forced to make a humiliating peace.

In fact, there was more hope than there appeared to be. Although her cities and ports were soon aflame by night, Britain found her voice. In her hour of danger Winston Churchill, one of the few remaining orators, took over the reigns of government at the head of a coalition, and it soon began to be realized that the Channel was a formidable tank ditch. More than that, the Royal Navy, though it was now stretched well beyond its theo- retical limit, upheld all its majestic traditions, while British air- men showed that they could not only protect their country by day, but by night could inflict ever increasing damage upon the enemy by bomb, mine and direct attack on the invasion armada which Hitler was building up in the style of Napoleon.

The war soon extended to Africa, and raged mercilessly on and under the Western Ocean, and Hitler, so far all-victorious, was soon faced with the choice of whether to risk what even Napoleon had not dared venture, or whether, like his predecessor, to turn his back upon the islanders. By the winter of 1940 there was little doubt as to how he would proceed.

Early in the following summer Hitler's deputy, Rudolf Hess, flew alone to Britain in a Messerschmidt, parachuting down into the Scottish countryside with a general plea for peace. He did not know, or did not disclose, Hitler's eastern plans, though Sta- lin, with his suspicious nature, long believed that his mission was part of a deep negotiation or plot between Britain and Germany which had miscarried. When in the course of a later visit to Moscow, Mr. Churchill explained the simpler truth, Stalin would not credit it. "When I make a statement of fact within my knowl- edge," said Mr. Churchill, "I expect it to be believed." Stalin grinned genially, saying: "There are lots of things which happen even here in Russia which our Secret Service do not necessarily tell me."

1 3 . The great explosion

In the early summer of 1941 the shape of the future and thus the destiny of mankind lay largely in the hands of four men, two of whom, Adolf Hitler and Winston Churchill, were at the head of countries at war with each other. The others, Franklin Roosevelt and Joseph Stalin, watched from the wings, Roosevelt and his nation increasingly sympathetic to Britain, Stalin equally anxious to do what service he could for Hitler, short of an open war with Britain, in which he could not, for all his imponderable strength, usefully take part.

Hitler had announced that the British lion was licking his wounds, which was true enough of the intervals between her offensive-minded air attacks, her pressure upon Germans and Italians in remote theatres of war, and keeping open the sea lanes. Stalin boasted that, whatever might be in store, he intended to "help pull no Imperialist chestnuts out of the fire." With Finland and its setbacks behind him, he was well placed, content to see the Germans employed in a struggle which seemed to be getting them nowhere, though there were prospects that Britain's life line across the Atlantic might in time be severed, and if that should happen, who would care less than Joseph Stalin? Japan was likely to be a major factor in any new shift of world power, but Stalin had already come to an understanding with the Mikado's government, and foresaw no development in that quarter which need cause him anxiety. His Secret Service might not tell him everything, but he was satisfied from reports from Far Eastern areas that Japanese aspirations were south, in the rich territories controlled by Americans, British, Dutch and French. Ribbentrop had already informed the Japanese Ambassador to the Reich that Germany was "not interested" in Dutch colonial possessions. It was an invitation to a free hand in Java and elsewhere, and France, which was in German chains, could certainly do little to defend Indo-China.

To those in beleaguered Britain, study of the map yielded no comfort whatever. There were those, like the present writer, who spent nights in an observation post on a hilltop overlooking the wealds of Kent and Sussex, whence had come the timbers for the old sailing navy, who watched the bombers disappear into the darkness on their missions to Germany, and who reflected, as many would have done at the time, that the best hope for the future lay in two letters, *u s*. These stood for the "us" who were around in the villages and in the more distant cities, where searchlights moved in white arcs, where shell burst glowed briefly in the sky and over which enemy bomb hatches opened to scatter destruction. The letters stood also for the distant, friendly but as yet uncommitted United States, and for the chillier United Soviets. If these forces ever coalesced, victory was certain—one day; but by what combination of circumstances could that miracle come about? What contingency could range America and Russia on the same side, and in alliance with Great Britain?

In war mistakes by opponents bring decision as often as wise actions nearer home. Charles XII destroyed the Swedish empire by his marches against Peter the Great, Russia being saved as much by Charles as by herself. Napoleon destroyed his fleet in 1805 by ordering its admiral into the Mediterranean in the face of Nelson off Cádiz, and ruined a great army in Russia by repeating some of the errors of the King of Sweden. The cardinal example was now preparing, for Hitler, unwilling to postpone any longer an exploit which would crown his life, believing that his U-boats, his air attacks and the massive defences on the Channel coast would immobilize Britain and slowly wither her spirit, collected himself for the greatest explosion of all, the attack on Russia, to which he gave the title of Operation Barbarossa. Thus far, in the course of over five years' aggression, he had not met a single reverse, while his only setbacks had been at sea, where he had just lost his monster battleship, the *Bismarck,* and in the air above hostile territory. He believed himself to be a military genius, and everything supported such a notion. He had complete faith in the Wehrmacht. His country was already full of prisoners of war, mainly French. He had no fear of blockade, and was there not good evidence, from Finland, of the current state of the Red Army?

Barbarossa was a curious title for this supreme aspiration. The historical Barbarossa or "Red Beard"—Hitler himself had a small black moustache—had been a Holy Roman Emperor who in the twelfth century made five separate expeditions into Italy for purposes of its subjugation, the last of which was a failure. The Emperor himself was drowned in a river during the course of the Third Crusade, having gone to war by land to avoid the perils of the sea, an apt enough parallel in its way. Legend said that Barbarossa slept in a cavern in the Kyffhäuser with his companions about him, his beard around a stone table, waiting until the needs of his country would once more summon him forth.

Whatever the German regiments knew of the Teutonic myth, Barbarossa sounded well enough at a time when the soldiery, parading through the Fatherland and conquered territories with their aptly named goose step to the sound of bands, their spirit and their belief in their Führer at an all-time peak, were aflame for still bigger worlds to conquer. Hitler promised them *Lebensraum,* more and more living space, and they were the master race. The world had already seen what they could achieve, but this was nothing to prospects before them. Mighty and once Holy Russia, from a line which would run from Archangel to the Volga, could become German after a short, fierce struggle. The balance of power in the Baltic, which over the centuries had been so often finely poised, would be settled for good, Sweden and Finland falling completely into the German orbit, since Hitler would control their trade. The idea was by no means as preposterous at the time as it may sound years later, and that it did not actually come about was due to no statesmanlike preparations on the part of Joseph Stalin. For once, and for perhaps the only time in his life, he was outwitted by a man as unscrupulous as himself.

Stalin, at the time of Hitler's assault, was five years younger than Churchill, and three years older than Roosevelt, but he had enjoyed supreme power for longer than either of them, and his nature and experience should have prepared him for any trick. The lengths to which he had been prepared to go in the case of Finland and the Baltic states might have served to show him alive to the danger to which he was exposed, yet this was not so. Stalin believed that time was on his side, and that he would have at least one more summer and winter to prepare for any contingency. In this matter France's fall had been too quick, Finland's too slow. If any season was ripe for what he attempted, Hitler chose not unwisely, though he did not quite know his man.

Stalin's portraits are alike in conveying the impression of outstanding concentration and command. Films of his movements show hands, arms and posture of an appropriately bearlike character. He was born in Gori, a town in Georgia. His names were Iosif Vissarionovich Dzhugashvili, but out of a consideration for posterity which he shared with Lenin and with Hitler's father, he changed his patronymic to something at once more manageable and more memorable. Stalin was the son of a shoemaker who died when Joseph was still a boy, and his mother educated him with a view to priesthood in the Georgian Orthodox Church. This was a career which did not appeal to a young man who by the age of nineteen was a convinced Marxist and an embryonic troublemaker everywhere he worked or studied.

Stalin was soon well known to the police, and one of his spells of prison led him to Siberia, where he employed his leisure in translating some of Lenin's works from Russian into Georgian. He met Lenin personally in Finland in 1905, and from that time onwards was to be found at Marxist Congresses in Sweden, Germany, England and elsewhere, listening, learning, reading voraciously. Immediately before the First World War, Stalin became editor of *Pravda*, which was later to become a principal journal of the Revolution, and during the early stages of the struggle he was in exile in Turukhansk, close to the Arctic Circle, where he taught himself to fish with homemade tackle. He was released in time to join Lenin after his journey from Germany to Petrograd.

As Commissar of Nationalities in the Revolutionary Government, Stalin had the duty to proclaim the independence of Finland, which did not prevent the protracted attempt to Bolshevize the country. During the course of the Civil War he served with distinction at Tsaritsyn, a town afterwards renamed after him, and at the defence of Petrograd. At one stage in the war, which Trotsky was conducting as War Minister, Stalin wrote to Lenin: "I need military powers and shall myself, without any formalities, dismiss army commanders and commissars who are ruining the work . . . and of course, not having a paper from Trotsky is not going to deter me."

In 1922, Stalin was made Secretary-General of the Communist Party, a position which enabled him to see every document sent to the attention of the Supreme Soviet. It was a post which, in the hands of an able man, offered the certainty of always being at the seat of power at the right time and the chance to influence higher deliberations. When Lenin died, early in 1924, he left a letter advising Stalin's removal on account of his "rudeness and abuse of power," but the warning was set aside, and by the end of the decade Stalin had become master of Russia, though not at first in name. Until his death in 1953 he was in fact as absolute as any Tsar.

Stalin, at the head of so vast a country, thought on an appropriate scale. One of his earlier decisions was that as Russia was in most respects half a century at least behind the more advanced nations, she must industrialize herself within a decade. Over the years he increased the urban population by forty-five million people, and at monstrous cost in suffering and human life, turned twenty-five million small holdings into 100,000 collective farms, an operation which he described to Mr. Churchill as terrible. He found Russia working with wooden ploughs and left her with atomic piles.

It was against this formidable will, supported by a nation almost as numerous as grains of sand on a seashore, that Hitler was to let loose his obedient soldiers.

II

Stalin had gone to extraordinary, almost ridiculous lengths to please the Germans. Hitler had suggested an Arctic base on Soviet territory, and Stalin made every effort to meet his request, though time in this case did not allow the proposal to be implemented. Rubber was in short supply in the Reich, and in the days of the Twilight War the Russian Navy put their latest icebreaker at the disposal of a ship routed via Siberia to load rubber at an eastern port. As the war spread, a series of special trains, with lines cleared for them, rushed rubber into German-controlled territory, so that Hitler would run no risk of loss of the precious commodity at the hands of the British on the high seas. If the Germans had asked for the moon, Stalin would have done his best to annex it for them.

Signs were not lacking of what was about to befall him. Sound intelligence came through sources in the United States of Hitler's intentions as early as the winter of 1940, but the report was pigeonholed in the Kremlin. German pressure in the Balkans, an area about which Russia was always sensitive, grew ever stronger, and when Yugoslavia had been added to Hitler's other gains a note was struck which should have alerted the most unwary. Rumania was the next country marked down for German infiltration, but in this case Russia, which had never relinquished her claim to Bessarabia, bordering the Ukraine, had forestalled the Germans by occupying the territory at the time when France was in collapse. Northern Bukovina was also swallowed up, the Red Army thereby reaching the Danube. Stalin, for the first time, had trespassed beyond the line of partition agreed before the advance into Poland.

Warnings from his own side affected Stalin as little as those from elsewhere, for his mind was made up. A Soviet intelligence report confirmed German troop concentrations in areas dangerous to the Soviet, as well as the fact that the Czech works at Skoda had been ordered by Berlin to halve their Russian deliveries. Stalin wrote in red ink on the document that this was "an English provocation," and that the perpetrator must be sought out and punished. When the news was found to be true, the agent who had channelled it to the Kremlin, knowing his fate if he persisted in bringing embarrassing facts to the attention of his master, sensibly invited his informant to a picnic. Secret Service was not always encouraged. The more vital the news, the greater the need to suppress it.

In the Baltic, where advantages won by blood or diplomacy might have been expected to be made much of, Russia's "sacred

inertia" seemed to have overcome her. The building of fortifica-
tions, started in Estonia and Latvia immediately before the war
with Finland, were suspended. The new naval bases were never
properly equipped, and even at Viborg, which had been acquired
at such cost, positions of strength were neither camouflaged nor
fitted with signal arrangements of any but a primitive kind, nor
were they organized for the use of field troops. Stalin, who had
made so much of the need to close the Gulf of Finland by batteries on the northern and southern shore, did nothing to ensure
their proper co-ordination. Although he was now in a perfect
position to bar and bolt any advance upon Leningrad, he left
the door ajar.

In March 1941, German troops moved into Bulgaria, a fact
which increased Russian nervousness only imperceptibly, imply-
ing either iron nerve at the top, or an atmosphere of Cloud-
Cuckoo-Land. Three months later what was about to happen
had become so patent to well-informed people that Maisky, the
Soviet Ambassador in London, was told that in the event of a
German attack, Britain would be prepared to send a mission to
Moscow to discuss urgent *economic* needs. The word is stressed,
in view of Stalin's later pressure for an "immediate second front."
Next day the Soviet newspaper *Izvestiya* made the solemn pro-
nouncement: "In the opinion of Soviet circles, rumours of Ger-
many's intention to break the pact and begin an attack on the
U.S.S.R. are devoid of all foundation . . . Rumours that the
U.S.S.R. is preparing for war with Germany are lies and provocations."

One week later Colonel General Halder was able to note:
"Tactical surprise of the enemy has apparently been achieved
along the entire line." It was scarcely credible—yet it was true.
At midnight on 21 June, Timoshenko sent warning telegrams to
the staffs of his military districts, ordering a state of combat readiness for dawn next day. Red Army commanders had therefore
some three hours of darkness in which to prepare to meet the
most formidable fighting machine in the world. In the state of
Russian communications, many units certainly did not receive
even this much grace.

Shortly after midnight the Berlin–Moscow international express passed quite normally through Brest-Litovsk. Two hours

later the German general Guderian, who had personally observed unoccupied Russian defence positions on the eastern bank of the river Bug, watched the taillights of Luftwaffe aircraft disappear overhead as they headed across the frontier to bomb targets in the Soviet rear. And when dawn came, German wireless operators intercepted plaintive Russian signals: "We are being fired on, what shall we do?" Headquarters replied tartly: "You must be insane! And why is your signal not in code?"

The chronicles of war afford no more astounding spectacle of incompetence and surprise. Even the more experienced Russian officers must have believed *Izvestiya* implicitly, and when the test came upon them like a thunderbolt, they were required to think and act with lightning speed, and with a resolution which might have taxed the character of Gustavus Adolphus. The omens were unpropitious. Britain and France had shown poorly against German military preparedness. Britain was in a slow and painful process of redeeming herself. Would Russia be given the time? Moreover, would the regime which had already cost her people so much suffering on account of a remotely brighter future survive the tests which lay before it, which it had brought upon itself?

The momentous news was learned by Mr. Churchill at Chequers, where it had been expected daily. At dinner the evening before the German attack, Mr. Winant, the American Ambassador, was present. Mr. Churchill remarked that he thought Hitler was counting on enlisting right-wing sympathies in Britain and the U.S.A., but that he was wrong. Mr. Winant agreed. Afterwards, when he was walking on the lawn with his secretary, the Prime Minister was asked whether for him, an arch anti-Communist, support of Russia would not be bowing down in the house of Rimmon. Mr. Churchill replied: "I have only one purpose, the destruction of Hitler, and my life is much simplified thereby. If Hitler invaded hell, I would make at least a favourable reference to the devil in the House of Commons!"

III

Unlike the Germans, the Russians appear to have had no agreed over-all plan for a war which would be waged on their own territory, but although Stalin's boast of three hundred divisions ready in the field to meet the Germans did not correspond with the truth, they had a preponderance in numbers of available men, in tanks and even in aircraft, until staggering losses, mainly on the ground, quickly gave the Luftwaffe a superiority which it was not to lose until an advanced stage in the war.

The Germans disposed of three great army groups—north, facing the Russian Baltic Military District, centre and south, the latter responsible for a line running from Vlodava to the mouth of the Danube, and augmented by Rumanian divisions. There could be no immediate possibility of lessons being drawn from the Napoleonic campaign of 1812, for Hitler attacked on a vast front, not with a single thrust, his ultimate objectives being Leningrad, Moscow and the Ukraine. If he secured Leningrad and Moscow before the winter, his position would be infinitely superior to that of any other invader in history. East of the Ukraine lay oil fields which would afford him all he needed, and their possession would cripple his adversary. Count Rostopchin, a military adviser to Tsar Paul I, once commented that the Emperor of Russia would always be "formidable in Moscow, terrible in Kazan, invincible in Tobolsk." Hitler was aware of the infinite, absorbing spaces of the Russian hinterland, but he believed that by standing on a line deep within European Russia he would have everything at which he aimed, and that in the process his opponents would be obliterated as a military and political factor with which he need seriously reckon. Russia had been rendered helpless once before, at a time when Bismarck's empire was fighting on two fronts. Hitler could not imagine the possibility of another front in Europe before he had achieved his ends. When he had done so, there would be no need to fear it. As for the little matter of Africa, his troops, under the leadership of Rommel, were proving a match for an army whose men and supplies had to be convoyed over immense distances.

Hitler had one surprise which no commander could have found unwelcome. This was the scale of his initial success. In the early months of his advance he took over two million prisoners and accounted for five thousand aircraft, on the ground or above it. Victories of this scale, almost always the result of encirclement, overshadowed even the lightning destruction of the French

Army. Hitler's propaganda machine, urged to unparalleled activity under the direction of Goebbels, announced, even before summer was over, that the elimination of the Red Army as a fighting force was accomplished. At one stage at least this was the serious view of the German High Command. Huge areas of the Ukraine soon came under Hitler's control, and had his political department been conducted with sense instead of with short-sighted barbarity, it might have won friends where it created dangerous partisans.

Caught completely off balance, the Russian radio did not even admit a state of war for some hours, while the voice of Stalin himself was not heard for days—until he had made the adjustment which he had expected his front-line troops to achieve within minutes. When it came, it spoke of a patriotic war, and it enjoined all good Russians to fight to the last man. They were to harry and destroy. When encircled or cut off, as they increasingly were, they were told to create confusion behind the enemy lines. When retreating, they must leave the land a desert. Their ancestors had done just that, with notable results. Stalin was prepared to mobilize history, and even the Orthodox Church, to serve the needs of the moment.

The Russians had their orders. Disobedience meant death, and to make sure that he was understood, Stalin had one or two generals shot, together with their chiefs of staff. Betrayed by stupidity in Moscow, beset by the Germans, they met the fate of equally good men who in peacetime had gone the same way, and of countless peasants who had resisted a reorientation of their lives. Cases were actually known of soldiers fighting their way out of encirclement, only to be arraigned and sometimes sent to prison on suspicion that they had been released by the Germans and sent back as spies. It was hard to do right under Stalin!

Having placed his nation in such a dilemma, retaining absolute control, Stalin now faced his own test. If he could keep his nerve under protracted and increasing trials, he might yet save his country as well as his regime and his own position. Time might or might not be in his favour. Space certainly was; moreover, he was not alone. Churchill had made the intentions of Britain as clear to the world as was his custom, and if a wavering and shaken Russian people could derive comfort from the fact

that resources of a land which had for years been blackguarded
by Moscow were at their disposal, they were welcome to take it.
The spectacle of Communists in Britain and elsewhere turning
jubilantly in favour of a war towards which they had hitherto
been opposed would have been comical had not the times been
so grave. At best, the defeat of a man in command of matériel
such as Hitler enjoyed must be a matter not of months but of
years. It could be brought about only at the expense of infinite
life and treasure, and with the aid of hard thinking.

IV

The Russian Baltic fleet should have been well placed to conduct not merely a defensive war from its bases old and new, but
to attack the Germans where they were weakest. On paper Russian strength was formidable. To oppose such units as Hitler
could spare from the North Sea and the Atlantic, there was stationed at Kronstadt and elsewhere a considerable fleet, including
ninety submarines, over half a force of some 170, which, at the
outbreak of war, was the largest of its kind in the world. They
had two battleships, two modern cruisers, at least forty destroyers
and well over a hundred motor torpedo boats, mine layers and
smaller vessels. Against this assembly the Germans mustered ten
mine layers, thirty-eight motor torpedo boats and a handful of
U-boats. Such was Russian efficiency, training and enterprise
that it was quite enough. No greater gesture of contempt for the
maritime prowess of an enemy could have been made, and it was
justified. In this respect history was repeating itself.

Stalin had at one time shown some interest in the Red Navy.
It was true that the Baltic commander in chief had disappeared
at the time of the purges, and that Stalin's ideas had then inclined more to building up a Pacific fleet than to expanding the
Baltic flotillas, but that he was unaware of the importance of the
northern sphere was disproved by every action since the pact
with Hitler. Any zealous Russian admiral, unfettered by too rigid
control from inland, could have dominated the Baltic, made
Scandinavian ore supplies to Germany next to impossible and
put the fear of Peter the Great into Admiral Raeder. Yet the semi-

atrophy which had permeated the navy of Nicholas II afflicted its Red successors, who made no better showing. Its strategy was made subordinate to that of the army, and as the army was soon in confusion and retreat, Baltic units followed suit. The Germans were quick to counter submarine activity by mine-laying operations on a bold and successful scale. Within a fortnight of the beginning of their land offensive, their Baltic sea traffic was normal, which was a terrible indictment of a navy upon which much had been spent.

Memel had given Hitler an advanced base, and he was soon in possession of Libau, Russia losing within days what had been acquired by intrigue and blackmail extending back to the weeks before the Polish war. There was no possibility that the British would be able to give support in a sea with which they had at one time been so familiar. Such material aid as could be afforded would need to come via the Arctic, through some of the stormiest and most uninviting areas of the world. The ironic suggestion that ships traversing that dreaded northern route should be manned by the elements who clamoured so loudly for a "second front" was, alas, not practical, and seamen of the Royal and Merchant navies who survived to bring munitions to Russia found a welcome at Murmansk and elsewhere as icy as the seas they had crossed. It was not always easy to help Stalin, and such services as were possible were frostily acknowledged. He had shown no sympathy whatever for Britain in her lonely life-and-death struggle, and although he was now busily "pulling imperialist chestnuts from the fire," it was with fingers which did this in self-defence.

v

The first directive from the Russian High Command to troops in the field read strangely, though it established innocence of aggressive intentions. The soldiers were ordered to "liquidate" the enemy in areas where forces had crossed the Soviet line of demarcation, but "unless given special authorization, ground troops will not cross the frontier." The warning was superflous. They would have no opportunity of doing so until increasingly grim years passed. "Aviation blows will be mounted to a depth of 100-150 kilometres into German territory," ran the next announcement. Again it was too late. The Luftwaffe were doing their job to such purpose that all possibility of retaliation vanished. The final instructions were among the oddest. "Memel and Königsberg will be bombed," said the order, but "there will be no flights over the territory of Finland or Rumania without special instructions."

Instructions about Finland must have been given with unusual speed, for shipping off Turku (Abo) was attacked on the morning of the German assault, without a declaration or warning of any sort. Three days later Helsinki, Turku itself and other centres were the object of attention, the Red Air Force losing twenty-six bombers, which was an indication of the scale. In view of such wanton sorties, it is clear that in no single aspect of the conduct of their war did the Russians show greater stupidity. They had not been provoked by Finland, or even remotely threatened. The country was recovering from a trial which had already cost a nation of only four million people some 25,000 dead. The Russians knew the spirit of the Finns, and if they had wished to drive them straight into the arms of the Germans, they could not have taken more effective steps.

It was at this stage of affairs that Mannerheim, once more persuaded to assume responsibility for the defence of his country, showed his statesmanlike qualities as well as military perception. It was obvious that the Finns must fight. It was soon clear how the initial stages of the war were going, and it was possible that Russia would be dismembered, to Finland's advantage. Mannerheim was urged by the German High Command to take part in offensives against Leningrad, as well as against a line running south from Murmansk, by which route Russia must draw most of the aid she could hope to receive by sea. He refused. "Finland," he said out of experience and knowledge, "was never made a present of her liberty," and he knew from the outset of the renewed struggle that it would take every nuance of diplomacy, and cost much blood, to preserve the country as a living entity. "Germany will live on," he wrote later to Hitler, "even if fate should not crown your aims with victory. Nobody could give such an assurance regarding Finland." His idea for a Scandinavian combination, which he always believed could have saved Norway if not Denmark from invasion, had not been realized. Once again Finland would have to play what in the last resort was a lone and dangerous game, in which it might become necessary, in course of time, to change sides.

It was for this reason that the Murmansk offensive became a German commitment, the objective of an army which was already in Lapland, installed during the occupation of Norway. By limiting his aims to regaining what had been lost in the Winter War, Mannerheim, fully backed by the Finnish Government, set himself a task within his country's capabilities, at the same time allowing no accusation that Finns had taken advantage of the situation in which Russia found herself.

Few commanders would have been so firm in the face of increasing German demand, particularly when his country depended on German supplies and arms. Mannerheim held to the directive throughout the war, and as the chances of German success receded, it became ever more justified. Only a soldier of splendid achievements would have enjoyed such prestige as to hold the continuous respect of the Wehrmacht, a respect which extended from Hitler downward. Hitler could have pressed the Finnish President to replace the field marshal, if necessary on the ground of age. He had the sense to realize that Mannerheim, even with limited aims, would be of more help against the Russians than a commander of less skill who was willing to fall in with plans which, though useful to the Germans, might be fatal to the Finns. It was something for the Germans to have the Finns on their side, and a comradeship which had been begun years before in the War of Liberation was extended.

Stalin soon demanded that Britain declare war on Finland, in much the same way in which Napoleon had manoeuvred Sweden into belligerent status in a distant age. In view of the admiration with which Finland was regarded not merely in Britain but throughout the world, decision was delayed as long as possible, and it was not until 6 December, 1941, nearly six months after the German attack, that Churchill yielded, after courteous letters had been exchanged between the British Prime Minister and the Finnish commander in chief, who were acquaintances of standing. "It is difficult to see what England gained by this declaration," wrote Mannerheim. The simple fact was that she could not avoid it. Russian suspicion of her ally was seldom stronger than during the opening winter of her war. Britain's chivalrous delay had increased it. As in the Napoleonic instance, it was a formal rather than an actual state, and it was never even required of the United States, which almost simultaneously with the British declaration was attacked by the Japanese at Pearl Harbor.

Hitler, to whom the Far Eastern move came as a surprise, took the opportunity to go to war with a country which was already helping Britain actively in the Atlantic, and which had already sent representatives to Moscow to arrange for sinews to be supplied from her immense arsenals. The three greatest powers were now united against Germany, against what remained of the power of Italy and against a Japanese Empire the strength of which soon astonished Asia. The miraculous combination of forces had been realized, and it was only a matter of time, and of the best use of resources, before victory was assured and a reordering of the world came about. It had taken over two years to involve all the greatest powers, but serious extension was impossible. The protagonists were lined up, and only Italy would succumb before the end of the struggle. Even so, such was the strength and resilience of Germany, so extensive were her conquests, so efficient her organization and so multitudinous her slave labour that it was over three years before she was overcome, and not much short of four when atom bombs and more conventional military pressure forced the surrender of Japan.

VI

Anyone who has attempted the German, and to a lesser degree the Swedish, documentations of the Thirty Years' War, unfolding as they do in involved and archaic language all the details of atrocity, devastation and sheer unreason which follow in the wake of armies, may have wondered whether any further refinement of misery was possible, and may have tried to console himself with the reflection that such inhumanity and suffering belong to a remote age, when standards were lower and men knew less. Such mitigation is impossible in considering the Second World

War, during which all the agonies of devastated seventeenth-century Germany were repeated on a vaster scale, with equal lack of justification. As the armies rolled onwards and the Russians, retreating, bought time with space, leaving a charred countryside, ruined homes, scattered and desperate people, Hitler and his administrators, accelerating their drive to eliminate "subversive and useless elements," began to consider means for that policy of mass death which has no precise parallel even in German history.

As early as 1940, Hans Frank, the Nazi Governor General of Poland, said in a public interview: "If I wanted to put up a poster for every seven Poles shot, all the forests of Poland would not be able to produce enough paper to make them." Six months after the mounting of Operation Barbarossa, he added: "We have about two and a half million Jews in the territory of the Government General. If we include those intermarried with Jews, and so on, the total is about three and a half millions. We can't shoot three and a half million Jews, nor can we poison them, but we shall be able to take measures of some kind finally to liquidate them." As the master race drove east, on their seemingly invincible progress, the camps and gas chambers were laid out, mainly in Poland, and Hitler made sure of earning lasting hatred for himself not only everywhere his troops advanced, but everywhere Nazis had control. German "thoroughness" was no mere boast. Four million people are believed to have died in Auschwitz-Birkenau camp alone, the commandant himself agreeing to a figure of at least two and a half million, for the Germans began to make themselves such a name in Europe as would indeed endure for a thousand years, though not quite in the way Hitler intended. Pity is generally bestowed on the defeated, whatever their deserts. It is not an emotion which Germans could ever expect from others, though they are apt to lavish it liberally upon themselves.

In the meanwhile they had their months of military triumph. The three great thrusts—towards Moscow, towards Leningrad and towards the Caucasus, enjoyed, at first, unbroken success. "I do not say we shall conquer the Soviet Union," said Hitler in October 1941, "we have done so already." From his headquarters near Goldap, in East Prussia, he was able to play soldiers to his heart's content: to plan grandly; to see ideas realized; to telephone commanders in the field and give personal orders with a certainty and speed denied to every previous invader; to dream himself into mastery, ultimately, of the world. No critics came near the presence; if they did, they were sent away with the conviction that the Führer was right after all, and that doubts and fears were cowardly or childish. Who could cross this genius, a corporal in the First World War, a leader greater than Napoleon in the Second? The rules, so it seemed, had all gone by the board. The times were unique.

It is improbable that any German at that high stage of events bestowed a second's thought on the folk tales of Joel Chandler Harris or the fate of a certain Brer Rabbit at the hands of the Tar Baby—yet the parallel was not absurd. Hitler struck, and struck again, into yielding material, and when he struck, there he stayed. His refusal to yield ground became ever more rigid as the limits of his occupation and his communications stretched until they reached from the Atlantic to the ancient lands of Muscovite princes, from Lapland to the Balkans. If he could keep what he held, and on his own terms, he need fear nothing; he would have fulfilled his own hopes. From his earliest days as Chancellor the generals had urged caution, and he had rightly defied them. Was it likely at this stage, when Leningrad was about to undergo siege, when the roofs of Moscow were almost within sight from his tank turrets, when his divisions were driving along the shore of the Black Sea, that anything could stop him? Hitler was no Wallenstein, subject to irrational fear of his own fate and the slave of horoscopes. He was master of the machine, and the German machine had no equal.

And yet, Leningrad, though invested in the early months of war, where two and a half million people became trapped, and where even by the autumn numbers died of disease and starvation, did not surrender. In Moscow, Stalin, experienced at war, and the most levelheaded man in the city, from which most other members of the government fled, collected troops whence he could, and with Zhukov's help checked the great drive at the outskirts of the capital. More than this: the regime held together. Somehow fear of their fate if they surrendered, added to Russian love of country, inspired fresh armies in place of those which had been routed. Finally, there was the weather. In 1939 it had befriended the Finns. In the winter of 1941 it turned against the Germans, freezing them in their tracks, bringing relief, in the nick of time, to hard-pressed defenders.

A wiser man than Hitler would have withdrawn, to strike anew when conditions became more promising. That was not Hitler's way, and his decision cost him the end of the first round. He failed, as the German Army had failed before Paris in 1914, when Helmuth von Moltke uttered the ominous words: "We have had success, not victory. Victory means the annihilation of the enemy's power of resistance." Moltke was echoing Nelson, a master of war, who said, though he seldom had them, that "only numbers annihilate." Vast as the German numbers were, by failing to annihilate when they could—and it may actually have been impossible—they allowed the Russians time as well as the space of which they had so much. The combination of space and time meant doom for Hitler. Complete reversal of the fortunes of war would take long and cost much, but if the Russian regime remained firm, and if the Russian soldier continued to fight, it was inevitable.

VII

Any hope which may have been entertained within Leningrad that effective support might be looked for from the Kronstadt fleet soon proved vain. After their early capture of Reval the Germans were able to control the entrance to the Gulf of Finland, while in order to ensure its destruction, if the Baltic Red fleet should attempt a sortie in strength, Admiral Raeder ordered the newly completed battleship *Tirpitz* into the area. This vessel, together with the smaller *Scheer* and four modern cruisers, patrolled for a week or two between Libau and the Aland Islands, and represented the most powerful naval force ever seen in Baltic waters. Their presence was enough. Russian surface ships and submarines were confined within an ever closer area, limiting their offensive and even their training activities to a minimum, and by the time the ice hardened, Red sailors, except for those who manned the large-calibre guns which were sometimes effective in support of land operations, fought mainly ashore, helping to defend both the beleaguered city and the pocket which the Russians held at Oranienbaum, on the shore of the gulf facing Kronstadt. The Russians withdrew from Hangö during the first autumn, so enabling the Finns to take the offensive by sea in support of their Allies.

Typical of the fighting in the sea approaches to Leningrad was the fate of the island of Hogland, lying near the main shipping channel. The Russians had occupied it during the Winter War, but by December 1941 it was once more Finnish. A month later the Russians, knowing its importance, drove the Finns out, only to see them return in March 1942, with strength enough to keep it throughout the war.

During the course of 1942 the Germans, with Finnish help, erected a submarine net between Porkkala and Nargon, and any possible threat—it had never seemed likely to be serious—from the Russian underwater arm disappeared. Try as they would, and some of the Russian captains were bravely persistent, the submariners never once succeeded in breaking through the barrier, and thus the whole fleet was rendered useless. As the war lengthened, oil supplies became critically low, and more and more naval men were drafted ashore. The Baltic fleet never recovered. Once the vanguard of the Revolution, then disgraced, then revived, the squadrons proved by their record in war that if naval operations are subordinated to military, and if admirals and captains are allowed no freedom to exercise initiative, the nature of Baltic configuration, together with natural conditions such as the certainty of ice for a substantial part of each year, renders effort and expense to equip such a force nugatory. A Baltic fleet has always needed to be handled boldly, as a succession of Danish, Swedish, Dutch, Russian and British admirals showed in the past; otherwise it may as well not exist. A "fleet in being" in most seas, and at most times, has been a matter of consequence. It was not so in this case. The *Tirpitz* and the *Scheer* soon moved west, the *Tirpitz* to serve as a mobile fortress off the coast of Norway and the *Scheer* to train for operations against convoys using the Arctic route to Russia.

The first impetus of the invasion checked, the Germans held mainly to the line they had gained in their thrusts for a full year

of war. Here and there salients were pinched out. Pressure on
Leningrad increased and relaxed, while deaths in the city from
starvation and disease rose to 600,000, and cannibalism was not
unknown. The Russians, with great difficulty, kept a link of some
sort open across Lake Ladoga, while the Finns, admitted even
by Hitler to be bearing a heavier burden of war than the Germans, held their advanced positions in the Karelian Isthmus and
waited for the inevitable counterattack.

In the south the drive towards the Volga and the Caucasus
was decided, in Russian favour, at Stalingrad, in one of the turning points of the war. Stalingrad, once called Tsaritsyn and now,
since the dictator's posthumous disgrace, again renamed, had
been the scene of Stalin's most successful military operations as
a younger man. After a battle of attrition lasting many weeks—
German soldiers called it "the bone mill"—when Hitler employed
eighty divisions in a gambler's throw for his prize of oil and grain,
his generals gradually lost the initiative, and on 30 January, 1943,
the tenth anniversary of the founding of what Hitler called the
Third Reich, Field Marshal Paulus made final preparations to
surrender. By the second day of February, 91,000 Germans became prisoners of war. As Stalingrad had already cost their
army 142,000 dead, the immense early Russian losses were beginning to be avenged.

A year later the Germans were in slow but fairly general retreat,
and were certain of pressure not merely by way of Italy, which
they were defending after Italian collapse, but from France as
well, for the day of full-scale invasion from the west was almost
upon them. Hitler had three secret weapons by which he hoped
to blunt its edge, two of them developed in the Baltic. The first
was the schnörkel, the tube fitted to U-boats which enabled
them to recharge their batteries when submerged, only the small,
almost invisible snout comprising the air intake being above the
surface. Had Doenitz been given more time, a submarine force so
equipped could have menaced Channel traffic. The second was
the pilotless aircraft, or V-1, which was discharged in great numbers, though without accuracy of aim, over southeast England,
and in particular over London. The third was the V-2, or explosive rocket, capable of a very high trajectory. This was developed
at Peenemünde, in Pomerania, once famed as a landing place of

Gustavus Adolphus. As the rocket with atomic warhead is now the basis of much strategic planning, and as the rocket has since produced its own select race of astronauts, it is not the least claim of the Baltic, which has seen so much warlike preparation, that upon its coast opened a new era in military thought.

Hitler had proclaimed, early in his war with Britain, that he possessed a decisive weapon in the magnetic mine, though he was mistaken. In June 1943 he visited Peenemünde, there to see and discuss what he believed to be the most important brain child of his experts. By the end of that month intelligence reports and aerial reconnaissance made it clear to the Allies that the time had come to bomb the establishment of whose work Hitler boasted that it would raze London to the ground.

On the night of 17 August, the Royal Air Force struck by moonlight with a force of 571 heavy bombers, their target being buildings on a narrow strip of coast which were protected by a smoke screen. Although forty bombers were lost, mainly to fighters, the results were highly satisfactory. Constructional drawings just completed for issue to the workshops were destroyed, and the start of large-scale production was retarded. The parent factory was hit; there were casualties among the directing staff; manufacture was transferred elsewhere, and experiments were transferred to a Polish area beyond the normal range of British bombers.

The new weapon, which in practice did little serious damage and none of vital consequence to the war, was first tried out in January 1944. One day, shortly afterwards, a rocket fell on the bank of the river Bug and failed to explode. Polish intelligence agents got to the place before the German technicians, rolled it into the river, waited till the enemy had given up the search, then salvaged and dismantled it under cover of night. On 25 July a Polish engineer was picked up by an aircraft landing secretly and was flown back to England, carrying essential parts of the new weapon. It was his last service to his country, for on his return to Poland he was caught by the Germans, and shot at Warsaw.

While events of such consequence to the future were taking place in Pomerania and in Poland, far away to the north the Russians were at last able to relieve their pocket at Oranienbaum, to free Leningrad from all immediate threat, to cross the pre-war Polish boundary and to increase the weight of their attacks on the Finns. On 9 June, 1944, three days after the British and Americans had landed in Normandy in the most intricate and successful amphibious operation ever planned, the Russians prepared to take a final revenge on their small neighbour. Massing three to four hundred guns every half mile (as against two hundred at the height of crisis at Stalingrad), the Red Army began the biggest barrage of the Second World War, the noise of which could be heard, at its pitch, 170 miles away. They were prepared to lose 100,000 men to gain Helsinki, and by August 1944 the end was in sight. Mannerheim then took office as President, being called once more to the highest post because, as had been the case when he became Regent in 1918, he was the only man likely to win terms for his country. These were as harsh as everyone knew they would be. They included a demand that the Finns drive out the 200,000 Germans still in Lapland, the loss of Arctic Petsamo, which had been Finnish since 1920, and the payment of a crippling indemnity. The Finns had no choice but to accept or be blotted out. They lost all and more than they had regained in their phase as German co-belligerents, and 55,000 killed in action was the final price of their continued independence.

Russia's successes, so delayed yet so decisive, had been won regardless of cost in human life, which, from the first, had been expended with a prodigality which no Western nation could have contemplated.

In the earlier stages of the war coercion had at times been necessary and fully applied. Wavering troops found that weapons in Party hands behind them were as lethal as German machine guns ahead, for the Russians employed much the same methods recorded as in use by Frederick the Great, who had observed: "If my soldiers once began to think, no one would remain in the ranks." As the war progressed, as suffering increased and as the rank and file, through whose wonderful qualities Russia has always won her battles, realized that this was indeed a patriotic war, coercion became less and less necessary until, with success, the need for it disappeared altogether. It is significant that although the commissar dual-command system was applied with full rigour in the first year or so of campaigning, after the victory at Stalingrad it was relaxed, and political officers, as a general rule, once more became "assistants."

"Experience shows," wrote General von Mellenthin with the wonder of a veteran hardened to warfare in most of its manifestations, "that the Russian soldier has an almost incredible ability to stand up to the heaviest artillery fire and air bombardment, while the Russian Command seems unmoved by the bloodiest losses. The stoicism of the majority of Russian soldiers and their mental sluggishness make them quite insensible. The Russian soldier values his own life no more than his comrades'. To step on walls of dead, composed of bodies of his former friends and companions, makes not the slightest impression on him and does not upset his equanimity at all. Without so much as batting an eyelid he stolidly continues the attack or stays in the position he has been told to defend. *Life is not precious to him*."

VIII

Once the Russians were back in Poland, their progress was swift—at one stage they advanced 450 miles in five weeks—and vast numbers of Germans, soldiers and civilians, were isolated in huge pockets, to be rifled at leisure. By the end of January 1945 the Brandenburg frontier had been crossed, and all Germans east of Danzig were cut off. The city itself, together with Gdynia, fell in March, and the Red Army was soon within a hundred miles of Berlin. In April patrols of Russians joined forces with their western allies on the Elbe and elsewhere, and on the 30th of that month, with his capital surrounded, Hitler committed suicide, naming Admiral Doenitz as his successor.

Even in the final stages of war, with their armies pressing down the Baltic coast, the Russian Navy made little use of wide-open opportunity. The largest evacuations in history were allowed to take place with little interference, no less than two million refugees being carried in German ships from the Baltic territories under Russian domination to what was considered to be the greater safety of the west, the more sanguine German officers hoping, against all reason, the British and Americans would be open to an offer of a separate peace, after which their own units would be reorganized to continue the fight with the Russians. On German showing, the mine laying and other activities of the Royal Air Force were in fact more damaging to their Baltic sea traffic than any efforts by the Russians, equipped though the Red Navy now was with an air arm more considerable in numbers than anything seen before.

Doenitz and the nucleus of a new German Government functioned for a few days in the once Danish town of Flensburg, but unconditional surrender had always been insisted upon by the Allies, and on 7 May, 1945, a general cease-fire was ordered in Europe, after which the whole of Germany came under Allied military control. Next day the first British naval units, the cruisers *Birmingham* and *Dido,* together with four destroyers, re-entered the Baltic. After passing the Skagerrak, where many mines were cut, the squadron closed the Swedish coast, and it was then led through the territorial waters of that country by Swedish vessels. Arrival at Copenhagen on the evening of 9 May was a moving event to British and Danish alike. British ships of war, which had not at all stages of history been welcomed in that famous harbour, were greeted rapturously. Denmark and her former constituent country Norway were once more free.

Britain, which had once so relied upon Baltic products for her naval stores, had not been wholly excluded from its waters even during the darker days of the Second World War. For instance, in the winter of 1943 there had been a clandestine operation on some scale which had enjoyed a reasonable measure of success. This consisted of the evasion of German patrols in Danish and Norwegian waters by a number of motor gunboats flying the Red ensign. They were organized by Sir George Binney, and their names, *Gay Corsair, Gay Viking, Hopewell, Master Standfast* and *Nonsuch,* recall the best buccaneering tradition.

The object of Binney's venture was to bring cargoes of ball bearings and other special products from Göteborg, and in the upshot nine successful round trips were made from Hull. In each ship's saloon was a portrait of the British Prime Minister, and in each captain's cabin hung a picture of Sir Francis Drake. Only one ship, *Master Standfast,* was captured by a patrol boat, which seems to have deceived her captain into the belief that she was Swedish, not German. The others, besides their valuable cargo, brought sixty-seven Norwegians to Britain in an episode reminiscent of the feats of Lieutenant Agar in the Gulf of Finland a quarter of a century earlier.

IX

It was in the Baltic, on 1 September, 1939, that the *Schleswig-Holstein's* guns, as they fired at the Poles of the Westerplatte, shattered an uneasy peace and began Europe's descent into the most terrible conflict on record. Nearly six years later the Danish island of Bornholm, immediately south of Sweden, was the scene of one of the last, and certainly one of the more fantastic, episodes in the history of Baltic warfare. Bornholm, which had been restless under the Hanseatic League, and whose inhabitants had murdered a Swedish garrison in the time of Charles X, had been assigned to the charge of a stubborn German commander, who refused to submit to the general order to surrender. His headquarters at Nekso were thereupon bombed by Russian women pilots—the Russians used women in combatant roles on a scale unknown elsewhere—who did much damage to property, and the island was later occupied by Stalin's forces. Thwarted in Jutland, where they made at least one attempt at parachute landings, the Red troops had at least this small share in the war as it had spread to Scandinavia.

The dominant Russian part in the postwar transformation of the Baltic radically altered every previous pattern. It is so large a matter as to warrant scrutiny apart from any broad survey of the course of the struggle itself. As it was the subject of personal negotiation, and as these negotiations have been recorded in detail, it is possible to trace a reasonably full pattern of argument and decision, particularly as concerns Poland and East Prussia. This latter territory, from which the Hohenzollerns derived their kingly title, vanished from the map completely. In its way this was neither inappropriate, since it had nurtured a race of warriors who had long disturbed the European peace, nor unprecedented.

It was a fate which had overtaken those mysterious earlier inhabitants—the Old Prussians, or Borussi—racially akin to the Letts, whose very language died before the end of the seventeenth century.

14. Prelude to Stalin's North Europe

To those with a sense of the past, with at least some knowledge of the Congress of Vienna in the earlier years of the nineteenth century and of the deliberations at Versailles in the twentieth, it came as no surprise to find that just as the Second World War had opened in Poland, so, almost as by tradition, that country provided cause for dissention among the leaders of what Mr. Churchill called the "Grand Alliance." It was over the settlement of Polish frontiers and the line of the Baltic shore that some of the most prolonged and least satisfactory negotiations took place.

The words of Stalin, Roosevelt and Churchill, representing their countries, carried as much weight in determining the immediate future shape of Europe as had the more protracted deliberations of Wilson, Clemenceau and Lloyd George a quarter of a century earlier. Moreover, they were of instant consequence. There was no peace treaty, so there was no delay in implementing their decisions.

The triumvirate was dispersed, even before the European war ended, by the death of Roosevelt, while Mr. Churchill's own government did not survive until the end of the war with Japan. Stalin alone was left of the originals and as no living power could remove him, so nothing could prevent the Red Army standing on the line he wished. He became the arbiter of Europe in a sense to which there has been no parallel since Napoleon. Of the three leaders, only he represented a European land power, and in the last resort there was no one who could bar his way, however outrageous his demands, short of starting a third war, which was unthinkable. The conflict had already cost fifty million dead, soldiers and civilians, and there were myriads in the Far East to be added to the account.

Lloyd George had made himself memorable at the time of Versailles with a remark to the effect that giving Silesia to the Poles would be like giving a clock to a monkey. It was not the sort of sally to endear him to the nation he was helping to reconstruct, but Lloyd George, like many statesmen before him, was intent on building up a Poland with a chance to endure. The attempt was unsuccessful, and the establishment of a free, lasting democratic Poland may then, on a long-term view, have been almost impossible, considering the future strength and aims of Germany and Russia. It was never Stalin's idea. He visualized a one-party Communist Poland, completely under Russia's domination, and although he made verbal concessions from time to time in favour of "free elections" and other political aims popular with his allies, these were gestures which meant as little as most of the paper treaties which over the centuries have gathered dust in the official archives of nation states.

For America at that particular time Poland was almost a secondary question, provided her status as a nation was restored. At conferences when the question of her reconstitution was discussed, Roosevelt was often preoccupied (and most naturally) with the far and more urgent problem of Japan. The war with that power was absorbing a high proportion of his nation's manpower and resources, and as he once wearily remarked, Poland had been a headache for five hundred years and might continue to be. Even Germany's frontiers seemed a matter which might be settled at more leisure, once her military defeat was in sight, though it had been agreed that the European war and its consequences should be, for all parties concerned, first priority, a strategy which was honourably pursued to the end.

Britain's case was singular. Although her historical ties with Poland were tenuous, she had had the help, throughout the war, of Polish units considerable in size and proven in value. More than that, she had actually gone to war on behalf of a Poland she had guaranteed but could not help, and it had become her duty to honour a pledge which might well have cost her almost everything. If Poland's integrity were not restored, Britain would have fought her war in vain.

The story of Mr. Churchill's struggle with Stalin on behalf of the Poles, in which he was loyally backed by the American President, decided the pattern of power in the Baltic certainly for a generation and possibly for much longer. It has its ironies, since Churchill himself did not give the original Polish guarantee, though he supported it as a private member of Parliament. The Polish question forms an important ingredient in his protracted and complex dealings with the Russian dictator, and it is among the incidental compensations of the Second World War that he, alone of the principal participants, was given time and opportunity to tell the story in his incomparable way. It is through his account, supplemented in the final stages by the memoirs of Roosevelt's successor, Truman, that ordinary men and women, directly or indirectly affected by the greater decisions of the war, may see, step by step, how policy evolved, and how, with the irresistible advance of the Red armies which Hitler's diplomacy and military rashness loosed upon Europe, an enormous stretch of territory was made to afford scope for Russian control.

Present-day Europe is largely of Stalin's creation, and in whatever light he may now be regarded in his own country and elsewhere, that is the size of his achievement. He alone succeeded, where every other statesman in history, with the same ambitions, met check. Stalin became the heir of a line of Tsars of whom his own favourite, not unnaturally, was Peter the Great. He took an ample revenge upon Hitler for attacking him unprepared, but it was not only Hitler and his successors who suffered. The process by which Stalin had his way has its own sinister fascination, though it can scarcely serve as a warning, since it is unlikely that time will greatly modify the pattern he ordained. The world is grouping into ever larger political systems, and the more it does so, the less scope is there for those dramatic, sometimes beneficent changes and reversals of which the past is full, the result of combinations by smaller and more flexible states.

II

Stalin, in the course of a complimentary after-dinner speech, once called Winston Churchill the sort of man born once in a hundred years, and the phrase was as true as he ever spoke. Churchill's passion for the study of foreign affairs, and for warfare in general, was combined with an experience of affairs which was unrivalled both in span and in variety. He was in a position, as political head of the largest navy Britain had ever assembled, to influence events at the time of the opening of the First World War, and if he was called to the same post in 1939, too late to halt a train of events at which he had unavailingly protested, he was not too late to save his country in the hour of her greatest need. It is even conceivable that had his plan for the forcing of the Dardanelles been carried to success in 1915, it would have shortened the earlier war, saved the Tsarist regime from collapse, prevented the return of Lenin, postponed the enlightenment of the Russian Revolution and forbidden the rise of Stalin. That is conjecture; what is certain is that he was almost the unlikeliest man then living to be acceptable as an ally to the Russian dictator, and that in point of fact they got on with each other excellently in a personal, if not in a political way. Had they not done so, the path to victory would have been even thornier than it was, and the arrangements of 1945 perhaps even more startling.

Having welcomed a Russian alliance as soon as the German assault began, Churchill very soon found it more of an immediate burden than a general relief, for although the Red Army had, perforce, to bear the shock of a land attack to which Britain might be immune, and although the Luftwaffe, employed mainly eastwards, eased their attacks on British cities and ports, Moscow instantly began to clamour for help and supplies from a country which was itself almost under siege, and to whom every shell, ship and man-at-arms was precious. It cost Stalin nothing to urge a second front in Europe. If one had been opened prematurely, and with disaster, he would have shed no tears, since even an abortive attempt would have drawn forces away from the eastern front, and he could view British misfortunes, however serious, with equanimity. But Britain's prestige was one of her principal remaining assets; her responsibilities were world-wide, and she would not be drawn. The word "evacuation," with the examples of Norway, Dunkirk, Greece and Crete before her, and with a succession of humiliations against Japan to come, had an ominous sound. When, in good time, British soldiers landed in Europe, they must be there to stay.

Aside from that matter, which was eventually somewhat eased by British success in Libya (almost concurrent with the agony of Stalingrad) and by later Anglo-American landings in French North Africa, there was the ever delicate question of Poland and the Poles. This arose acutely soon after Operation Barbarossa was in train, when the Russians were faced with the question of what they should do with their many Polish prisoners of war, some of whom, general officers included, had been handled very roughly. When Germans and Russians had been friendly, the Poles, except for the comparatively few who had been able to make their way, via Rumania, first to France and later to England, had had no chance to help their own country. Now that the giants had fallen out, it was possible that they could be of use, or at least that their hereditary foe would release them for service elsewhere.

They had also been encouraged—at any rate, those who were in a position to study the terms—by the publication, on 14 August, 1941, of what became known as the Atlantic Charter, the declaration by President Roosevelt and Mr. Churchill of what were the aspirations of the one and the war aims of the other. This served as the equivalent of President Wilson's Fourteen Points of January 1918. It included the phrases that the President and Prime Minister:

> . . . desire to see no territorial changes that do not accord with the freely expressed wishes of the people concerned.
> They respect the right of all peoples to choose the form of government under which they will live; and they wish to see sovereign rights and self-government restored to those who have been forcibly deprived of them.

The other clauses, strongly reminiscent of the Wilson document, stated that the two countries concerned sought for themselves no territorial or other aggrandizement; that they would "further the enjoyment by all States . . . of access, on equal terms, to the raw materials of the world which are needed for their economic prosperity"; they desired "improved labour standards, economic advancement and social security"; they hoped to see established "a peace which will afford to all nations the means of dwelling in safety within their own boundaries, and which will afford assurance that . . . men . . . may live out their lives in freedom from fear and want." The latter clause was the basis of President Roosevelt's "four freedoms," those of speech and worship, with freedom from want and fear.

Final points emphasized that such a peace should be made as would "enable all men to traverse the seas and oceans without hindrance," and that "pending the establishment of a wider and more permanent system of general security," disarmament of aggressor nations was essential. Few of the aspirations, and only one of the freedoms, were of a kind which would have been subscribed to by those in the Kremlin, and in spite of the fact that Russia and the China of Chiang Kai-shek gave their formal adherence to the Charter when Russia and the United States were at last both at war with Hitler, the shape of Europe barely three years later shows that armaments, ruthlessly used, were more eloquent than the most gracious words. Yet, although many of its ideas were to be set aside or unrealized, the declaration expressed the intentions of liberal-minded men, one of whom was engaged in a conflict not of his own seeking and the other about to become so. Moreover, deeds have always lagged behind words, sometimes painfully so. In the American Declaration of Independence, dated 1776, it is stated, in the fine style of that day: "We hold these truths to be self-evident, that all men are created equal, that they are endowed by their Creator with certain unalienable Rights, that among these are Life, Liberty and the pursuit of Happiness." Nearly a century later America's own most painful war was fought largely because one at least of those "self-evident" truths was not yet reality.

It was significant that in the meetings which were held in London just before the signing of the Atlantic Charter between General Sikorski, representing Poland, and Mr. Maisky, representing Russia, the objects of which, so far as the Poles were concerned, were to obtain recognition from the Russians that the Partition of 1939 was null and void, and liberation for Poles then in the Soviet Union, no success whatever was achieved in the first aim. In the frigid atmosphere in which negotiations were conducted, not much headway was made even in the second.

Britain, for her part, refused to recognize changes effected in Poland since the opening of the war. In December 1941, when Mr. Eden, as Foreign Secretary, saw Stalin and Molotov in Moscow, Stalin was adamant in purpose and utterly confident that he would achieve his aims, whatever might then appear to be the state of the military situation. So far as the Baltic was concerned, he suggested that East Prussia be transferred to Poland, Russia, by implication, compensating herself elsewhere, and he pressed for the recognition by Great Britain of the *future* frontiers of the U.S.S.R., including the absorption of the Baltic states and rectification of the Finnish demarcation as established after the Winter War. This was coupled with fierce appeals for unlimited supplies and impossible military action.

When the British Goverment learned of the demands, opinion was unanimous that they were directly contrary to the Atlantic Charter, and that under no circumstances would they be given support, certainly not without prior agreement with the United States. Even to raise the question was then, so Mr. Churchill thought, inexpedient. To do so publicly would be to rally all Germans around Hitler.

III

In August 1942, with characteristic courage, Mr. Churchill set off on a journey to Moscow, first to meet Stalin in person, and then to tell him the unpalatable truth, that it would not be possible to open a land front in northern Europe for some time to come. Mr. Churchill had no illusions about the difficulty of his mission or about the fact that he could expect to find little enthusiasm for himself. Long before, he had been an interventionist, and he took pride in deriving from a class of society inimical to the Marxist. "I pondered on my mission to this sullen, sinister Bolshevik state I had once tried so hard to strangle at its birth," he wrote, "and which, until Hitler appeared, I had regarded as the mortal foe of civilized freedom." Of his personal safety he was soon assured, for he noticed at once that the glass in the windows of his official car was two inches thick, surpassing all records in his experience; and he was quick to understand that Stalin's general security methods were as thorough as his hospitality. Churchill was useful, and Stalin did not intend that any harm should befall his guest if he could prevent it.

The official meetings were as bleak as Mr. Churchill had expected; nevertheless, he made an impression, and Stalin liked him personally well enough to invite him later to his private apartments, where he saw the dictator devour an entire suckling pig, noted the way he received reports from the battle fronts and was told of the stresses which had been involved in turning Russian agriculture over to collective farming, about which he had particularly asked. He was also assured that the Caucasus would be defended so strongly that the Germans would never reach them. The generals who accompanied Mr. Churchill were unconvinced, but Stalin was right.

The ice had been broken; henceforward the statesmen would meet and correspond as men who understood each other better: tough and ruthless, but not without humour, and not without mutual appreciation. Taunts about the British being afraid to face the Germans in battle had been parried with wise self-control; recrimination had been confined to the Russian side; information about Anglo-American plans had been freely given, though with scarcely any reciprocation, and Mr. Churchill then flew back to Cairo. Shortly afterwards the results of a raid in strength on the German-held coast at Dieppe, designed to test the defence and the capabilities of existing Allied landing craft, began to become known. The operation taught many lessons which were invaluable later in Normandy, and it proved Mr. Churchill's point that a large-scale assault, mounted prematurely, would merely invite another cheap success for Hitler.

Only eight months had passed since the Stalin-Churchill meeting when a crisis occurred between the Russians and the Polish Government in London. This made it almost certain that Sikorski, who as the leading Polish statesman—he had been Prime Minister of his country as early as 1923—had hitherto been acceptable to Moscow, would henceforward become *persona non grata*. Relations between the countries, difficult at the best of times, would then become increasingly so, and it was in fact soon clear that the Russians would in due course break off all diplomatic relations with the Government in Exile. This was probably inevitable, but they would scarcely have chosen this particular occasion.

After the overrunning of Poland in 1939, many thousands of Polish officers and men had given themselves up to the Russians, with which country Poland was not formally at war, and they were interned. Many were handed over to the Germans, by agreement, to serve as forced labour, but under the Geneva Convention prisoners of officer status could not be so treated, and of some 14,500 Poles held by the Soviet Union in three camps in the Smolensk region, no less than 8,000 were commissioned. Many were members of the intelligentsia, university professors, engineers and others who had been mobilized as reservists. After April 1940 silence descended upon the camps. No scrap of information emerged about a single internee, not one of whom was ever seen again.

After the German invasion of Russia relations with Poland changed overnight. The Russians planned to raise forces among the Poles to fight the enemy, and men such as General Anders, who had been treated with a harshness not stopping short of brutality, were released, equipped and asked to set about organizing new divisions. When Anders and others requested the immediate release of the prisoners of Smolensk, they were met with silence or evasive replies, and not a single man who had ever been in the area reported for duty. The Germans quickly occupied the territory in which the camps had stood, and the war rolled on.

Early in April 1943, General Sikorski saw Mr. Churchill, and told him he had proof that the Russians had murdered their prisoners, who had been buried in mass graves in the forests of the Katyn area. His evidence was considerable, his indignation appropriate to the misdeed. "If they are dead," said Mr. Churchill, "nothing you can do will bring them back." Sikorski said that although that was so, he could not restrain his people, and that his government had already released the news to the press, at the same time inviting the International Red Cross in Switzerland to send a delegation to Katyn to conduct an enquiry on the spot. The action itself was as natural as the way of handling it was unwise, for the Germans, who were themselves expert in mass murder, had already charged the Russians with the deed, which was in the nature of a peccadillo compared with their own exploits in the same field. They, too, proposed an international enquiry.

The Red Cross authorities announced from Geneva that they could not undertake investigation until a request to the same effect had come from Soviet sources, and as the Russians remained silent, the Germans, conducting their own enquiries, claimed that they had discovered upwards of 10,000 bodies and that the evidence of documents found upon them, together with the age of the trees planted over the graves, showed that the murders took place in the spring of 1940, when the area was within Soviet control.

By September 1943 the Russians had reoccupied Katyn, and an exclusively Russian committee produced its own report some four months later. Their claim was that the camps had not been evacuated in time, owing to the speed of the German advance, and that the Poles had fallen into German hands, upon which they had been "eliminated." "When we remember the confusion caused by the German advance," commented Mr. Churchill, the fact "that the guards of the camps must have fled as the invasion came nearer, and all the contacts afterwards during the period of Russo-Polish co-operation, belief seems an act of faith."

The episode, at least to those who find acts of faith in Russian favour dauntingly acrobatic, accounts for Stalin's advocacy of the "elimination" of the whole German officer class. At the time of revelation it caused a wave of shock throughout a world which, though hardened to war, had not yet been made familiar with the full circumstances of the death camps established in occupied Europe. It had two results, one beneficial to the Allied cause and one less so. The Russians continued to release Polish fighting men, chiefly via Persia, to be re-equipped to fight elsewhere, but it was clear that the breach between the Polish Government in London and that in Russia was final, a matter which became of increasing importance as a postwar settlement grew nearer. General Sikorski himself, to the immense loss of his country and his allies, was killed in an air crash not far from Gibraltar in July 1943, and one who was described by Count Raczyński, Polish Ambassador in London, as a statesman possessing a realism rare among his compatriots could no longer give skill and experience to reordering his country.

IV

In October 1943, Mr. Churchill prepared notes for consideration at a meeting of the Allied Foreign Ministers which was to take place in Moscow, one which was hopefully designed to prepare the way for a postwar settlement, though it fell out differently. Nothing new was proposed, but Mr. Churchill reasserted that "nations . . . subjugated by Nazi or fascist violence during the war should emerge at the peace conference with their full sovereign rights, and that all questions of final territorial transference must be settled at the peace table, due regard being paid to the interests of the populations affected." He recalled the "principles of the Atlantic Charter, noting that Russia's accession thereto is based on the frontiers of 22 June, 1941," that is to say, after absorptions of Finnish and Polish territory. "We should welcome any agreement between Poland and Russia," he added, "which, while securing a strong and independent Poland, afforded to Russia the necessary security for her western frontier." He said: "We consider that the future structure of Germany and the position of Prussia as a unit of the German state should be subject to an agreed policy among the three great powers . . ."

As matters turned out, the meetings, under Molotov's chairmanship, largely sidetracked general questions of foreign affairs, and hinged upon the theme of a second front in northern Europe, Stalin being incurably suspicious that this might be postponed or abandoned by Britain and the United States, leaving the Russians to continue to endure the main pressure of the land war. Mr. Eden, in a talk with Stalin, emphasized that his Prime Minister was "just as keen on hunting Hitler" as Stalin was. Stalin acknowledged that this was so, but caused a general laugh by saying that Mr. Churchill had a tendency to take the easy road for himself and to leave the difficult jobs to the Russians!

The real beginnings of discussion started in the following

month at Teheran, where for the first time Stalin met his principal allies outside the frontiers of his own country, and where for the first time he saw President Roosevelt. The opening plenary session, which took place in the Soviet Embassy on 28 November, had no formal agenda, but represented, in Mr. Churchill's words, "probably the greatest concentration of worldly power that had ever been seen in history." In the hands of the three assembled statesmen lay "perhaps the shortening of the war, almost certainly victory, and beyond any shadow of doubt, the happiness and fortunes of mankind." The meeting ranged over questions of military offensives in all theatres of war, and discussed the possibility of Turkey's participating. Suggestions about the future of Germany, Poland and countries which were within the Baltic sphere were confined mainly to semi-official meetings, of which the first took place after dinner on the day of the first session.

At Churchill's request, Stalin gave his views on the future of Germany, which, he was sure, would soon recover from defeat. After Versailles, said Stalin, Germany restored her strength quickly, and although he did not recall Clemenceau's famous remark that the treaty had ushered in a "a stern and just peace" which would "rage for many years," it was clear that he felt that the time factor had been badly misjudged. When Churchill asked how soon Stalin expected a German revival after the current holocaust, the answer was "within fifteen to twenty years." Churchill said that the world must be made safe for fifty, otherwise "we should have betrayed our soldiers." It all came back, he said, to the question of whether Britain, the United States and Russia could maintain close friendship and supervise Germany in their mutual interest. "There was control after the last war," said Stalin, "but it failed." "We were inexperienced then," said Churchill. "The last war was not to the same extent a national war, and Russia was not a party at the peace conference. It will be different this time."

Mr. Churchill felt that Prussia should be isolated and reduced, and that Bavaria, Austria and Hungary might form "a broad, peaceful, unaggressive confederation." "All very good," said Stalin, "but insufficient." "We are trustees for the peace of the world," said Mr. Churchill. "If we fail, there will be perhaps a hundred years of chaos. . . The three powers should guide the future of the world. I do not want to enforce any system on other nations. I ask for freedom and the right of all nations to develop as they like. We three must remain friends in order to ensure happy homes in all countries."

Later the talk turned to Poland, and again Mr. Churchill took the initiative. Britain had declared war on account of Poland, he said, which was therefore important to his country. Nothing was obviously more important to Russia than the security of her western frontier, about which Britain had given no pledges. Personally Churchill thought that Poland might move westwards, "like soldiers taking two steps 'left close.'" If Poland trod on some German toes, that could not be helped, "but there must be a strong Poland. Poland is an instrument needed in the concert of Europe." Stalin cautiously agreed that the Polish people, with their culture and language, could not be extirpated.

"Are we to try to draw frontier lines?" asked Churchill. "Yes," said Stalin. Churchill pointed out that neither he nor, he believed, President Roosevelt had any mandate on the subject, but he hoped that the three of them could "form some sort of policy which we could recommend to the Poles and advise them to accept." Stalin asked whether this would be done without Polish participation, and Mr. Churchill said he thought, in the first place, "Yes," and that "when all was informally agreed between us, we could go to the Poles later." Mr. Eden, who was also present, recalled being struck by a remark of Stalin's that he thought the Poles could go as far west as the Oder. He saw hope in that, and was much encouraged. Mr. Churchill concluded: "I demonstrated with the help of three matches my idea of Poland moving westwards. This pleased Stalin, and on this note our group parted for the moment."

A few days later, at a formal conference, President Roosevelt, in what was in effect the first direct American intervention in the current affairs of a Baltic land, expressed the hope that the Polish and Soviet governments would resume diplomatic relations, "so that any decision taken could be accepted by the Polish Government." Stalin asked with what government he would have to negotiate; he did not like the one existing in London or their friends in Poland, who, he alleged, were "in contact" with the Germans, and killed Partisans. The Western statesmen, he said, could have no idea of what was going on in the country at that moment. He differentiated entirely between Poland and its government abroad, with which he had severed relationship, "not from caprice, but because it had joined with Hitler in slanderous propaganda against Russia." What guarantee was there that this would not happen again?

Mr. Churchill asked if Stalin was prepared to expatiate on frontiers, and Stalin suggested that those of 1939 were "ethnologically the right ones." Eden asked if this meant the Ribbentrop-Molotov line. "Call it whatever you like," said Stalin. Molotov remarked that it was generally called the Curzon line, after proposals made by the British statesman as a result of discussion when Poland was being re-created. Mr. Eden argued that there were important differences. Mr. Churchill, with his flair for ocular demonstration, which had already been indicated by his play with the matches, produced a map showing the so-called Curzon line, the 1939 line, and the line of the Oder. Stalin was not impressed with the accuracy of the Churchill map and emphasized that, for instance, Lvov—the former Lemberg—should be on the Russian side. He said he did not want any Polish population, and if he found any district inhabited by Poles, he would "gladly give it up." When there had been more detailed discussion of the maps, Mr. Churchill said he "liked the picture" of the prospect of the Oder line, and that he would "say to the Poles that if they did not accept it they would be foolish," and he would remind them that but for the Red Army they would have been utterly destroyed.

Roosevelt asked Stalin whether he thought a transfer of population on a voluntary basis would be possible, and Stalin agreed that it probably would be so. Upon this, the discussion turned to Finland.

v

The recording of such exchanges as occurred at Moscow, Teheran and elsewhere between the heads of state during the Second World War was important not only because of the unique character of these exchanges, but because they resulted in a prospect for Europe, and in particular for the Baltic world, which might have been ordained earlier had Russia, in addition to the United States, Britain and France, been represented in chief at Versailles. And since there has not even yet been a treaty, such as all three statesmen, or certainly the Western representatives, anticipated, European demarcation still rests upon what was agreed, or what was afterwards occupied. No record comparable in scope can be found in which to account for the remaking of earlier Europes, for Mr. Churchill was right when he said that the power assembled at Teheran was unique in its force. It was, moreover, of a kind which may never be seen again, since in the case of each country concerned, resources were then mobilized on the basis of total involvement.

Even as early as Teheran, Mr. Churchill was haunted by the fear, natural enough as a result of American disengagement after the First World War and of her nonparticipation in the League of Nations, that the United States would withdraw her troops from Europe once victory was achieved, and that a war-worn Britain might then be faced with the still expanding might of Russia, unable to prevent her from refashioning the political map wherever she wished to do so. Such a state of affairs must, he believed, result in a third great war, or in such an undisguised descent into pure power politics that the principle of free association would disappear, perhaps forever.

This natural fear was at the root of much of Mr. Churchill's whole perplexity over the future of Europe. The fact that the United States, in the event, found it necessary to continue her forces on the European Continent long after fighting ceased makes it harder to remember the difficulties then facing all British statesmen. France was still prostrate, and there was no guarantee that the United States would learn a lesson from world history.

Finland provided an excellent test of Russian methods and sincerity, and as the United States was not directly involved, the subject gave Roosevelt the chance to enquire if he could "do anything to help to get the country out of the war." Stalin's answer was that he had recently heard, by way of Sweden, that the Finns feared that the Russians would turn the country into a Soviet province. His answer to this was that they had no wish that way unless the Finns forced them to do so. The Finns had suggested negotiation on the basis of the 1939 frontier, "with some corrections in favour of the Soviet Union." Stalin did not believe that the wish to negotiate was serious, and he thought that some leading Finns still believed in a German victory, which at the time he spoke was indeed the case. Roosevelt asked if it would help if the United States Government advised the Finns to go to Moscow. Stalin answered that they were "ready enough to go to Moscow, but it would not do much good if they went with their present programme."

When the question of an indemnity arose, Mr. Churchill said he imagined "that the harm the Finns did to Russia by improper attack far exceeded what a poor country could supply." He added: "There is still ringing in my ears the famous slogan: 'No annexations and no indemnities.' Perhaps Marshal Stalin will not be pleased with me for saying that." Stalin replied with a broad grin: "I have told you that I am becoming a conservative."

On points of detail Stalin said firmly: "Nothing doing about Viborg," Finland's second-largest city, and the same obviously applied to the Karelian Isthmus. He added: "If Hangö presents a difficulty, I am willing to take Petsamo instead." "A fair exchange," said Roosevelt, and it was thus that Finland lost her Arctic outlet. Roosevelt said that he, too, believed the Finnish leaders were pro-German, but that if there were others they should go to Moscow, with a prospect of getting somewhere. "Anyone may come," said Stalin; "even the devil." He was not afraid of devils. But, he added, he would not budge from certain conditions—these were the restoration of the 1940 treaty, Hangö or Petsamo, compensation for war damage, a break with Germany and expulsion of German troops, and demobilization of the army. Churchill and Roosevelt persevered against the indemnity condition, but they did not convince Stalin, and the clause was insisted upon. The Finns were, in fact, "squeezed till the pips squeaked," and paid in full.

Churchill had remarked during the course of the session that he had been sympathetic to Finland at first, but that his feelings had changed. Stalin (who never missed a trick) told him, later on in the war, and in the course of a conversation over the dinner table, his own version of how the Winter War started. This pro-

vides an illuminating gloss on the facts. "It began in the following way," said Stalin in his deceptively simple way. "The Finnish
frontier was then some twenty kilometres from Leningrad"
(which, so Churchill noted, he often referred to as "Petersburg").
"The Russians asked the Finns to move it back thirty kilometres,
in exchange for territorial concessions in the north. The Finns
refused. Then some Russian frontier guards were shot at by the
Finns and killed. The frontier guards detachment complained to
Red Army troops, who opened fire on the Finns. Moscow was
asked for instructions. These contained an order to return the
fire. One thing led to another, and the war was on." He added
gravely: "The Russians did not want a war with Finland."

VI

The formal discussion on Germany produced some original
ideas. Roosevelt, who initiated the matter, agreed with Stalin
that he would like to see the country split up. Stalin said he
thought that Mr. Churchill would object, which was not in fact
so. Roosevelt produced a plan for dividing the country into five
parts, upon which Stalin, with the grin which he seems to have
reserved for his British ally, suggested that Churchill was not listening!

The American plan was to split Germany into the components
of Prussia; Hanover and Northwest Germany; Saxony and the
Leipzig area; Hesse-Darmstadt, Hesse-Cassel and the section
north of the Rhine; and Bavaria, Baden and Württemberg. The
components would be self-governing, but two other districts
would be administered by the United Nations—the Kiel Canal
and Hamburg, and the industrial Ruhr and Saar.

Neither Roosevelt nor Stalin took Mr. Churchill's point about
Prussia, which indeed he may have overemphasized. If so, it was
due to the belief, traditional in Britain, that German aggression
had its origin in Prussia and particularly in the Junker class. History showed much to support this view, but Mr. Churchill was
the only professional historian present. Roosevelt had no claims
that way, and Stalin, though the only member of the triumvirate

whose writings were considered as gospel throughout a vast territory, thought of German evolution in different terms.

"When one had to deal with large numbers of German troops," said Stalin, "one found them all fighting like devils, as the British and American armies would soon learn . . . Fundamentally there was no difference between North Germans and South Germans, for all Germans fought like fierce beasts." Roosevelt agreed. Mr. Churchill's more general doubt over the Roosevelt plan was that "if Germany were divided into a number of parts, as suggested by the President, and those parts were not attached to other combinations, they would reunite. It was not a question of dividing Germany so much as giving life to the cut-off bits and making them content not to be dependent on the Greater Reich. Even if that were achieved for fifty years it would be a lot."

Stalin thought that though "it was far better to break up and scatter the German tribes . . . they would want to reunite, no matter how much they were split up. In this he saw great danger, which would have to be neutralized by various economic measures, and in the long run by force if necessary . . . Germans would always want to . . . take their revenge. It would be necessary to keep strong enough to beat them if they ever let loose another war."

Before the conference broke up, Mr. Churchill considered it wise to bring the discussion back to Poland, since he alone of the statesmen had to satisfy or at least placate Poles in London who were on his doorstep, and they, as Count Raczyński was soon to point out, were contributing more to the Allied cause in the way of fighting men than most of the subsidiary Allies put together. The formula Mr. Churchill suggested was: "It is thought in principle that the home of the Polish state and nation should be between the so-called Curzon line and the line of the Oder, including for Poland East Prussia (as defined) and Oppeln; but the actual tracing of the frontier line requires careful study, and possibly disentanglement of population at some points." Mr. Churchill added: "We shall never get the Poles to say that they were satisfied," but he wished to be able to tell them that they were "being well looked after."

After some meditation Stalin said that the Russians "would

like to have the warm-water port of Königsberg," and then, said Mr. Churchill, "he sketched a possible line on the map that would put Russia on the neck of Germany." Subject to that proviso, he would be ready enough to agree to the suggested Polish formula. This unfolding of Russian plans must have satisfied Mr. Churchill at least to the extent that the city where the first King of Prussia had been crowned would be removed from the German map.

There was one remarkable silence at the Teheran and later conferences. Germany, Poland and Finland had all in turn been passed under review, but not the Baltic states, though *de jure* recognition of their separate entities was still widely maintained. Silence implied assent to Russian absorption, an attitude not shared by the many Poles, looking to the future, who saw hope in a Baltic association which might provide some sort of political buffer against Russia, though it was one which their statesmen, in the interwar years, had neglected to explore. The very idea was highly unrealistic, but it was natural enough among those who had not yet discerned the full intentions of Russia in re-creating her influence in Europe.

"In the circumstances," wrote Raczyński resignedly in the year of Teheran, "the game was bound to be lost by us whatever the Polish Government in Exile and the Polish armies might do, either in Poland itself or on the battlefields of the alliance." He added: "I personally had no illusions and few hopes. But I believed that the game should be played out to the end, to the last political card and to the last shot." It was a statement with which every patriot must have agreed.

VII

Warsaw's ordeal, one of a series which had begun long before the days of the Swedish kings and their fleeting triumphs, did not end with Hitler's bombardment in the opening days of the Second World War. A year later the German Government General ordered that an area of ten square kilometres should be declared a Jewish ghetto, into which 240,000 people were forced, six to a room. The number was then doubled, and to heighten the mortality rate, Frank reduced the food ration to 200 calories a day (the average Dane today consumes 3,400). Later still, when disease and starvation produced terrible and inevitable epidemics, Hitler ordered infected houses to be burned, and this led to a rising. It was just the pretext needed for systematic destruction of ghetto buildings and the transfer of survivors to the extermination camps.

Hardly had the tragedy ended when, on 1 August, 1944, Partisans in the city, on orders from the Polish Government in Exile and encouraged by propaganda from the Russians, whose armies had by then advanced to within striking distance, openly rose against the garrison. This action was premature. When it came to the point, the Russians gave no support to the insurgents, and put every difficulty in the way of supplies being dropped by Allied aircraft. After sixty-three days of bitter fighting, waged even along the subterranean sewer passages, the rising was suppressed, at the cost of 200,000 Polish lives. This dark episode, together with the fermenting of trouble by Communists in Greece, a country in which Britain was admitted to have special interests, was the background to the next Stalin-Churchill conversations. By the time they took place, the Allied armies had achieved a firm lodgement in Europe and the future lines of military occupation of Germany had been agreed. In so far as the Baltic area was concerned, the Russian zone was to include the entire littoral to a point slightly east of Lübeck, the British occupying a line running from Lübeck to the Danish frontier, and the greater part of West Germany. The Americans, a proportion of whose share was to be ceded, by arrangement, to the French, took in Bavaria and Württemberg, and they were also given the use of the ports of Bremen and Bremerhaven.

It was not only in affairs of Poland and Greece that the Russians were baring their teeth, and were to continue to do so. By their insistence on a right of veto, and on the exclusion of lesser powers from the Security Council's deliberations in the organization which was to evolve into the United Nations, they were showing increasing intransigence in every sphere where their influence was established, or even invited. Field Marshal Smuts, the South African leader, to whose wisdom Mr. Churchill and Roosevelt paid respect, uttered the warning, as early as September 1944, that "the more firmly Russia can establish herself in the saddle now, the further she will ride in the future and the more precarious our holdfast will become."

It was with these facts in mind that despite an immense burden of public business in England and elsewhere, Mr. Churchill determined on yet another visit to Moscow, for Stalin, on the plea of precarious health or the needs of his own country, could never be drawn farther from home than Iran. "I felt acutely the need to see Stalin," said Mr. Churchill, "with whom I always considered one could talk as one human being to another." This was true, and he could sometimes bring Stalin to make apparent concessions, but such were immediate events that even Mr. Churchill, despite his natural buoyancy, could scarcely have gone to Moscow with very high hopes. What he met with was a personal triumph, clearly stage-managed by his host, and a treatment in the whole matter of Poland which was of a piece with the Russian attitude to the Warsaw rising, which had been felt both in Britain and the United States to have been a gross betrayal.

Mr. Churchill and Mr. Eden reached Moscow early in October, and their visit related almost entirely to the affairs of Poland and the Balkans. The points at issue were respective spheres of influence in Europe, and in particular the relationship between what the Russians called the "Lublin Polish Committee," which they wished to represent their country, and the still official Polish Government in London. Roosevelt's Ambassador, Mr. Averell Harriman, was kept in close touch with progress, and Roosevelt and Churchill had themselves now reached a stage of understanding where, in their cabled interchanges, they spoke of Stalin as U.J. or Uncle Joe. Stalin got to know of it in due time, and at first was furious, till a wag suggested that he himself was not unaccustomed to using the expression Uncle Sam.

On 13 October, an unlucky day, Mr. Mikolajczyk, the Polish Prime Minister, who had been flown from London, was invited to consider two matters: *de facto* acceptance of the Curzon line, with interchanges of population where necessary, and a friendly discussion with the Lublin Committee, so that a united Poland might be established. The same evening, Mr. Churchill and Mr.

Eden met the Lublin Poles for the first time, and saw them for what they had always felt they were: mere pawns of Russia. "They had learned their part so carefully . . ." said Mr. Churchill, "that even their masters felt they were overdoing it. For instance, Mr. Bierut, the leader, spoke in these terms: 'We are here to demand on behalf of Poland that Lvov shall belong to Russia. This is the will of the Polish people!' "

Here, indeed, dependence assumed grotesque forms. Lvov had been well within the 1939 Polish boundaries: it is now well within the territory of the Ukraine. When Mr. Bierut's observation had been translated from Polish into English and Russian, Mr. Churchill looked at Stalin "and saw an understanding twinkle in his expressive eyes, as much as to say: 'What about that for our Soviet teaching.' " A contribution by another Lublin gentleman, Osóbka-Morawski, was, thought Mr. Churchill, "equally depressing."

Matters got no better as the autumn days went by. The Poles, that is, Mr. Mikolajczyk and his colleagues, were willing to accept the Curzon line "as a line of demarcation between Russia and Poland," but the Russians insisted on the formula *"as a basis of* a frontier." Mikolajczyk declared that he would be repudiated by his own people if he agreed, while Stalin, at the end of a long talk, declared that he and Molotov were the only two of those he "worked with" who were favourable to dealing "softly" with Mikolajczyk. Stalin said that had Mikolajczyk been willing to accept the Russian terms, he would have been willing to see him at the head of a new Polish Government. Mr. Churchill thought that difficulties of all sorts would arise in any attempt to fuse the London and the Lublin Poles, whom he was coming to regard as "a kind of Quislings." Behind the immediate talk loomed the shadow of still more trouble in London for Mr. Churchill. His Cabinet colleagues, and Parliament, would never willingly approve of surrender to Lublin, particularly after the disaster of the Warsaw rising, and he began to suspect that even Stalin was subject to pressures about which he did not know. Mr. Churchill observed of the dictator when he returned home: "Behind the horseman sits black care." The two men never talked together more easily, yet they seldom had a more intractable subject.

Such gleam of hope as remained in favour of a satisfactory settlement lay in the fact that President Roosevelt was elected for a fourth term of office, and that he had proposed a triple meeting in the very near future at a resort on the Black Sea.

I5 . Decisions at Yalta

Yalta, a place once associated not with power politics but with Anton Chekhov, was the appointed rendezvous of the three statesmen who had guided the world war. It was "a sheltered strip of austere Riviera," said Mr. Churchill, "the villas and palaces, more or less undamaged, of an extinct imperialism and nobility." It was to serve as the final staging point before the surrender of Germany, and it saw the last international meeting at which Roosevelt was present, for he had not long to live. The magnificent struggle which he had begun over twenty years earlier, when he had been stricken with paralysis, was nearing its close, and every picture taken at or about the time of the conference shows plainly and tragically that his physical powers were ebbing, though his grasp and courage remained as memorable as ever.

Mr. Churchill had not spoken merely for Great Britain in the tedious matter of the Polish disagreements. Whatever divergencies of view there may have been in other spheres of foreign politics, there were none over Baltic lands. The Western ideal would have been a series of states, independent of, even if friendly with Russia, stretching from Germany to the Gulf of Finland. That was a legacy of Versailles, and of the influence the Royal Navy had once been able to exercise, but it had been dissipated. Roosevelt and Churchill recognized the facts accordingly, yet if, as had been proposed at Teheran, Poland was boldly to shift west, then it was more vital than ever that she should not become

simply a puppet state. For this reason exchanges between Roosevelt and Stalin at the end of 1944, preliminary to the Yalta Conference, had as much importance as the exchanges between Mr.
Churchill and Stalin at Moscow.

On 5 January, 1945, clean against the wishes of their allies,
the Russians recognized the Lublin Committee as the Provisional
Government of Poland. It was a step which made useless all Mr.
Churchill's efforts at Moscow. Stalin justified his action to Roosevelt on the ground that "radio communications with Mikolajczyk's
government intercepted by us from terrorists arrested in Poland
—underground agents of the Polish *émigré* government"—an offensive designation which was to be applied henceforward to the
London Poles—"with all palpability prove that the negotiations
of Mr. Mikolajczyk with the Polish National Committee served
as a screen for those elements who conducted from behind Mikolajczyk's back criminal terrorist work against Soviet officers and
soldiers on the territory of Poland." There was much more of this
strip talk, the purport being that Roosevelt would do well to recognize the men of Lublin without more ado.

Roosevelt answered at once and to the point. He had by then
heard that Mikolajczyk had resigned, as the result of what he
saw to be inevitable, which was a fact that did not improve matters in London or elsewhere, since Stalin had at least been willing
to talk to him. "I must tell you with a frankness equal to your
own," said the President, "that I see no prospect of this government's following suit and transferring its recognition from the
Polish Government in London to the Lublin Committee in its
present form . . . The fact is that neither the Government nor
the people of the United States have as yet seen any evidence
. . . that the Lublin Committee as at present constituted represents the people of Poland. I cannot ignore the fact that up to the
present only a small fraction of Poland proper west of the Curzon
line has been liberated from German tyranny, and it is therefore
an unquestioned truth that the people of Poland have had no
opportunity to express themselves in regard to the Lublin Committee."

Every word that Roosevelt wrote was sensible and just, but
it was too late. He had telegraphed to Stalin on 30 December. On

New Year's Day 1945, Stalin answered that five days earlier the Presidium of the Supreme Soviet had told the Poles, "in reply to an enquiry," that it proposed to recognize Lublin. Russia could not retract without loss of face, and she was not interested in retracting at all. Even before the conference opened, the principal decision had been arrived at unilaterally, and the most the Western Allies could now hope for was some reconstitution of the personnel of the Polish Committee. A formula might be found to patch matters up, but it was plain that this would scarcely be more than a pattern of words.

II

Yalta was notable for the cordiality of the purely personal contacts between the statesmen; for the extremes of Russian hospitality—on one occasion someone casually remarked that there was no lemon peel in the cocktails; next day a lemon tree loaded with fruit was growing in the hall—for the excessive security precautions—the hills behind the resort were filled with Russian troops inconspicuously disposed, while on the waters of the Black Sea were Allied destroyers and transports—and for the iron purpose with which, behind a mask of geniality, the Russians pursued their ends.

Stalin and Churchill, both old campaigners, confessed their zest for military affairs, which Stalin said occupied him almost exclusively. In that particular sphere matters were so well in hand that at the first plenary session, which began on 5 February, the future of Germany was discussed as a matter of urgency. There was even a special reference to reparations, with which Russia—as had been the case with Finland—seemed excessively concerned. Her statesmen had not shared in the disillusion resulting from the 1919 policy of "making Germany pay."

At the very first meeting, Roosevelt made a statement at which Mr. Churchill's heart must have sunk, and at which the Russians, if they realized its full significance, must correspondingly have rejoiced. He said that while the United States would "take all reasonable steps to preserve peace," this would not be "at the expense of keeping a large army in Europe, three thousand miles from home. The American occupation" would be "limited to two years."

"Formidable questions rose in my mind," said Mr. Churchill as he looked across the table at his colleagues. "If the Americans left Europe, Britain would have to occupy singlehanded the entire western portion of Germany. Such a task would be far beyond our strength." President Roosevelt did not add prophecy to his other gifts, and the reason which lay behind his announcement, which in the circumstances was precipitate, was that he believed that the idea of the United Nations could be made to work, and that the Russians were sincere in their wish for partnership. Stalin helped him. Not ordinarily loquacious—he was a pipe smoker and a fisherman, which are characteristics of the contemplative man rather than the rhetorician—he made more than one speech which impressed his hearers.

"I am talking as an old man," he said, though he could give Mr. Churchill five years. "That is why I am talking so much. But I want to drink to our alliance, that it should not lose its character of intimacy, of its free expression of views. In the history of diplomacy I know of no such close alliance of three great powers as this, when allies had the opportunity of so frankly expressing their views. I know that some circles will regard this remark as naïve.

"In an alliance the allies should not deceive each other. Perhaps that is naïve? Experienced diplomatists may say, 'Why should I not deceive my ally?' But I, as a naïve man, think it best not to deceive my ally even if he is a fool. Possibly our alliance is so firm because we do not deceive each other; or is it because it is not so easy to deceive each other? I propose a toast to the firmness of our three-power alliance. May it be strong and stable; may we be as frank as possible."

There were those present who believed that the frankness had been mainly on one side, throughout the war and before it; and an audience which, even in the circumstances of a speech made after the hospitality of the Yusupov Palace, could have believed the speaker to be naïve, either diplomatically or in any other direction, could have known nothing of Russians, or of the evolution of the U.S.S.R.

III

Poland—Poland—Poland. The theme recurred at every plenary meeting but the first, and the British record contains an interchange on this topic of nearly 18,000 words, painstakingly translated by devoted and highly skilled interpreters. Their role in all the interchanges was important, for although President Roosevelt's successor came to suspect that Stalin knew English— he had indeed attempted at one time to learn the language, but had given it up in despair—the time taken by translation was invaluable to a suspicious man, not glib with his Georgian speech, who liked to ponder before he spoke, and who had none of Mr. Churchill's wealth of expression, which was capable at times of rising to an eloquence reminiscent of Burke, or of Roosevelt's persuasive way of addressing an audience on any subject to which he gave his mind. Churchill's speeches had been clarion calls to a commonwealth. Roosevelt's "fireside chats" were the means by which he had taken a whole nation into his confidence for more than a decade. Stalin could offer nothing comparable, and perhaps, by contrast, his occasional outbursts were all the more impressive. The case of Poland, whose problems, as Mr. Churchill put it, were "ancient, multitudinous and imperative," was in point.

By the time of Yalta the Lublin Committee had not only been recognized by Moscow, but were styled the "Warsaw Government" by the Russians—and no irony was intended. Feeling against this body was fierce in London, not unnaturally, and although charges were freely made that the Polish Underground was sabotaging the advance of the Red Army across Poland, both official access to and information about Poland were denied to the Western powers, who were therefore in no position to judge the truth of the allegations.

On the other hand, what was undeniable was that in Italy and on the western front some 150,000 Poles were fighting valiantly for the final overthrow of the German Army, the Polish Corps having played a particularly distinguished part at the battle for Cassino. These troops represented the cream of the free Polish nation. Their political leaders were in London, and it was this fact which, all questions of justice apart, gave their case so strong a claim on time and attention.

The immediate questions, often as they had been raised before, were still unresolved. These were: how to form a satisfactory Provisional Government; how and when to hold free elections; how to agree on the new frontiers; and how to safeguard the rear areas and lines of communications of the advancing Soviet armies.

President Roosevelt spoke of five or six million Poles in the United States, mostly of the second generation, who would, he thought, be in favour of the Curzon line. They realized they would have to give up eastern Poland, and would be glad of compensation in East Prussia. It would make it easier for him to persuade them that the settlement was fair if the Russians would grant some concession, perhaps Lvov, as a counterbalance to Königsberg. But more important even than frontiers was a permanent government. General opinion in the United States was, he said, against recognizing the Lublin Committee, because it represented only a small section of the nation. He hoped to see a government of national unity, drawn perhaps from the five main political parties. Mr. Churchill agreed, though he recognized Russia's wish for Lvov. "If, however, she made a gesture of magnanimity to a much weaker power, such as the President has suggested, we should both admire and acclaim the Soviet Union. But a strong, free and independent Poland is much more important than particular territorial boundaries."

It was not until after an adjournment that Stalin spoke, and when he did so, it was with an appeal to history. There was an echo of the voice of the Tsars and Empresses who had fought in Poland, fought with Poland, and had at last broken Poland up. If, said Stalin, Poland was a question of honour for Britain, for Russia it was a question both of honour and security: of honour "because the Russians have had many conflicts with the Poles, and the Soviet Government wished to eliminate the causes of such conflicts: of security, not only because Poland was on the frontiers of Russia, but because throughout history Poland had been a corridor through which Russia's enemies had passed to attack her." Swedish—French—Germans—all had passed that way.

"During the past thirty years," he continued, "the Germans twice crossed through Poland. They passed through because Poland had been weak. Russia wanted to see a strong and powerful Poland, so that she would be able to shut this corridor of her own strength. Russia could not keep it shut from the outside. It could only be shut from the inside by Poland herself, and it is for this reason that Poland must be free, independent and powerful. This is a matter of life and death for the Soviet state." The Soviets, he said, did not want to assimilate Poland, like the Tsars. They wished for friendship.

As for the Curzon line, continued Stalin, that had not been a Russian invention. It had been drawn up by Curzon, Clemenceau and representatives of the United States at a conference to which Russia had not been invited. Lenin had not agreed with it, and now it was actually suggested that Russia should take less than Curzon and Clemenceau had conceded. "That would be shameful," said Stalin. "When the Ukrainians come to Moscow they will say that Stalin and Molotov are less trustworthy defenders of Russia than Curzon or Clemenceau. It is better that the war should continue a little longer, although it will cost Russia much blood, so that Poland can be compensated at Germany's expense." Mikolajczyk, he recalled, had been delighted when he heard in October that Russia proposed that the western frontier of Poland should be extended to the Neisse. "There are two rivers of that name," said Stalin, "one near Breslau, and another farther west." It was the western Neisse that he had in mind. He asked the conference to support his proposal.

Stalin went on to say: "We could not create a Polish Government unless the Poles themselves agreed to it." Mikolajczyk, when in Moscow, had found some measure of agreement with the Lublin Committee, yet the moment he returned to London he had resigned his office. "The Polish Government in London were hostile to the very idea of the Lublin government, and described it as a company of bandits and criminals. The Lublin government had paid them back in their own coin, and it was now very difficult to do anything about it." He himself felt that the

London government, whose agents had "killed 212 Russian soldiers," had done "much evil." On the other hand, the Lublin
Poles had been "helpful," and as it was "vital for the Red Army
to have safe rear areas," as a military man he would only support
the government which could guarantee to provide them.

By the time Stalin had finished the hour was late, and the
President suggested an adjournment, though not before Mr.
Churchill stated that his information differed vastly from Stalin's,
and that he believed the men of Lublin would not be supported
by more than a third of the people. "On the facts at my disposal,"
he ended, "I could not feel that the Lublin government had a
right to say that they represented the Polish nation."

No doubt Mr. Churchill was right; nevertheless, Stalin had
delivered one of the most impressive speeches he ever made, and
although the battle was to continue not for days but for weeks
and months, the issue had already been decided by the power
which, in this instance, had the greater strength. Henceforward
the struggle would be in the nature of a face-saving rear-guard
action. There was no hope of victory, and not much prospect of
convincing the most innocent that Russia had not won the first
round in what would become the Cold War.

IV

"We ought to do something," said Roosevelt on 7 February,
"that will come like a breath of fresh air in the murk that exists
at the moment on the Polish question." It was a wish which no
doubt found an echo everywhere in the assembly, and when the
President asked Stalin if there was anything to add to his speech
of the day before, Molotov produced a formula which moved an
inch or two in the Western direction. It was true that the western
Neisse was indicated as a Polish boundary, a matter which was
not readily acceptable, but Molotov's memorandum included
the phrases: "It was considered desirable to add to the Provisional
Polish Government some democratic leaders from Polish *émigré*
circles"—as the word "*émigré*" was objectionable to both West-

ern statesmen, "Poles abroad" was substituted—and: "It was considered desirable that the enlarged Provisional Government should be recognized by the Allied governments."

Concerning the western Neisse, Mr. Churchill made the point that while he was in favour of moving the frontier westwards, "it would be a great pity to stuff the Polish goose so full of German food that it died of indigestion." If Poland took East Prussia and Silesia as far as the Oder, that alone would mean moving six million people. Stalin's answer to this difficulty had the merit of simplicity. He said: "There are no Germans in those areas, as they have all run away."

Stalin never talked nonsense, and his jokes were rarely on subjects of such importance. What he actually meant, though the matter could scarcely have been apprehended by his hearers, was that Germans in the territory concerned had been outlawed. People had become as the beasts, with no rights at law, a conception of such savagery as had not been known to Europe since the Middle Ages. Proof of this statement may be found in the terrible pages of Hans von Lehndorff, who has described what happened when, in due course, the Russian advance reached the area of Königsberg; how they treated the historic city which was Stalin's particular prize; its men, its women and the property they looted from the splendid old houses.

Later in the discussion Stalin made two other statements, equally astonishing. He said that Bierut and Osóbka-Morawski, the Lublin leaders, had not left the country during the German occupation, "but lived all the time in Warsaw and came from the Underground movement. That made a deep impression on the Poles, and the peculiar neutrality of people who had lived under German occupation should be borne in mind." He thus made staying in Poland, instead of fighting the country's battles outside it, into a cardinal virtue, and capped the matter by the statement that it was "a great event in Poland that the country has been liberated by Soviet troops, and that this has changed everything. It is well known that the Poles did not like the Russians, because they had three times helped to partition Poland. But the advance of the Soviet troops and the liberation of Poland has completely changed their mood. The old resentment has disappeared, and has given way to good will and even enthusiasm for the Russians."

Listening to this speech, Mr. Churchill may well have recalled a story related of the Duke of Wellington. A stranger came up to him and said: "Mr. Jones, I believe." "Sir," said the Duke, "if you believe that, you will believe anything." For the fact had already made itself apparent that wherever the Red Army advanced, the population fled if it could and hid if it could not. There was no recorded instance of spontaneous welcome, except among creatures ready to be used as Russian tools, hoping to be able to exercise a semblance of power, not for their country's benefit but for their own.

As for elections, Stalin was prepared for these, though he noted that none had as yet occurred in France, in spite of the fact that General de Gaulle was recognized as head of a Provisional Government. Mr. Churchill emphasized the difficulty which the Western governments were having in getting the barest information out of Poland. That facilities should be given for political observers seemed, in the circumstances, fanciful. "The elections," said the President, "must be above criticism, like Caesar's wife. I want some kind of assurance to give the world, and I don't want anybody to question their purity. It is a matter of good politics rather than principle."

By 11 February a formula had been agreed upon which represented a considerable achievement on the part of the drafting committees. There was "a common desire to see established a free, independent and democratic Poland." A Provisional Government would be organized, "on a broader democratic basis, with the inclusion of democratic leaders from Poland itself and from Poles abroad." This government should "be pledged to the holding of free and unfettered elections as soon as possible on the basis of universal suffrage and secret ballot." When the new government had been formed, the United States and Great Britain would establish diplomatic relations and would exchange ambassadors, "by whose reports the respective governments will be kept informed about the situation in Poland." The eastern frontier "should follow the Curzon line," with some digressions of five to eight kilometres in favour of Poland. "The final delimitation of the western frontier," it concluded, "should await the peace conference."

Lesser incidents of Yalta include some observations worth preserving. Roosevelt recalled that in 1933 his wife visited a school in the United States. "In one of the classrooms she saw a map with a large blank space on it," he said. "She asked what was the blank space, and was told they were not allowed to mention the place—it was the Soviet Union." This, said Roosevelt, was one of the reasons why he wrote to President Kalinin, the nominal, though never the actual head of the Russian political organization, asking him to send a representative to Washington to discuss the opening of diplomatic relations. "That," he said, "is the history of our recognition of Russia."

Mr. Churchill told Stalin that there would be a general election in the United Kingdom after the defeat of Hitler. Stalin thought that Mr. Churchill's position was assured, "since the people would understand that they needed a leader, and who could be a better leader than he who had won the victory?" Mr. Churchill explained that there were two parties in Britain, and that he belonged to only one of them. "One party is much better," said Stalin with deep conviction.

Roosevelt compared the British constitution, which was unwritten, to the Atlantic Charter: "The document did not exist, yet all the world knew about it." Among his papers he had found one copy "signed" by himself and Mr. Churchill, but strange to say, both signatures were in his own handwriting! Mr. Churchill replied that the Charter was "not a law, but a star."

When the Prime Minister returned home, he found that although the House of Commons in general gave support to the attitude taken at the Yalta Conference, there was intense feeling about the country's obligations to the Poles, and a group of some thirty members spoke in deprecation of the published formula. "There was a sense of anguish," said Mr. Churchill, "lest we should have to face the enslavement of a heroic nation." This resulted in abstentions from voting and even in resignations, although the government secured an overwhelming majority. Mr. Churchill himself summed up the dilemma in sentences to which there is no satisfactory answer. "It is easy," he said, "after the

Germans are beaten, to condemn those who did their best to hearten the Russian military effort, and to keep in harmonious contact with our great ally, who had suffered so frightfully. What would have happened if we had quarrelled with Russia when the Germans still had two or three hundred divisions on the fighting front? Our hopeful assumptions were soon to be falsified. Still, they were the only ones possible at the time."

I6. Stalin's North Europe

"Nations touch at their summits." Bagehot's aphorism was never truer than of the time of the war, and had the leaders been able to meet regularly and frequently, with the chance to talk frankly, it is possible, though by no means likely, that divergencies would have lessened. As it was, the Yalta Conference had only to disperse for the business of Poland to flare up with all the acerbity which was inseparable from it. Moreover, it was soon seen to be part of a pattern, and the realization that their predecessors had been right to treat the Soviets as diplomatic pariahs was forced upon men who had either schooled themselves to good will towards Moscow or had possessed it from the beginning. Russia's methods differed scarcely at all from those of Hitler; the Soviets were as indifferent as the Germans to more civilized usages, and they had the advantage of an additional weapon which they employed without scruple: they were leaders in a way of life which had as its aim the betterment of the "workers of the world." This lent a spurious sanctity to their aims, and to much of their language. Stripped of camouflaging nonsense, the closing stages of the war beheld Russian imperialism advancing with great strides, led by men with working-class roots who used their toughness to keep their country dominant, themselves in power and the rest of the world at a disadvantage.

Catherine the Great had once said: "It is futile to fight ideas with guns." The Soviet leaders had both ideas and guns, and as their ideas appeared more dynamic than the tempered liberty which was the inheritance of the West, they gained ground, as a result of the war, which restored the acquisitions of Peter the Great and influence beyond the dreams of their predecessors. Their "window upon the west" became a portal. Instead of the modest aperture which Peter the Great had secured at such cost, they were masters of territory they intended to instruct, not to learn from.

Warning of the future came in the obstruction met with by the Western Allies when they asked for facilities for their Polish observers; in the fist-banging insistence with which Stalin's envoy, Mr. Vishinsky, forced a subversive government upon Bucharest; and when virtually all Polish candidates for office who were suggested to the Lublin Poles were rejected. "If we did not get things right," wrote Mr. Churchill, "the world would soon see that Mr. Roosevelt and I had underwritten a fraudulent prospectus when we put our signatures to the Crimea settlement." Memoranda went back and forth between London and Washington, arguing the tactics to be pursued, though never the aim of the policy, which was firm and established. The only factor hidden from London, though not unguessed at, was the state of the President's health. That had become grave, though it was reasonably well concealed.

It was now that Russian partiality for the veto made itself apparent, Molotov being expert at this game. It was applied at San Francisco, where the embryo United Nations was already forming, and where the Russians were manoeuvring to gain a seat for Poland in addition to the two they had already secured for constituent Soviets. It was to be applied to every awkward question posed by Allied Foreign Ministers and ambassadors. United protest was at last made directly to Stalin on 1 April, to which he replied blandly that he blamed the British and American ambassadors in Moscow for "getting the Polish affair into a blind alley." By this he meant any road which did not lead straight into the Russian camp. As for observers, he added that the Poles could not be expected to accept such as were "unfriendly." "You are aware," he said, "that the Provisional Government puts no obstacles in the way of entrance into Poland by representatives of other states which take up a different attitude towards it. That is the case, for instance, in regard to representatives of the

Czechoslovak Government, the Yugoslav Government and others." By "others" Stalin meant any others which had been "liberated" or were about to be liberated, by the Red Army.

President Roosevelt died at Warm Springs, Georgia, on 12 April, 1945, at the age of sixty-three. Almost until the end he had been at full stretch. He had been in office longer than any other American President in history, and his New Deal had brought relief to a country which had then been in crisis. His aims had been so opposed to that of the state with which he and Mr. Churchill were increasingly contending that they are worth recalling as those of a man who, in common with millions elsewhere, was opposed to all that state capitalism stands for. "Every man," said Roosevelt early in his great career, "has a right to life, and this means that he has a right to make a comfortable living. Every man has a right to his own property, which means a right to be assured, to the fullest extent, of the safety of his savings." Not only had he led his country to a dominant economic position, but to military victory, for he would be survived by Hitler for only a few weeks, and the Empire of Japan, in its wartime expansion, would not outlive him many months. He was one of the rare American Presidents whose statue adorns London—and with reason, for he helped to sustain Britain in her darkest hour.

Of the clouds which were descending upon the affairs of Europe he was well aware, but it was left mainly to Mr. Churchill to try to ensure, now that Russia was seen to be becoming a mortal danger to the free world, that the front against her should be as far east as possible; that Western status in Berlin (which was an enclave within the Russian zone) should be as secure as possible; that Vienna should be regulated by the Western powers at least on an equality with the Soviets; and that the entrance to the Baltic, historically the trust of Denmark, though modified by German control of the Kiel Canal, should not be allowed to fall within the Soviet orbit. It was known that Stalin had designs that way which had caused difficulties in the days when Molotov and Ribbentrop were in council. It was the duty of the northern group of armies, tactically commanded by Field Marshal Montgomery, to make sure that Denmark, and the land immediately south of it, including Kiel, was acceptably secure.

II

No one was better aware than Stalin that the Germans would continue to resist in the east as strongly as possible, while allowing the armies facing the British and Americans to retreat in the certain knowledge that the civil population in occupied areas would be reasonably used. Until the very last moment he feared that the Western Allies might make if not a separate peace, then separate arrangements for surrender, or might wish to revise the zones of occupation. As agreed in September 1944, these were exceptionally favourable to the Russians, and they appeared increasingly so at a stage when the rapid advance of the Western armies would have enabled them to occupy areas in Czechoslovakia and Austria before the Russians could reach them.

Stalin also considered that now that Roosevelt was gone, and a new and inexperienced successor was in office, there was some chance that the united stand which had been taken up by the West about Poland might be shaken, or at the worst that the transitional period between the President's demise and a successor's assumption of the full control of policy might give him opportunities of which he would take every advantage. His hopes were ill founded.

Inexperienced as Mr. Truman was, he was guided well, and on the Polish question, which was one of the first with which he was faced, there was not the slightest shift from the line which had been agreed upon at Yalta. Mr. Harry S. Truman, son of a Missouri farmer, was an altogether simpler man than Roosevelt, but this gave him strength. He had been called upon to exercise power at a moment of supreme crisis, and his directness saved him from errors which a subtler politician might have fallen into.

On 13 April, the day after Roosevelt's death, the State Department presented their new chief with a memorandum which for accuracy and masterly concision equals anything he can have read. It was drafted by Edward R. Stettinius, and the portions which concern the affairs of countries of Europe, beginning with Great Britain, include the summary: "Mr. Churchill's policy is based fundamentally upon co-operation with the United States.

It is based secondly on maintaining the unity of the Three Powers, but the British Government has been showing increasing apprehension of Russia and her intentions. Churchill fully shares this Government's interpretation of the Yalta Agreements on Eastern Europe and liberated areas. He is inclined, however, to press this position with the Russians with what we consider unnecessary rigidity as to detail." The last sentence (reminiscent of a schoolmaster's report) was amplified in one which followed. "The British long for security, but are deeply conscious of their decline from a leading position to that of the junior partner of the Big Three, and are anxious to buttress their position vis-à-vis the United States and Russia both through exerting leadership over the countries of Western Europe and through knitting the Commonwealth more closely together."

As regards the Soviet Union and Poland, the document bore out Mr. Churchill word for word. Intransigence everywhere—coupled with a Soviet request for a large "postwar credit." Over Poland the Soviet authorities were spoken of as "consistently sabotaging Ambassador Harriman's efforts to hasten the implementation of the decisions at the Crimea Conference . . . Because of its effect on our relations with the Soviet Union and other United Nations, and upon public opinion in this country, the question of the future status of Poland and its Government remains one of our most complex and urgent problems both in the international and the domestic field." It was not many days before Truman himself was so sure of the truth of this opinion that he said to one of his principal advisers that it was his view that "unless settlement of the Polish question is achieved along the lines of the Crimea decision, the treaty of American adherence to a world organization will not get through the Senate. I said I intended to tell Molotov just that in words of one syllable."

Meanwhile things had been going from bad to worse within Poland itself. In March the Underground had been invited by the Russian political police to send a delegation to Moscow to discuss the formation of a united Polish Government on the lines of Yalta. This had been followed by a written guarantee of personal safety, and it was understood that the party would later be allowed, if negotiations were successful, to travel to London to discuss matters with the Government in Exile.

On 27 March, General Leopold Okulicki, then commanding the Underground army, together with two other leaders and an interpreter, had a meeting with a Soviet representative in the suburbs of Warsaw. They were joined at a further meeting next day by eleven others, representing major political parties. One other leader was already in Russian hands. It was all a trap, and not a man returned from the second rendezvous. On 4 May, Molotov, who had by then gone to San Francisco, admitted that the Poles in question were being held in Russia. A little later Stalin denied that they had ever been invited to Moscow at all. On 18 June all were tried for "subversion, terrorism and espionage." Nearly all were found guilty, and were sentenced to varying terms of imprisonment. This was, in fact, the liquidation of the Polish movement which had fought so heroically against Hitler. "The rank and file," said Mr. Churchill, "had already died in the ruins of Warsaw."

The line of divergence grew stronger and stronger, until it was becoming a wall with no loopholes. But Poland was not only a country in dispute: she represented a principle which must at all costs be defended. Agreements freely arrived at between nations must be honoured in the spirit and the letter. The opportunity to make the matter clear came when Molotov met Mr. Truman for the first time. If he had ever supposed that Truman would be easier to deal with than Roosevelt, he was soon disillusioned. "I said," the President reported of their conversation, "that the United States Government was prepared to carry out loyally all agreements reached at Yalta and asked only that the Soviet Government do the same. I expressed the desire of the United States for friendship with Russia, but I wanted it clearly understood that this could only be on a basis of the mutual observance of agreements and not on the basis of a one-way street."

"I have never been talked to like that in my life," said Molotov. "Carry out your agreements," said the President, "and you won't get talked to like that again."

III

By 2 May, Field Marshal Montgomery had brought his forces as far east as Wismar, renowned in the days of the Swedish wars,

and thus, in his own words, had "sealed off the Danish peninsula with about six hours to spare, before the Russians arrived."
Various attempts by Himmler and others had been made at a
separate agreement with the British or Americans, but all were
disregarded, and a general surrender took place on the 7th. In
due time the Russians advanced to the line opposite Lübeck
which had been agreed at Quebec. They then reached their far-
thest agreed limit on the Baltic coast, occupying their share of
East Germany.

The sea entrance to the Baltic had been saved, and the Royal
Navy was soon minesweeping in its waters, but if the Russian
Navy were ever rebuilt, and it became one of Stalin's immediate
objectives to do this, there was now no power which could hope
to prevent Russian mastery of the northern sea. They had the
use of every port between Wismar and Viborg for which rivals
had struggled over the centuries, and they were under their unfettered control. It was a historical opportunity for the country to
develop as a major maritime nation in Europe, and given international control of the Kiel Canal, even command of the entrance
to the Baltic did not appear to be of great consequence. It is significant that the Russian sphere included what remained of Peenemünde, and there is little question that the victors benefited
from German technical advances made in the workshops of this
area, as well as from the scientists they quickly suborned to serve
their cause.

A slight easement occurred in the inter-Allied tension after
the celebrations of Victory-Europe Day on 8–9 May, and as it
was obvious that there would have to be another meeting of
the leading statesmen, Truman sent Mr. Harry Hopkins on a
special mission to Moscow, to try to reach some preliminary understanding with Stalin. A fresh mind on Poland might, so Truman thought, break the deadlock. He was right. Although by
that time what Mr. Churchill described in a May cable as an
"iron curtain" had descended upon the Russian front, and although he himself was still oppressed by the knowledge that on
Roosevelt's showing, American sojourn in Europe would be
strictly limited, he agreed that Hopkins seemed to have worked
a change in Moscow, and persuaded the London Poles to allow a restored Mr. Mikolajczyk to resume negotiations with Lub-

lin. In the upshot a Provisional Government was set up which, at the President's request, was recognized by the West on 5 July. It was a date which, either by intention or not, carefully avoided the one on which American independence is traditionally celebrated.

"We were as far as ever from any real and fair attempt to obtain the will of the Polish nation by free elections," wrote Mr. Churchill. He added more cheerfully that "there was still a hope —and it was the only hope—that the meeting of 'the Three' now impending, would enable a genuine and honourable settlement to be achieved. So far only dust and ashes had been gathered, and these are all that remain to us today of Polish national freedom."

One of Hopkins's early discoveries was that Stalin had genuine difficulty in understanding Western interest in Poland as a matter of principle. Suspicious by nature, he found it almost impossible to credit that the Western politicians were not "ganging up" on this subject for some reason which he—self-described as a naïve man—had not fathomed. "The Russian Premier is a realist in all his actions," reported Hopkins to his chief, "and it is hard for him to appreciate our faith in abstract principles. It is difficult for him to understand why we should want to interfere with Soviet policy in a country like Poland . . . unless we have some ulterior motive. He does, however, appreciate that he must deal with the position we have taken."

Stalin's experience did not include practical knowledge of how Western democracy worked, and he was persistently wrong in his estimate of, for instance, the reaction of the postwar British voter to the leadership of Mr. Churchill. That Mr. Churchill himself was almost equally wrong is not to the point, for his varied life had accustomed him to the not very palatable truth that he might be. He now met with adulation everywhere he went. He was still realizing a lifelong ambition of exercising supreme power in an immense continuing crisis, and it seemed against all likelihood that he would not be able to complete his work, particularly when foreign affairs, in which he could claim far more perception than most statesmen, were likely to occupy his countrymen with the gravest matters.

The immediate prospect was of talks in Germany, for the

statesmen were to meet in July at a place which Truman noted was called Babelsberg, a suburb of Potsdam. A superstitious man might have been worried at the name, but this was not so in the case of the President, one of whose greatest assets being the uninhibited zest which he brought to bear on tasks which had vexed his predecessor. He was fresh and vigorous, and his impression of the impact of these tasks upon himself and upon his colleagues would be of great importance. The deliberations were, so it was hoped, to indicate a settlement of Germany; to agree upon a procedure for a peace conference; and to decide at what stage and on what terms Russia was to join in the war against Japan, which appeared to be approaching its final stages.

There was one further matter, of the highest secrecy, and at that time known only to Truman, Churchill and their principal advisers. The atom bomb, which had been developed at fabulous cost during the years of the war, was at last almost ready to be dropped on Japan, and the signal was awaited. It was not yet certain whether it would be successful as a strategic weapon, and its immediate effects could only be guessed at. If it proved as terrible as the scientists predicted, it would transform the balance of power, it would lie like a shadow over the lives of every man and woman living, and over the human race so long as it endured upon the earth. When Mr. Churchill was shown a code message of three words, "Babies satisfactorily born," he knew the best and the worst. The test bomb had been successfully detonated at the top of a pylon a hundred feet high. Devastation within a one-mile circle had been absolute.

It was not many months before every intelligent man and woman deduced that for the rest of their lives they would have to depend, as never before, on the sanity of politicians (a rope of straw in the light of history), and would realize that at any moment an intolerable flash, a tremor equal to the severest earthquake, would be the last impressions they received before—if they were among the luckier ones—life ended there and then. Many incidents are spoken of as "unique in history"; sometimes they have indeed been so. This test explosion was unique in the sense that it signified that man's ingenuity, harnessed to the service of war, had produced the ultimate nightmare, a missile which would produce, at its kindest, mass death on a scale unprecedented, and an existence for survivors whose sufferings would be of a kind which even science did not dare predict. Peenemünde and the atom bomb between them would produce a new climate in world politics; meanwhile there was Potsdam.

IV

At one time, though only during a brief phase, Truman thought that his role at Potsdam might be as a moderating influence between Stalin and Churchill. "I judge," telegraphed Lord Halifax from Washington, "that American tactics with the Russians will be to display at the outset confidence in Russian willingness to co-operate. I should also expect the Americans, in dealing with us, to be more responsive to arguments based on the danger of economic chaos in European countries than to the bolder pleas about the risk of extreme-left governments or the spread of Communism. They showed some signs of nervousness in my portrayal of Europe . . . as the scene of a clash of ideas in which the Soviet and Western influences are likely to be hostile and conflicting." The analysis was probably correct in its assessment of current feeling in America, but Babelsberg, living up to its name at least in respect of the multitude of voices, proved somewhat different from what Truman could have expected.

The President and Prime Minister met on 15 July, after there had been a general understanding that the conferences would have to be interrupted in two days' time, when the British representatives, who included Mr. Attlee, then at the head of the Labour Party, would need to return to London to learn the result of the general election. Personal harmony was at once established. Mr. Churchill was delighted with Truman's "gay, precise, sparkling manner and obvious power of decision," and he found him full of generous sympathy for Britain. When economic questions were discussed between them, Truman said: "If you had gone down like France, we might be fighting the Germans on the American coast at the present time. This justifies us in regarding matters as above the purely financial plane." Truman added, after the two had lunched together, that it had been the most enjoyable luncheon he had had for many years. On the face of it, it seemed unlikely that there would be any more divergencies between Truman and Churchill than had been the case with Roosevelt and Churchill.

On 18 July, Stalin and Churchill dined alone together except for their interpreters, and they conversed "from half past eight in the evening to half past one in the morning." Their personal acquaintance, tried in the fire of war, was three years old, and they spoke with a freedom and equality which Stalin probably found with no other living man. He addressed fellow Russians, even the favoured Molotov, like subordinates. Most of them cringed, and none ventured to contradict. Candour was no doubt refreshing, but there was a great deal of courtesy, too. For instance, Stalin had by now warmed to the idea of the British monarchical system, and was disappointed not to have met King George, while Churchill for his part expressed welcome of Russia as a future power by sea. "Russia," he said, "has been like a giant with his nostrils pinched by the narrow exit from the Baltic and the Black Sea." Matters would no doubt be different in the future.

Mr. Churchill said how anxious people were about Russia's general ambitions. "I drew a line," he wrote afterwards, "from the North Cape to Albania, and named the capitals east of that line which were in Russian hands. It looked as if Russia were rolling on westwards. Stalin said he had no such intention." Russian losses, he continued, had amounted to five million killed and missing, and he was actually withdrawing troops, who were badly needed at home. The Germans, said Stalin, had mobilized eighteen million men, apart from industry, and the Russians twelve million. These figures must have been "round" indeed, for what most historians of the war agree upon is that on the eastern front Russia had a preponderance in numbers almost throughout, and won her battles by her traditional mass methods.

Truman and Stalin met the following day, Stalin calling upon the President about eleven o'clock, apologizing for being late, saying that his health was not so good as it used to be. He had had a mild heart attack, though the fact was not generally known. Truman asked his guest to lunch. Stalin refused, but Truman insisted. "You could if you wanted to," said the President, and Stalin stayed.

"I was impressed with him," wrote Mr. Truman, "and talked to him straight from the shoulder. He looked me in the eye when he spoke, and I felt hopeful that we would reach an agreement that would be satisfactory to the world and to ourselves. I was surprised at Stalin's stature—he was not over five feet five or six inches tall. When we had pictures taken, he would usually stand on the step above me. Churchill would do the same thing. They were both shorter than I. I heard Stalin had a withered arm, but it was not noticeable." It was actually the left, and Stalin concealed the fact with practiced skill. "What I specially noticed," said Truman, "were his eyes, his face and his expression."

The sketch was amplified on later occasions. In formal conference, Truman found that while Churchill was "great in argument . . . Stalin was not given to long speeches. *He would reduce arguments quickly to the question of power, and had little patience with any other kind of approach.*" In twenty words, the President summed the man and matter up completely, and never had cause to alter his judgement. "In politics," said Stalin himself at one of the plenary sessions, "we should be guided by the calculation of forces."

v

Although a large part of the business of the conference had no bearing on Baltic affairs—since the Far East, the Balkans, Italy, Turkey, the Black Sea, world organization, reparations all came under review—yet Poland remained, and if one thing was more certain than another, it was that Poland would provide grounds for argument. A reconstituted Provisional Government had indeed been recognized by the Western powers, but there still remained the question of free elections. By this time Truman was beginning to understand that few nations, apart from Britain, the Scandinavians, and such others as cherished a tradition of well-ordered democratic government, spoke the same language as he did about elections, but quite apart from this the Russians, with tactless ingenuity, had introduced a completely new complication. Without prior consultation of any kind, they had given the Poles an "occupation zone" of their own. This extended from Stettin along the Oder and its continuation, the western Neisse, so that the Baltic area from north of Königsberg to the eastern bank of the Elbe contained first Russian-, then Polish-administered areas, then Poland as newly constituted, then a farther Polish-administered area, and finally East Germany, which was in Russian hands. Much of Germany's grain came from the area which the Poles had been given, and it appeared that the Western Allies would be left not only with wrecked industrial zones, but with a starved and swollen population. Britain had already paid some 120,000,000 pounds to finance the Polish armed services in the Allied cause, and to relieve Poles who had sought refuge during the war. Was she now to be burdened with the cost of feeding Germans driven from their country because the Poles, anticipating a treaty, had illegally occupied it?

Stalin said that the Western powers should appreciate the position in which the Poles found themselves. They were taking revenge on the Germans for the injuries the Germans had caused them in the course of centuries. Mr. Churchill pointed out that if what Stalin said was true, and there were no Germans left in the areas in question (his own information differed), then Polish revenge took the form of throwing the Germans into British and American zones to be fed. "Frustration," he commented, "was the fate of this conference."

This applied to some extent to other Baltic matters; for instance, there were the relics of the German fleet. At Gdynia the battlecruiser *Gneisenau*, mined and bomb-damaged, had fallen into Russian hands. British bombers had sunk the *Scheer* in Kiel Harbour and her sister ship, the *Lützow*, at Swinemünde. The *Schleswig-Holstein* and the *Schlesian* had been scuttled. At Kiel were the cruisers *Emden* and *Hipper*, forlorn and stranded. The *Prinz Eugen*, *Nürnberg* and *Leipzig* were in Danish ports, almost the only major units that could still steam. Stalin complained that his representatives were not allowed to see the ships, nor had they ever been given a list of surviving vessels. He asked for such a list, and for permission to inspect. Churchill answered that it was quite possible this could be managed, "but the British would want reciprocal facilities to be given them to see German installations in the Baltic." It was natural enough that the intended victims of rocket attacks should wish to see what had hit them, also the damage, done by their own airmen, which had prevented them from being hit harder. Churchill understood that the Russians had obtained forty-five U-boats at Danzig, and he suggested an interchange of inspections. Stalin said that all the submarines were damaged and "out of use," but that he could arrange for the British to see them. "All we want is reciprocity," said Churchill, and there the matter rested.

Mr. Truman observed a characteristic of Mr. Churchill's noted by many others. It was often his way to make long statements, and then to agree to what had already been done. This, thought Truman, was for purposes of record, "for use later by the British when the peace treaties were really and actually negotiated." He said that "on several occasions when Churchill was discussing something at length, Stalin would lean on his elbow, pull on his moustache and say: 'Why don't you agree? The Americans agree, and we agree. You will agree eventually, so why don't you do it now?' Then the argument would stop."

It was, however, Stalin who made a speech about Königsberg. This was the one occasion when the ghost of the Baltic states threatened to disturb the assembly. Stalin said that the question of Königsberg had been discussed at earlier conferences, since Russia felt the need of at least one ice-free Baltic port. "The Russians," he said, "had suffered so much at the hands of Germany that they were anxious to have some piece of German territory as small satisfaction to tens of millions of Soviet citizens. This had been agreed to by Roosevelt and Churchill, and he was anxious to see this approved at the conference."

Mr. Truman said that he concurred in principle, although it would be necessary to study the population affected, and other related questions. Mr. Churchill's only remaining consideration was that of the legal occasion of transfer. "The Soviet draft on this subject," so he pointed out, "would require each of us to admit that East Prussia did not exist, and also to admit that the Königsberg area was not under the authority of the Allied Control Council in Germany. The draft would commit us to the incorporation of Lithuania into the Soviet Union." All these matters really belonged to the final peace settlement, but he wished to assure Stalin of his continued support of the Russian position in that part of the world. Stalin noted that the matter would be finally settled at the peace conference, and added that Russia was satisfied that the British and American governments approved.

It was in the course of the same session—when the question of the freedom of the Dardanelles was under discussion—that Truman delivered himself of one of his rare general statements. He thought that the straits "should be a free waterway, open to the whole world, and that they should be guaranteed by all of us. "I have come to the conclusion," he said "after a long study of history, that all the wars of the last two hundred years have originated in the area from the Black Sea to the Baltic, and from the eastern frontier of France to the western frontier of Russia. In the last two instances the peace of the whole world has been overturned—by Austria in World War I and by Germany in this war." He thought it should be the business of the conference, and the peace conference which was to come, to see that this did not happen again. To that end he was presenting a paper proposing free access to all the seas of the world by Russia and by all other countries. He was proposing the solution that the Kiel Canal, the Rhine-Danube waterway, the Black Sea straits, the Suez and Panama canals "be made free waterways for the passage of freight and passengers of all countries. " Churchill agreed, and Stalin said he would read the paper attentively.

He would also have listened attentively to the news which Truman gave him about the "new bomb" had he had the slightest notion of its fundamental importance. As it was, the matter was handled in a way which gave no grounds for accusation that the Russians had been "kept in the dark," and as information about the successful test was still of a kind which was "top-secret" in a very top-secret aspect of war, it could best be conveyed by word of mouth. "I think," said Truman to Churchill, "I had best just tell him after one of our meetings that we have an entirely novel form of bomb, something quite out of the ordinary, which we think will have decisive effects upon the Japanese will to continue the war."

It was on 24 July that the matter was broached, and Mr. Churchill saw it all happen. "After a plenary meeting had ended," he said, "and we all got up from the round table and stood about in twos and threes before dispersing, I saw the President go up to Stalin, and the two conversed alone, with only their interpreters. I was perhaps five yards away, and I watched with the closest attention their momentous talk. I knew what the President was going to do. What was vital to measure was its effect on Stalin. I can see it all as if it were yesterday. He seemed to be delighted. A new bomb! Of extraordinary power! Probably decisive on the whole Japanese war! What a bit of luck. This was my impression at the moment, and I was sure he had no idea of the significance of what he was being told. Evidently in his intense toils and stresses the atomic bomb had played no part . . . his face remained gay and genial, and the talk between these two potentates soon came to an end. As we were waiting for our cars I found myself near Truman. 'How did it go?' I asked. 'He never asked a question!' he replied."

The President's own account is typically brief, and entirely bears out Mr. Churchill's version. "On 24 July," he noted, "I casually mentioned to Stalin that we had a new weapon of unusual destructive force. The Russian Premier showed no special interest. All he said was that he was glad to hear it, and hoped we would 'make good use of it against the Japanese'!"

The sequel came quickly. Atom bombs were dropped on Japan on 6 and 9 August, and war ended almost immediately afterwards, Russian declaration of co-belligerency being a last-minute matter of form, so that the country could enjoy the advantages of participation. Even before the destruction of Nagasaki and Hiroshima, the Japanese had put out peace feelers through the Russians, for they were in a desperate state both in a military and an economic sense. Although the bombs made no difference to the outcome, and may have saved but few Allied lives, the mere fact of their existence altered the whole pattern of the future.

VI

As at Yalta, there were revealing personal incidents at Potsdam, which was by far the most important conference of its kind ever held in what was virtually the Baltic area, since the nearest

NORTH EUROPE 1945

DENMARK

Bremerhaven
Lübeck
Rostock
Hamburg
U.S. CONTROL
Bremen
Wittenberg
Stettin
Danzig
RUSSIAN
Berlin
INTERNATIONAL OCCUPATION
Warsaw
Brunswick
Magdeburg
POLISH ADMINISTERED AREA
RUSSIAN Königsberg ADMINISTERED AREA
PRUSSIA
POLISH ADMINISTERED AREA
POLAND
ZONE
Leipzig
Dresden
Breslau
Cologne
Kassel
Erfurt
FRENCH
Karlsbad
Cracow
Mainz
Frankfurt
Würzburg
Prague
ZONE
Nuremberg
Pilsen
CZECHOSLOVAKIA
FRANCE
Karlsruhe
AMERICAN
Regensburg
Budejovice
Stuttgart
ZONE
FRENCH
RUSSIAN
INTERNATIONAL OCCUPATION
ZONE
Munich
Linz
Vienna
ZONE
Salzburg
Budapest
FRENCH ZONE
Innsbruck
SWITZERLAND
BRITISH ZONE
Klagenfurt
HUNGARY
ITALY
YUGOSLAVIA

0 50 100 150
MILES

International boundaries 1937 —·—·—
Zonal boundaries — — —

seaport was Stettin, now to be Polish. These incidents may be described collectively as the "musical glasses."

Truman was musical, so was Stalin, and on one particular evening an American sergeant, Eugene List, played Chopin's Waltz in A-flat major, Opus 42, together with several nocturnes. "Churchill," said Truman, "did not care much for that kind of music, but Stalin was so delighted that he rose from the dinner table, walked over to Sergeant List, shook his hand, drank a toast to him and asked him to play more." The President added: "I took a hand in the musical programme, and when I was asked to play the piano, I offered Paderewski's Minuet in G, one of my favourites." This Polish emphasis was not accidental. "I had been told previously that Stalin was fond of Chopin," said Truman, "and asked Sergeant List to brush up on his Chopin. He sent for the score of the waltz and practiced it for a week before the dinner." Stalin reciprocated by sending to Moscow for his two best pianists and two women violinists. "They played Chopin, Tschaikovsky and all the rest," said Truman. "They were excellent."

More in Mr. Churchill's line were the glasses. Once, when seated next to Stalin, Mr. Truman "noticed that he drank from a tiny glass that held about a thimbleful. He emptied it frequently and replenished it from a bottle he kept handy. I assumed it was vodka, and I wondered how Stalin could drink so much of that powerful beverage. Finally I asked him, and he looked at me and grinned. Then he leaned over to his interpreter and said: 'Tell the President it is French wine, because since my heart attack, I can't drink the way I used to.' "

There was, however, another occasion, one of the last upon which Stalin and Churchill met. Churchill had also noted Stalin's way of drinking from thimble measures. "Now," he said, "I thought I would take him on a step, so I filled a small-sized claret glass with brandy for him and another for myself. I looked at him significantly. We both drained our glasses at a stroke and gazed approvingly at each other."

Mr. Churchill, a future "honourary citizen" of the United States, had become a member of that free-masonry, independent of class and race of those who, all questions of politics and governments apart, supremely value the Russians as a people. It needs to be added that Stalin improved the shining hour by suggesting a base which would strengthen his position at the egress to the Black Sea, for he felt acutely the advantages held at that time by the United States as regards the Panama Canal and by Britain as regards Suez. Churchill contented himself with saying: "I will always support Russia in her claim to the freedom of the seas all the year round." This was wise of him, since destiny so willed it that he took no further part in discussions at this level. "I hope to be back," he said to Stalin before he left for England. Stalin remarked that judging from the expression on Mr. Attlee's face, he did not think he was looking forward to taking over Churchill's authority! Mr. Attlee had a way of keeping his thoughts to himself. When he returned home, it was to learn of his party's triumph at the polls and, in consequence, of Mr. Churchill's immediate resignation from executive office.

This event appeared to be a shattering blow not only personally, but to those with whom Mr. Churchill had worked in Europe. Truman wrote afterwards to his mother to say: "Mr. Stalin has been unable to leave his house for a couple of days, I really think he's not so sick but disappointed over the English elections." But in fact, whatever shade of political hue may be favoured, it was perhaps the most refreshing sign of political vitality which Britain had shown for a generation. Mr. Churchill was that rare creature, a world statesman, yet for some ten years before the war he had been refused office by the leaders of the party to which he belonged, and it had been those leaders who had brought the country not merely to war, but close to ruin. The verdict, as a party verdict, was fair, and by party Mr. Churchill had to be judged. Only Stalin now remained of the three men who, over the years, had guided their people to victory.

One of the major compensations of the election was that it gave Mr. Churchill time in which to compose that blend of personal memoir and historical narrative, spanning the prelude, course and immediate aftermath of the war, upon which every future student must draw and to which every reader stands indebted. Posterity may enjoy the Duc de Saint-Simon on Louis XIV and Churchill on Stalin and Roosevelt. There are those who see in their pages the mature felicity of historical narrative.

VII

In so far as the immediate future was concerned, the pattern of power in the Baltic had already been decided. Russia had won all she wished for. Her word was law between Finland and Lübeck. Subservient Poland commanded a stretch of coast between Stettin and the Gulf of Danzig which could ensure her such maritime facilities as she had not enjoyed for centuries. The Scandinavian states remained separate; and by postponing and perhaps preventing a peace treaty, Russia had seen to it that Germany remained impotent, as an aggressive factor, for at least a generation. On this subject Stalin may be given the last word. "The West," he said later to Djilas, "will make western Germany their own, and we shall turn eastern Germany into our state."

On the Baltic littoral as elsewhere, East and West still stand poised, each now possessed of weapons of limitless destructive power; each distrustful; each convinced of the ultimate value of differing ways of life. Mankind has solved many problems which once seemed intractable. The greatest—survival; general political freedom, including that of speech, press and assembly, which is actually embodied in the Soviet Constitution, though the fact is seldom recalled, and true comity among nations have still to be mastered. Force has never proved a satisfying answer, as all history shows. Gustavus Adolphus, Charles X and his grandson Charles XIII, Frederick of Prussia, Bismarck, William II and Hitler, all in their turn had their hours of glory, but their achievements have faded. Mannerheim saved a nation; Pilsudski helped to restore one; but the men of ideas prove strongest of all, for humanity needs hope, not trophies.

The enchanting Danes, who once ruled Norway, the serious Swedes, the resilient Finns, the all-enduring Russians, the unpredictable Poles, the obedient Germans look out upon the Baltic from their various windows and points of vantage. If few heads lie easy, there are signs—as yet they are no more—that the future may be less devastating than the past.

Sovereign rulers
1630-1945

DENMARK-NORWAY
Christian IV (1588-1648)
Frederick III (1648-1670)
Christian V (1670-1699)
Frederick IV (1699-1730)
Christian VI (1730-1746)
Frederick V (1746-1766)
Christian VII (1766-1808)
Frederick VI (1808-1814 . . .

DENMARK
Frederick VI . . .
    (1808-1839)
Christian VIII (1839-1848)
Frederick VII (1848-1863)
Christian IX (1863-1906)
Frederick VIII (1906-1912)
Christian X (1912-1947)

NORWAY
Haakon VII (1905-1957)

SWEDEN
Gustavus II Adolphus
    (1611-1632)
Christina (1632-1654)
Charles X Gustavus
    (1654-1660)
Charles XI (1660-1697)
Charles XII (1697-1718)
Ulrika Eleonora
    (1718-1720)
Frederick I of Hesse
    (1720-1751)
Adolphus Frederick
    (1751-1771)
Gustavus III (1771-1792)
Gustavus IV Adolphus
    (1792-1809)
Charles XIII (1809-1874 . . .

SWEDEN-NORWAY
Charles XIII . . .
    1814-1818)
Charles XIV John (Bernadotte) (1818-1844)
Oscar I (1844-1859)
Charles XV (1859-1872)
Oscar II (1872-1905[7])

SWEDEN
Gustavus V (1907-1950)

POLAND
Sigismund III (1587-1632)
Wladislaus IV (1632-1648)
John II Casimir (1648-1668)
Michael Wisniowiecki
    (1669-1674)
John III Sobieski
    (1674-1696)
Frederick Augustus I
    (1697-1733)
[Stanislaus Leszczyński
    (1704-1709]
Frederick Augustus II
    (1733-1763)
Stanislaus II Poniatowski
    (1764-1795)

RUSSIA
Michael (1613-1645)
Alexis (1645-1676)
Theodore (1676-1682)
Ivan V (1682-1689) Joint Tsar
Peter the Great (1682-1725)
Catherine I (1725-1727)
Peter II (1727-1730)
Anna (1730-1740)
Ivan VI (1740-1741)
Elizabeth (1741-1762)
Peter III (1762)
Catherine II (1762-1796)
Paul I (1796-1801)
Alexander I (1801-1825)
Nicholas I (1825-1855)
Alexander II (1855-1881)
Alexander III (1881-1894)
Nicholas II (1894-1917)

ELECTORS OF BRANDENBURG-PRUSSIA
George William (1619-1640)
Frederick William (The Great Elector) (1640-1688)
Frederick III (1688-1701 . . .

KINGS OF PRUSSIA
Frederick I . . . 1701-1713)
Frederick William I (1713-1740)
Frederick II (The Great) (1740-1786)
Frederick William II (1786-1797)
Frederick William III (1797-1840)
Frederick William IV (1840-1861)
William I (1861-1871 . . .

GERMAN EMPERORS
William I . . . 1871-1888)
Frederick III (1888)
William II (1888-1918)

Events in the narrative

1630—Gustavus Adolphus intervenes in the Thirty Years' War.

1631—Swedish victory at Breitenfeld.

1632—Gustavus defeats Tilly.

Death of Gustavus at Lützen.

1643—Swedish invasion of Denmark.

Battle off Kolberg Heath saves the Danish islands.

1645—Treaty of Brömsebro advantageous to Sweden.

1648—Peace of Westphalia establishes Sweden in West Pomerania, Rügen, Wismar, Bremen and Verden.

1655—Charles X Gustavus takes Warsaw and Cracow.

1657—Sweden and Denmark renew war. Charles X Gustavus marches across the ice to threaten Copenhagen.

1658—Treaty of Roskilde frees Sweden from Danish rule in Scania.

Copenhagen under siege, relieved by a Dutch fleet at the Battle of the Sound.

1660—Death of Charles X Gustavus and the Peace of Oliva, which confirms Swedish conquests and marks the limit of her expansion.

1676—Danish-Dutch fleet under Cornelius Tromp and Niels Juel defeats the Swedes off Öland and an invasion threatens the reconquest of Scania.

1679—Charles XI frees Scania.

1699—Peter the Great and Augustus of Saxony secretly decide upon the partition of the Swedish empire.

1700—Defeat of the Saxons at Riga.

Defeat of Peter the Great at Narva by Charles XII.

1701—The Margrave of Brandenburg becomes King of Prussia.

1702—Charles XII becomes master of Poland (crowns his own candidate, Stanislaus Leszczyński, 1704).

1703—St. Petersburg founded on the Neva.

1704—Narva recaptured by Peter the Great.

1708—Charles XII invades Russia.

1709—Charles XII defeated at Poltava and flees to Turkish territory. Danish invasion of Scania.

1710—Danes defeated at Halsingborg.

1714—Charles XII returns to the north and defends Stralsund. Armfelt's army annihilated by the Russians in Finland.

1715—Charles XII overwhelmed at Stralsund and returns to Sweden.

1718—Charles XII killed at Frederikshald.

1721—Treaty of Nystad. Russia established in the Baltic Provinces.

1733—Stanislaus Leszczyński's bid to re-establish himself in Poland.

1734—Siege and fall of Danzig to Russian forces. Flight of Leszczyński.

1741—Sweden attempts to regain the Baltic Provinces, but loses Finland to Russia.

1743—Peace of Abo regains Sweden most of Finland.

1772—First Partition of Polish territory between Russia, Prussia and Austria.

1780—Armed neutrality of the Northern Powers to protect their sea traffic from belligerents.

1793—Second Partition of Poland between Russia and Prussia.

1795—Third Partition of Poland between Russia, Prussia and Austria extinguishes the ancient kingdom.

1796—Russia at war with the French Republic.

1800—Armed neutrality revived as a Northern League.

1801—The British fleet bombards Copenhagen.
Northern League dissolved after the assassination of Paul I.

1806—Napoleon's Continental System designed to ruin British trade, particularly with the Baltic lands.

1807—Treaty of Tilsit between Napoleon and Alexander I.
The British fleet returns to Copenhagen to remove the Danish fleet from enemy control.

1809—Russia occupies Finland.
Sir James Saumarez exercises control of the Baltic.

1812—Napoleon invades Russia.

1813—The retreat from Moscow.

1814—Bernadotte, Crown Prince of Sweden, lands in Pomerania and later moves against Denmark.

Norway ceded by Denmark to Sweden.

1815 Sweden cedes her possessions in Germany.

1848—Revolt in Holstein against Denmark.

1849—Battle of Eckernförde Fjord and the defeat of the Danes.

1854 Napier's expedition into the Baltic against Russia.

1855—Admiral Dundas bombards Sveaborg.

1857—Denmark relinquishes her ancient Sound Dues in consideration of a monetary payment by the principal maritime nations.

1864—Prussian and Austrian troops invade Schleswig.

Danes defeated at Düppel.

1866—Prussia annexes Schleswig-Holstein.

1871—The King of Prussia becomes German Emperor.

1898—Completion of the Kiel Canal for deep-water ships.

1905—Norway separates from Sweden.

Unrest in Russia and Finland.

1914—European war.

Battle of Tannenberg.

1917—Lenin returns to Russia. October Revolution.

1918—Finnish War of Independence.

President Wilson's Fourteen Points.

Baltic States declare their independence.

1919—Von der Goltz defeated in Latvia.

Reconstitution of Poland.

Restoration of North Schleswig to Denmark by plebiscite.

1920—Battle outside Warsaw checks Russian invasion of Poland.

1921—Suppression of rising by the sailors of Kronstadt.

1924—Failure of Communist *coup d'état* in Estonia.

1933—Hitler becomes Chancellor of the German Reich.

1939—Hitler takes Memel from the Lithuanians.

Stalin-Hitler pact.

The Germans invade Poland.

Russo-German partition of Poland.

The Winter War in Finland.

1940—The Baltic States forfeit their independence.

1941—Germans invade Russia.

1942—Stalingrad: the tide turns against the Germans.

1943—Rockets developed at Peenemünde.

Stalin, Roosevelt and Churchill meet at Teheran to discuss the war and the future state of Europe.

1944—Finland makes peace with Russia.

Zones of Allied occupation of Germany agreed.

1945—Stalin, Roosevelt and Churchill meet at Yalta to decide the future of Poland and other matters.

Defeat of the Germans and suicide of Hitler.

Death of President Roosevelt.

The Potsdam Conference decides the new dispensation in Europe.

Acknowledgements

While it would be pretentious and tedious to list all the works I have consulted, certain items stand out with such clarity as to demand appreciation. In necessary cases, I have given the date of a recent translation.

After the *Cambridge Modern History* in its original and newer versions, with bibliographies which include the principal studies in other languages than English, it is fitting that two works, published with an interval of over half a century between them by Dr. R. C. Anderson, should be given pride of place. *Naval Wars in the Baltic* (1910) and *Oared Fighting Ships* (1962) have been invaluable, especially the first, which assembles material elsewhere almost unavailable. Miss C. V. Wedgwood's *Thirty Years' War* (1938) is notable among other virtues for its portraiture and sweep, while Nils Ahnlund's *Gustav Adolf the Great* (Princeton, 1940) gives a detailed view of the Swedish hero. Charles E. Hill's *The Danish Sound Dues and the Command of the Baltic* (Duke University Press, 1926) treats an important subject fully, while R. G. Albion's *Forests and Sea Power* (Harvard, 1926) is a recognized classic. Ralph Davis's *The Rise of the English Shipping Industry* (1962) has useful Baltic material, and J. F. Chance's *George I and the Great Northern War* (1909) is still the fullest digest of its kind. Frans Bengtsson's *The Sword Does Not Jest: The Heroic Life of King Charles XII of Sweden* (1960) is a masterpiece, no less, and Ian Grey's *Peter the Great* (1962) is a modern portrait of a man, so well described in the pages of the Duc de Saint-Simon. For the earlier periods particularly, studies by Professor Michael Roberts and Ingar Andersson are as valuable as they are delightful.

The *Journals and Letters of Sir T. Byam Martin,* edited by Sir Richard Hamilton for the Navy Records Society (1898), are valuable for the Napoleonic Era, and I have also had profit from the papers of Mr. A. N. Ryan, of Liverpool University, published in the Transactions of the Royal Historical Society and elsewhere. Among a host of later works consulted, *The Formation of the Baltic States,* by Stanley W. Page (Harvard, 1959), treats political ramifications far more fully than I have attempted. I have used information from H. A. Grant Watson's brief *Mission to the Baltic States* (1962) and from Captain Augustus Agar's *Footprints in the Sea* (1961). Christopher Hill's *Lenin and the Russian Revolution* (1947) is sympathetic, and G. Katkov's *The Kronstadt Rising* (St. Anthony's Papers, 1959) is a full account of a grisly episode. Three other works are outstanding in factual survey: *The Soviet Navy,* edited by Commander M. G. Saunders (1947); *The Soviet High Command,* by John Erickson (1962), and *The Siege of Leningrad,* by Leon Gouré (1962).

Among memoirs, those of the Comtesse de Choiseul-Gouffier de Tisenhaus are useful for an earlier period, as are those of Sir Samuel Bentham. For later developments, works by Field Marshal Mannerheim, Count Edward Raczyński, Sir Winston Churchill and President Truman provide both basic material and chastening thought. Milovan Djilas's *Conversations with Stalin* (1962) is, I think, helpful to the understanding of a powerful character, and Hans von Lehndorff's *East Prussian Diary: a Journal of Faith: 1945-1947* (1963) illustrates the full extent of disintegration arising from war and savagery. Ludwig Dehio's *The Precarious Balance* (1962) is an admirable general study.

The author gratefully acknowledges the kind permission of Messrs Cassell to quote brief passages from Sir Winston Churchill's *The Second World War,* which is the essential authority for the British side of the struggle for the future of Poland. Further information of high value and importance has been provided more recently in the third volume of Lord Avon's memoirs, *The Reckoning.*

♆ INDEX